EDU                    TRA

SKILLS-BASED SOCIOLOGY

**Series Editors:** Tony Lawson and Tim Heaton

The *Skills-based Sociology* series is designed to cover all the key concepts, issues and debates in Sociology. The books take a critical look at contemporary developments in sociological knowledge as well as essential social theories. Each title examines a key topic area within sociology, offering relevant examples and student-focused pedagogical features to aid learning and develop essential study skills.

**Published**

THEORY AND METHOD (*second edition*)
Mel Churton and Anne Brown

RELIGION AND BELIEF
Joan Garrod and Marsha Jones

CULTURE AND IDENTITY
Warren Kidd

POLITICS AND POWER
Warren Kidd, Philippe Harari and Karen Legge

STRATIFICATION AND DIFFERENCE
Mark Kirby

CRIME AND DEVIANCE (*second edition*)
Tony Lawson and Tim Heaton

EDUCATION AND TRAINING (*second edition*)
Tony Lawson, Tim Heaton and Anne Brown

HEALTH AND ILLNESS
Michael Senior and Bruce Viveash

**Forthcoming**

THE MEDIA (*second edition*)
Marsha Jones, Emma Jones and Andy Jones

THE FAMILY (*second edition*)
Liz Steel, Warren Kidd and Anne Brown

---

**Skills-based Sociology**
**Series Standing Order ISBN 0–333–69350–7**
(*outside North America only*)

You can receive future titles in this series as they are published. To place a standing order please contact your bookseller or, in the case of difficulty, write to us at the address below with your name and address, the title of the series and the ISBN quoted above.

Customer Service Department, Macmillan Distribution Ltd, Houndmills, Basingstoke, Hampshire RG21 6XS, England

# Education and Training

## Second Edition

Tony Lawson

Tim Heaton

and

Anne Brown

First edition 1996
Second edition 2010

Published by
PALGRAVE MACMILLAN

Palgrave Macmillan in the UK is an imprint of Macmillan Publishers Limited, registered in England, company number 785998, of Houndmills, Basingstoke, Hampshire RG21 6XS.

Palgrave Macmillan in the US is a division of St Martin's Press LLC, 175 Fifth Avenue, New York, NY 10010.

Palgrave Macmillan is the global academic imprint of the above companies and has companies and representatives throughout the world.

Palgrave® and Macmillan® are registered trademarks in the United States, the United Kingdom, Europe and other countries.

ISBN 978–0–230–21792–8

This book is printed on paper suitable for recycling and made from fully managed and sustained forest sources. Logging, pulping and manufacturing processes are expected to conform to the environmental regulations of the country of origin.

A catalogue record for this book is available from the British Library.

A catalog record for this book is available from the Library of Congress.

10   9   8   7   6   5   4   3   2   1
19   18   17   16   15   14   13   12   11   10

Printed in Great Britain by
CPI Antony Rowe, Chippenham and Eastbourne

*To Phil, Emma and Laura*

# Contents

# Acknowledgements

Anne Brown would like to particularly thank Phil Brown for his guidance regarding the numerical and statistical material included in the book and for his input to Chapters 7 and 9. His general support during the updating and rewriting process is also appreciated. Thanks to Tony Lawson for his editorial work, to Anna-Marie Reeve for smoothly and professionally managing the whole process, as well as Keith Povey for his editorial input.

The authors and the publisher would also like to thank the following for kindly giving permission to reproduce material: Higher Education Statistics Agency for tables in Item E, Chapter 6; Personality Investigations Publications and Services for the 'Know Your Own IQ' material from H. J. Eysenck in Exercise 5.3, Chapter 5. Every effort has been made to contact all the copyright-holders, but if any have been inadvertently omitted the publishers will be pleased to make the necessary arrangement at the earliest opportunity.

# Chapter 1

# Introduction

## THE PHILOSOPHY BEHIND THE BOOK

The aims of this book are as follows; firstly, we wish you to take an active part in your own education. *Knowledge, understanding, interpretation, application, analysis* and *evaluation* are the central skills that new sociologists must demonstrate in any examination. Knowledge means showing you have learnt and have a good command of sociological concepts, evidence and theories and understanding is displayed in your accurate, clear usage of the material. Interpretation means that you should be able to look at different types of text, such as tables or newspaper articles, and be able to communicate your understanding of them. Application is the ability to take sociological and non-sociological material and use it in relevant ways to answer the questions set. Analysis means being able to demonstrate a detailed examination of the structure and composition of arguments, accounts, theories and evidence. Evaluation means being able to assess sociological debates and arguments through a consideration of evidence.

The best way of developing these skills is to practise them yourself. We have therefore designed a series of exercises that are tied to these skills, and if you carry them out you should be able to improve your performance in these areas. You will be able to identify the skills each exercise is designed to develop by looking out for the following symbols: [I] for interpretation, [A] for application, [AN] for analysis and [E] for evaluation. However we also want you to understand the interconnections between all the information in this book, so you will also find that there are *link exercises* for you to do. These will not only help you to perform skilfully, but also increase the sophistication of your understanding of the sociology of education and training.

Our second aim is to present you with sociological knowledge that is appropriate to and useful for your examination performance, as the ability to convey *knowledge* [K] and *understanding* [U] is another skill that all examinations include. We decided that what we did not want to do was to present the knowledge you easily could glean from elsewhere. But we do want you to be as up-to-date as possible with the material you are familiar with, so that you can apply it in the examination. We have therefore focused on developments in sociology during the 1990s and early years of the 2000s.

We have not attempted to tell you all there is to know about sociology in this period, because to develop your sociological skills you should be finding out for yourself what has been happening in society and sociology during this time. We have, however, tried to give you an overview of the debates that have been going on, and the sociologists who have been writing about education and training in this period. You will find that much of the material concerns the theories and ideas of the New Right and of the postmodernists, and how other sociologists have responded to these developments during this period.

Our third aim is to help you to pass your exams, so we have included a series of exam-type questions, sometimes with answers and sometimes not, but always there is some task for you to do yourself. We believe that if you carry out the activities connected to these questions you will help yourself to pass the examination. It may be that you will prefer to conduct these activities with a teacher, and she or he will be able to build on the ideas and activities to improve further your performance. However, you can also use the examination activities as supplements to your classroom work, as you go through the course, or as a revision aid as you near the examination.

The important thing to remember is that we cannot do it all for you. You will gain most from this book if you approach it in an active way, and are prepared to take the information and skills and apply them in the examination itself. If you just read the text and miss out the exercises, you will only be doing half of what is necessary to pass the exam. Therefore you should develop your own revision system that you know works for you, and use the material in this book accordingly to fills gaps in your knowledge, to learn key theories and debates, and develop skills that you can display when being assessed. A revision system works best when it involves you actively in identifying which areas you need to work on, asking your own questions about material and your understanding of it, using past exam questions to guide your revision, and making sure you know how to display the skills you will be assessed on. Actively summarising, condensing and abbreviating all the material you have learnt will go a long way in helping you internalise and remember the key content of your course.

## DEFINITIONS OF EDUCATION AND TRAINING

The Concise Oxford Dictionary defines the act or process of education as 'systematic instruction and/or the development of character or mental powers'. These are fairly vague notions which perhaps are of little help in trying to define education in the modern world. We know that children in many parts of the world receive little or no 'systematic instruction' but are still responsible for the economic well-being of their communities. On the other hand, in Western industrial societies, children are required by law to go to school and to receive 'systematic instruction' until the age of sixteen or, more commonly now, eighteen. In short, most people spend more or less the first twenty years of their lives in various types of school – nursery, primary, secondary, further, tertiary, higher. The corresponding illiteracy rates are very low in Western societies, at below 5 per cent. However, throughout Latin America and many nations in Africa, illiteracy is commonplace. These societies often have 'oral traditions' rather than communicating through the written word.

Ⓚ
### Exercise 1.1

Try to think of a definition for education that goes beyond the Oxford Dictionary one. Think about aspects of learning that could also be included related to relationships, emotional maturity, independence, working with others or problem solving.

There is thus an international or global dimension to education, in which competitiveness in a world economy is linked to the density of education and training that the populations of countries receive. The idea here is that, as economies become more sophisticated and interlinked, in order to compete with other areas of the world, a country needs to invest heavily in the skills and education of its people. With the massive changes that occur in economies through developments such as the internet and virtual reality, in order for a society to be economically successful it needs a highly skilled workforce (see Castells 1996).

There is another implication for education in the idea of a global economy. Whereas, in the past, education has been predominantly the preserve of the young, and adults tended not to become involved in education except as parents or teachers, the global economy demands that individuals become 'lifelong learners'. It is no longer sufficient that we learn to become adults through education or workers through training when we are young; we must continually be learning new skills and theories if we are to make our way in the world, both as individuals and as a society.

Education and training in a society is thus a valuable resource and, like all resources, become the object of conflict and competition, because there is a scarcity aspect to them. We have already noted how, in many parts of the world, there are low levels of skills and limited educational opportunities for many segments of the population. Yet many children and their parents will make huge sacrifices to obtain an education or be trained in a skill that has value in the workplace. In many developing countries, it is investment in education that is seen as a route to development and prosperity, but it is not everybody who is lucky enough to receive an education. Freire (1972), a Brazilian educator, developed literacy programmes for the poor to help them take control over their lives. His projects were supported by a left-wing government and became part of the Liberation Theology in Latin America. He argued that formal education was a means by which powerful groups in society could impose their value-system on the people, Freire was eventually imprisoned by a new right-wing government and went into exile. However, one of his key ideas was that education could transform the social order.

## Exercise 1.2

Imagine that you were given the power to create an education system. What would your main priorities be? How would decide what subjects to teach? How far does learning need to relate to societal norms and values?

This brings us to another aspect of education and training that must be taken into account. Access to education and training is not equal, nor has it ever been. Education and training is a 'site of struggle'. What this means is that social groups will compete with each other to gain education and training, and those that lose out are likely (but not inevitably) to be disadvantaged in the workplace and in the opportunities they have in life more generally. Education is therefore 'classed, gendered and racialized', as social groups compete for access to education and training, and to certain types of education and training. It has always been so. In the United Kingdom in the nineteenth century, education was the preserve of 'gentlemen'. This implied that, not only was education not for the lower orders or for women, but also that the aim of education was social as much as economic. That is, it was aimed at producing a well-rounded, erudite upper-class individual with a prescribed set of manners and a particular way of looking at the world. It was clearly an education and *not* training. As education, under economic imperatives, was made available to the lower orders (mainly the males), it was a different form of education that was designed for them, with much more training involved. Thus, basic literacy and numeracy (still a mantra in the twenty-first century) was seen as the proper form of education for workers, so that they could perform their work functions more effectively.

Similarly, education in the United States was not for slaves or, with the abolition of slavery, for black Americans, except for the most rudimentary provision. It was not accidental that the 1960s' Civil Rights Movement in America was concerned with access to schools and universities in the struggle for black emancipation. Alongside the right to vote freely, access to education on an equal footing with whites was seen as the most important step towards ensuring that black Americans would find a place in American society that would liberate them from racism and oppression.

On a contemporary theme, the issue of female access to education has been the dividing line between those who support the Taliban in Afghanistan and Pakistan, and those who adopt a more 'modern' approach to educational issues. The Taliban's destruction of schools for girls is not just some knee-jerk fundamentalist response, but a calculation that education can set people free to make decisions and choices with little regard to traditional authorities, and the Taliban see this as a dangerous and unacceptable development. The more liberal Middle-Eastern states such as the United Arab Emirates do provide education for girls and women, albeit separate from men. In some senses the cultural norms in such societies, which see the lives of men and women as separate spheres, lags behind the educational system, and once 'educated', women do not 'naturally' go out to find employment but rather return to the domestic sphere. Projects are beginning to emerge to encourage women to make this step into the world outside the home. On the other side, the courage of those who build such schools, and who teach and learn in them, suggests that the thirst for education is widespread and deep. This is a struggle over education of the most radical and life-threatening type. The next time you find yourself a little bored in an educational setting, think about the sheer privilege you are enjoying that others have died for.

## CONTENT OF THE BOOK

The content of this book is broken down into nine areas. In Chapter 2 we consider the background and context to the development of educational policies and systems in Britain in the 1980s and 1990s. In Chapter 3, we examine more recent developments in the curriculum that have occurred in the last part of the twentieth century and the first part of the twenty-first. Chapter 4 looks at the changes in policy and education systems that occurred in the 1980s, 1990s and 2000s, and the sociological research on them. The book then moves on to various explanations of differential educational attainment. Chapter 5 looks at class differences in educational performance. Chapter 6 addresses the debates on gender inequalities in educational achievement. Explanations of ethnic differences in educational attainment are covered in Chapter 7, and at the end of this chapter we draw together the social factors of class, gender and ethnicity, to explore the connections between and implications of looking at them together when we consider educational performance and underperformance. In the next two chapters, we go on to consider the role or function of schooling and training: Chapter 8 looks at the purpose of education and training from a functionalist perspective, while Chapter 9 offers a conflict analysis.

*Chapter 2*

# Educational Policy and Systems in Britain: The Background to Changes in the 1980s and 1990s

By the end of this chapter you should:

- be aware of how educational policy has been shaped by certain key objectives
- have a critical understanding of early educational policies in Britain
- be familiar with comprehensive schools and the conflicting views there are about them
- appreciate the arguments for and against private schools
- understand that educational policy since 1976 has been introduced for social, political and economic reasons

## INTRODUCTION

Chapters 2, 3 and 4 examine the significance of educational policies in Britain. Educational policies, like all social policies, are designed to bring about change(s) in society. As sociologists we are interested in the impact that social policies make on the behaviour of people and institutions. Educational policies are important for three reasons. First, they shape the education systems in which teachers, lecturers and students work. Second, they determine in part the degree to which societies can become meritocratic – that is, those who are talented rise in the social structure. Third, they shape what is taught in schools and colleges. In this chapter we provide an overview of the debates surrounding early educational policies, while Chapter 3 focuses on the issues that have emerged from policy developments in the 1980s, 1990s and 2000s. Attention is also given in this chapter to private-sector schooling. This exists outside state provision, and is not constrained by the same government educational policies that we shall be focusing on.

When reading Chapters 2, 3 and 4 it is essential that you do not treat them in isolation from the rest of the book. Subsequent chapters will examine differential educational achievement by social class, gender and ethnicity; and the role of education and training in society. All these can be understood and explained with reference to the educational policies discussed in these chapters, and it is essential that you are able to make the links. You will be helped to make the connections through a series of link exercises in subsequent chapters.

## IMPORTANT PRINCIPLES AND CONCEPTS OF THE EDUCATION SYSTEM

Reforms in the British education system since the Second World War have often had two objectives in mind:

1. To create a meritocracy through equality of educational opportunity.
2. To create a highly trained and efficient workforce by transferring vocational skills.

### Creating a meritocracy through equality of educational opportunity

A meritocracy is a situation where individuals are rewarded on the basis of merit or ability and effort, and not according to social background. The concept of meritocracy is important in the study of education because it provides the justification for the social system as it currently operates. This has also been described by sociologists as a system of achieved rather than ascribed status. If everyone is rewarded for their skills and abilities rather than who their parents are or were, then people will see their position in society, whether well-rewarded or not, as a legitimate position – that is, one that is deserved and therefore fair. Educational reform since 1944 has often been associated with attempts to make the education system, and therefore society, more meritocratic.

Equality of educational opportunity refers to the idea that education systems should provide the same opportunities for all students to achieve to their fullest ability regardless of their social background. It is important to

note the difference between reforms that are concerned with 'equality of educational access', such as the many 'widening participation' projects (such as
'Aimhigher', for example) designed to open up higher education to more
social groups, and 'equality of educational outcome', which might, for example, be concerned with encouraging female students to succeed in science
subjects. The creation of the Open University is an example of the former,
and the GIST (Girls into Science and Technology) project is an example of
the latter.

It is also important to recognise that this principle was part of the postwar
'social democratic consensus', in which the main political strands in Britain
were in broad agreement on the shape of social and educational policies. This
agreement focused on the creation of a welfare state as a way of eliminating
disadvantage and promoting equal opportunity. However this consensus was
not unchallenged: critics on the right were suspicious of what they saw as
egalitarian policies in the 1950s and 1960s, and critics on the left argued that
the reforms did not in fact produce equality of opportunity.

(A)

## Exercise 2.1

Discuss with another sociology student whether equality of educational opportunity exists in your school or college. Try to justify your decisions to each
other. You could begin by looking to see if your school or college has an equal
opportunities policy or statement (usually available on their website or in the
prospectus) and then consider whether this is achieved by reflecting on whether
males and females are offered an equal educational experience in your school or
college. You could also consider the subject options available, and what choices
male and female students tend to make.

## Creating a highly trained and efficient workforce by transferring vocational skills

The importance of schooling for the economy has long been recognized by
sociologists and politicians alike. They have argued that a society's economic
performance is linked to the skills and enterprise of its citizens. Though the
purpose of education may also include other aims, the transfer of marketable
skills from one generation to the next is a central part of economic success. The
role of the education system in this process is seen as vital, though it should be
remembered that there have traditionally been avenues other than schools for
the acquisition of vocational skills, such as apprenticeship schemes.

Ⓐ

## Exercise 2.2

In what ways do you think schooling can or does equip pupils with the necessary skills for employment? The following examples should help you to get started.

- Schooling teaches numeracy.
- Schooling develops interpersonal skills.
- Vocational or work-related courses or work experience.

## EARLY EDUCATIONAL POLICIES

### The 1870 Forster Act

This Act established state provision for elementary (primary) education. The introduction of a state system of education was a product of several factors. First, there was a need to create a literate workforce in Britain, one that would have the skills to produce goods as efficiently as the country's industrial competitors. Second, Val Rust (1991) argues that education systems were developed to fit the needs not just of modern industry, but also of modern society as a whole. That is, education systems were designed to promote a sense of national identity, unifying different groups within the modern nation-state and fostering a sense of citizenship. The main problem with the Act was that there was no provision for secondary education. Those secondary schools that did exist were fee-paying. Therefore the schooling system that prevailed served to divide children along class lines – the working classes were in effect denied a secondary education. Indeed, there was an explicit acknowledgement in the governments of the nineteenth century that education should mirror the graduations in society (see Chitty 1993).

### The 1944 Butler Education Act

This Act established compulsory and free secondary education for all (up to the age of fifteen), based on the principal of equality of educational opportunity. The 1944 Act created a tripartite (three-part) system of secondary education. The notion that there was a division between the academic, vocational and practical ability in children was based on research undertaken by the social psychologist Sir Cyril Burt (Livesey and Lawson 2005). These psychological notions about the nature of innate intelligence underpinned the development of the three different types of school. It was claimed that the three types of school would have 'parity of esteem' (equal status). Children were selected for each school on the basis of their '11-plus' exam and channelled into the schools most suited to their talents and abilities. The more academic went to grammar schools; those showing an aptitude for applied science and art went to technical schools; and the rest went to secondary modern schools for a practical education. The Act also established that education should be a partnership between central government, local government through the LEAs (local education authorities) and the schools. Though initially intended to create three types of secondary school, the system never really established technical schools, with the result that secondary education was bipartite rather than tripartite. By 1958, only 4 per cent of secondary schools were technical. The lack of technical schools can be seen as an important argument for the development of vocational education in secondary schooling during the 1980s.

(E)

### Exercise 2.3

To help you evaluate the 1944 Education Act, write down a list of problems, questions or issues you can think of concerning the principles on which the tripartite system of education was based. Here is one to get you started:

* Are there only three types of child? Where would the talented musician or sportsperson fit in?

## Evaluating the 1944 Education Act

The notion of 'parity of esteem' was never realised because the 11-plus was seen as a 'pass or fail' examination which decided a child's educational future. Those who 'passed' and went to the grammar school were likely to encounter a better quality of education in terms of resources and teachers. Hence there were (and still are in some areas of the UK, – such as Kent, which still have the 11-plus) differences in status between grammar and secondary modern schools, and the GCE (General Certificate of Education) O Level qualifications gained in grammar schools were more prestigious than the CSEs (Certificates of Secondary Education) taken in secondary moderns. O Levels were an academic qualification, whereas CSEs were of a more practical or applied nature. A further criticism is that grammar schools were often (but not always) single-sex and there were more boys-only schools than girls-only schools established.

---

### Exercise 2.4

This exercise will help you to develop a full understanding and critique of the tripartite system.

ⓐ 1. Find out which schools in your area were, or still are, part of the tripartite system of secondary education. Are there schools in your area that still have an entrance exam?

ⓘⓔ 2. Identify two arguments that have been made for the tripartite system of education and two arguments that have been made against it.

ⓐⓔ 3. Interview two people who were educated under the tripartite system of schooling. Senior staff at your school or college may have taken the 11-plus and been educated under the tripartite system. Find out the type of school they went to. Ask them whether they felt there was 'parity of esteem' with other schools in the area and get them to explain their answer. What arguments would they make for and against the tripartite system? (Do their answers match those you found for Question 2?)

ⓐ 4. The following is a question taken from an 11-plus paper. Ask five people you know to answer it and give the reason for their choice. You will probably find that there is an acceptable reason for each one to be chosen as the odd one out.

Which is the odd one out?
    House
    Igloo
    Bungalow
    Office
    Hut

The 'correct' answer is Office.

---

## THE COMPREHENSIVE SYSTEM: THE MID-1960s TO THE PRESENT DAY

Comprehensive schools are non-selective institutions that offer free schooling for all types of student under one roof (in 1987, 86 per cent of secondary schools were comprehensive). This system of schooling was introduced following intense criticism of the tripartite system; in particular, the way the selective basis of the system created 'wasted talent' among those who happened to 'fail' the 11-plus. There were more grammar school places for boys, which was partly the result of there being more single-sex schools before 1944. Also a proportion of girls who passed the 11-plus had their marks 'moderated' down to ensure a gender distribution in the grammar schools, otherwise girls would have been in the majority. Attacks on the selection process, based on what were seen as flawed IQ tests, were influential in convincing LEAs, whether Conservative or Labour, of the necessity for comprehensive schooling. It was also obvious that the grammar schools were filled by predominantly middle-class pupils. In particular, critics on the Left argued that the 11-plus was culturally biased in favour of middle-class children. The way forward at this time was seen as mixed ability teaching whereby children of different abilities and levels would be taught in the same classroom by the same teacher through differentiated methods which would cater for diversity in ability, pace and depth of learning of each child.

However, traditionalists were unhappy with the abolition of the grammar schools, which were seen as centres of excellence, and argued that comprehensivisation would only lead to a lowering of educational standards. Against this, social reformers argued that comprehensive schools would not only offer greater social equality, but would also better serve the economic interests of society by 'dredging the pool of talent' (Willis 1983). This meant that comprehensives would allow previously unrecognized talented individuals from the working class to be identified and given the opportunity to contribute to the economic success of society. Comprehensives were therefore seen by both left and right as an attempt to engineer social equality in society. They have subsequently been the focus of much research and comment, and have provided a battleground for those of different political outlooks.

Throughout the 1980s, Conservative governments introduced a number of policy changes that allowed state schools to 'opt-out' of local authority control, to manage their own budgets, employ staff, and to some extent control the entry of children to the school – these were known as Grant Maintained Schools, as they acquired their funding directly from central government. An argument against this 'fragmentation' of the comprehensive system was that it was privatization by the back door. The national curriculum was introduced in 1987 with GCSEs (General Certificates of Secondary Education) replacing O Level and CSE qualifications, and a new type of A Level was brought in. When Labour came to power in 1997 the government set about dismantling some of what had come to be seen as divisive changes and brought Grant Maintained Schools back under local authority control. However, parental choice and league tables had become embedded in educational discourse and remained as means of identifying the 'good' and 'bad' schools that had become characteristic of a two-tier state education system created under the Conservatives and based largely on social factors, such as social class. Additionally, Labour introduced the policy of creating 'specialist' schools, whereby bids were made for funding on the basis of a school becoming a centre of excellence in a particular field such performing or visual arts, sport, science and so on.

The equivalent development in further education was the introduction of COVEs (Centres of Excellence in Vocational Education). A feature of the education policy in the late 1990s and early 2000s was the development of City Technology Colleges, Academies and Trust schools partly sponsored by employers and religious or community groups. Once again, there were supporters and critics of these policies – those in favour, such as the New Left, closely aligned with New Labour, argued that they were necessary for the creation of a more 'personalized' education system, which would benefit more children and raise standards. Critics argued that the system was in disarray, with little evidence of improvements in standards of achievement over the years. See Chapter 3 (pages 28–36) for a more detailed account of these policies and changes to the education system.

## Exercise 2.5

One of the major arguments for comprehensive schools is that they 'mix' together children from diverse social backgrounds and therefore break down divisive social barriers.

(I) 1. Identify two other arguments for comprehensive schools.
(A) 2. Consider how the current education system might undermine the 'comprehensive ideal'.
(I)(A)(E) 3. What might the marking and moderation of the 11-plus tell us about the attainment of girls during the tripartite phase of the education system?

---

### Item A

**Exam Performance and Type of School**

A recurrent debate among politicians and educationalists is whether the type of school affects examination performance. One aspect of this is the relative merits of the private and public sectors in helping students to achieve, but there is little political controversy over the existence of the private sector in schooling. Much more contentious is the argument over whether grammar schools or comprehensive schools do better for their students. The situation is far from clear, precisely because like is not compared with like. Selective schools by their nature contain the more able academic students and therefore, to be fair, the figures for grammar schools should also include their equivalent secondary modern schools, where the non-selected school population goes. At A level the situation is even more confused. Because many students are able to go to Sixth Form Colleges, which until 2008 were independent of the local authority and who could set their own policies for

selection, there is a complicating factor in play. Some SFCs are open access, some are selective in certain subjects, and still others select students on the basis of their ability overall. Despite this complication, the situation in secondary modern schools at Advanced level is static. The percentage of candidates in secondary moderns attaining A grades rose by just 0.1 per cent, from 10.0 per cent in 2002 to 10.1 per cent in 2007. In contrast, the proportion of students in comprehensive schools getting grade A results increased from 16.5 per cent to 19.4 per cent between 2002 and 2007. In colleges, 15.2 per cent of candidates got A grades in 2002, compared with 18.9 per cent in 2007. Between 2002 and 2007, the A grade

Summary of GCSE/equivalent achievement by School Type

|  | Number of pupils | Percentage achieving | | | % entered for GCSEs or equivalent |
|---|---|---|---|---|---|
|  |  | Level 2 | Level 2 (E&M) | Any passes |  |
| Comprehensive | 540,962 | 59.7 | 44.9 | 98.8 | 99.5 |
| Selective | 22,466 | 98.6 | 97.5 | 100.0 | 100.0 |
| Modern | 27,360 | 53.9 | 35.7 | 99.0 | 99.8 |

|  | Number of pupils | Percentage achieving | | | % entered for GCSEs or equivalent |
|---|---|---|---|---|---|
|  |  | Level 2 | Level 2 (E&M) | Any passes |  |
| **All Maintained** | **601,128** | **59.9** | **45.7** | **98.9** | **99.6** |
| Independent | 48,031 | 88.3 | 59.5 | 99.3 | 99.0 |
| **All Schools** | **649,159** | **62.0** | **46.7** | **98.9** | **99.5** |

Notes:
Comprehensive schools include Academies and City Technology Colleges
All maintained includes hospital schools and PRUs
Independent schools included non-maintained special schools

*Source*: GCSE and Equivalent Results in England 2006/07 (revised). DCSF

pass rate for private schools rose from 41.3 per cent to 47.8 per cent. In grammar schools, it increased from 31.3 per cent of candidates to 37.1 per cent.

Figures for the academic year 2005/6 show that 59 per cent of pupils achieved five or more GCSEs at grades A*–C or equivalent, an increase of 14 percentage points since 1997/8; and 64 per cent of girls achieved five or more GCSEs at grades A*–C, compared with 54 per cent of boys. At A level, 37 per cent of students in schools and further education colleges achieved two or more passes, with 72 per cent of those entered for exams achieving passes at grades A–C. There are other factors, such as social class and ethnicity, which have an impact on attainment, with over three-quarters of children from the higher professional occupational groups achieving five or more A–C grades, while just under a third of children with parents from 'routine' occupations did so (see Chapter 4).

Note that these figures are based pon measures that the government uses for 'social status'. Later in the book we shall look in some detail at issues related to educational attainment, and the influence and interplay of social factors – see, in particular, Chapters 4, 5 and 6.

## Exercise 2.6

The following activity focuses on one of the main educational debates – about the effectiveness of different types of schooling on the success or otherwise of students.

Ⓘ 1. With reference to the table in Item A, what percentage of candidates passed English and Maths GCSE exams (Level 2) at comprehensive schools?

ⓘⒶ 2. Identify one implication for comprehensive school students of the differential educational achievement shown in Item A.

ⒶⒺ 3. As Item A indicates, the type of school that a student attends affects his or her chances of achieving at GCSE and Advanced level. Using information from Item A and elsewhere, assess the view that comprehensive schooling has failed to raise educational standards.

Ⓐ 4. Give some explanations for the improvement in attainment at GCSE level between 1997/8 and 2006/7.

For some interesting and up-to-date statistical material about exam results go to: http://www.statistics.gov.uk.

## PRIVATE SCHOOLS

Private schools – or, as they are often known, independent or public schools – exist outside the state sector and are not always required to follow government educational policies. For example, private schools do not have to teach to the national curriculum, nor make their pupils take the SATs. Most private schools tend to offer a traditional academic education (including subjects such as Latin) and charge fees for entry. In 1981, the government tried to make private education more accessible to low-income families by offering to pay all or part of a bright pupil's fees through the Assisted Places Scheme. Some New Right theorists support the Assisted Places Scheme because in their view the traditional academic curriculum of the private sector is superior to the 'progressive' curriculum of the comprehensive sector. They therefore saw the Assisted Places Scheme as part of a desired privatization process in the education system. However, the scheme has been criticized (Whitty 1989) for providing a taxpayer's subsidy to the private schools, while sending to them mainly middle-class children, rather than those from the less wealthy working class. It has also been argued that state financial support for private schools lends important ideological support to these schools (Walford 1993; and see Exercises 2.8 and 2.9 for the wider cases for and against private education).

---

### Item B

Private schools have usually attracted between 5per cent and 7per cent of the school population and were particularly popular during the 'boom' years of the early twenty-first century. However, with the 'credit crunch' of 2008 and the world recession, the impact on enrolments is uncertain. In 2009, applications for the most prestigious schools (known as the 'Headmasters' and Headmistresses' Conference schools – HMC') was up on the previous year by about 1.5 per cent. It is not known whether this increase is the same across the whole private sector, or whether it is at the expense of other private operators in the market place.

## Exercise 2.7

1. According to Item B, what was the increase in the percentage of applications for HMC private schools in 2009?
2. Referring to Item B, why might it be argued that the increase in applications for HMC schools is at the expense of other private operators?

## Exercise 2.8

Referring back to Item A (see p. 14), use any relevant information to make a case for independent (private) schools.

### Other arguments in favour of private schools

1. They give parents greater freedom of choice.
2. Many famous schools, such as Eton, are a precious part of the national heritage and culture.
3. They are not constrained by the national curriculum and have the freedom to experiment with new, 'progressive' methods of teaching. A good example of a private school that takes advantage of these 'freedoms' is Summerhill School in Suffolk.
4. They contribute to diversity in the education system, because they are themselves so diverse.
5. They provide opportunities for a specialised curriculum, so that particular talents can be developed.

---

### Item C

Ex-private-school students dominate the top jobs in British institutions, including the government, the civil service, the Church, the legal system, the armed forces and the financial system in the City. Furthermore, those who control these institutions come overwhelmingly from a few exclusive schools: for example, Eton, Harrow, Winchester and Westminster.

In 1992 the *Whitehall Companion* was published – a 1000-page directory containing biographies of the 980 senior civil servants. The *Whitehall Companion* reveals how far the mandarins of Whitehall share a similar social and educational background. Eight of the twelve biggest departments are run by permanent secretaries, all of whom are men, none of whom are from ethnic minorities, all but one of whom attended either Oxford or Cambridge University (the so-called 'Oxbridge' connection) and all of whom went to private, fee-paying schools.

Those who occupy the top jobs give their sons and daughters the unfair advantage of sponsored mobility. This is achieved by sending them to these same schools and by choosing new recruits for the top jobs from among those who have been to these schools. This restrictive, elite self-recruitment is known as the old school tie (or old boy) network.

*Source*: Adapted from M. Denscombe, *Sociology Update*, Leicester: Olympus Books, 1993.

## Exercise 2.9

Using Item C, in no more than fifty words make a case against private schools.

### Other arguments against public schools

1. Those from private schools who govern may not fully concern themselves with conditions in the schools attended by 93 per cent of the population, as their own children continue to be educated in private schools.
2. Comprehensive schools will not be truly comprehensive and non-selective until 100 per cent of pupils attend them.
3. Fee-paying schools split British society into two: those who can afford to pay and attend them, and those who cannot afford to pay and do not attend them. Thus the existence of private schools is divisive.
4. They are unfair in that they provide an education with small class sizes based on the ability to pay rather than talent.
5. In a society that claims to be a meritocracy, the existence of public schools gives an advantage to a small group in society.

## DEVELOPMENTS IN EDUCATIONAL THINKING AND POLICY SINCE 1976

### Background

The 'great debate' on education began in 1976, when the Labour prime minister at the time, James Callaghan, raised two issues of concern: work and standards.

### *Work*

Education was not geared up to the world of work. It was claimed that schools were failing to produce young workers with marketable skills, and that this was a major factor in the decline in Britain's industrial competitiveness (see Exercise 2.10). While Jim Callaghan saw this decline in relative terms, comparing the economic performance of Britain against that of its industrial competitors, sociologists in the 1980s and 1990s were more interested in the long-term changes that were happening in the world economy in the 1970s as an explanation for Britain's decline. The economic background to the 'great debate' has therefore been the focus of much sociological work, particularly from those sociologists who argue that there has been a fundamental change in the processes of production, under the impact of new technologies and new systems of working. Central to the development of a 'postmodern' economic system is the creation of a global market, through a high-tech information revolution that has made access to all parts of the world relatively easy.

It is therefore argued by postmodernists that traditional 'Fordist' methods of working, such as product standardization and a semi-skilled labour force, are inefficient in a global economy. Fordism emerged as the dominant way of organising production in the early part of the twentieth century. Its most significant features were the breaking down of tasks into smaller and smaller actions, so that the activities of workers could be closely controlled. Management consisted of co-ordinating the activities of large numbers of workers, often positioned along assembly lines, to achieve the most efficient production of large numbers of identical goods. Post-Fordists, such as Murray (1988), suggest that computer technologies have allowed industries to respond to a growing demand by consumers for diversity in goods, through organising work in different ways. For example 'just-in-time' systems of production are made possible through the use of computerized stock-control systems, so that large numbers of production components are not kept in warehouses, thus losing money for the entrepreneur through tying up capital. Instead, computers are used to order and deliver necessary parts only at the point in the production process when they are needed.

One result of post-Fordist production is a change in the way labour is used, and therefore in the type of labour needed by post-Fordist industries. Organisational hierarchies have been flattened, and workers are called upon to be much more flexible in the way they work, employing greater skills than the traditional Taylorist worker, who performed low-skill, repetitive tasks. As Britain's competitiveness in this global economy declined, there was perceived to be a need for a more highly skilled workforce. It was the lack of appropriate response from the education system to this need that underpinned the 'great debate'.

However, how far post-Fordist techniques have penetrated industry is a matter of much dispute. While it is clear that a global economy has taken shape, in which the market is worldwide, this does not mean that every firm, or even the majority of firms are post-Fordist. Indeed, Ainley (1993) argues that post-Fordist production techniques do not result in a universal demand for highly-skilled workers. Rather, post-Fordism polarizes the workforce into a core of highly-skilled and a periphery of deskilled workers – a dual labour market. The level of demand for a skilled workforce in Britain is therefore open to dispute.

## Standards

Educational standards were falling under the influence of 'progressive' teaching. Progressive education was an influential postwar development among British educators, according to New Right sociologists such as Marsland (1988). Progressive education placed the child at the centre of the educational experience and advocated a process of individualized learning, preferably through discovery methods. Critics argued that the employment of 'discovery learning' techniques in schools was holding back children through lack of teacher direction. Progressive education, it was claimed, undermined traditional morality through the promotion of values associated, for example, with feminism and anti-racism, and reduced access to the 'high culture' of Britain, represented by Shakespeare in the English curriculum. In the 1960s, the authors of the *Black Papers* (Cox and Boyson 1975) were calling for a return to traditional values and standards through restoration of the grammar schools and reversal of the postwar moves towards greater equality. The *Black Papers* represented the emergence of New Right ideologies with respect to education (see Exercise 2.10).

## Educational policy following the 'great debate'

The concern about relevance and quality in British education remained long after Callaghan's brief term in office. The Conservative governments of the 1980s and 1990s set out systematically to halt the alleged decline in British education through a series of sweeping educational changes. The policies introduced attempted to vocationalise schooling, and raise the performance and efficiency of individual schools by creating a climate of competition. It should be remembered that these policies were influenced by the work of the New Right 'think tanks', which had developed an ideological challenge to the social democratic ideas that had dominated both major parties since the Second World War. However, the New Right was itself divided: between a 'libertarian' wing, who were in favour of the free market in every sphere of activity, and an 'authoritarian' wing, who on social issues were concerned to establish social order and obedience, above the rights of individuals.

Simon (1988) claims that the whole package of reforms was introduced partly as an attempt to depoliticize the curriculum, widen parental choice and control, instil market forces into education, and enhance the powers of central government and individual schools in the control of education. This was to be achieved primarily through undermining the local education authorities' power to control schools, and introducing a national curriculum, which would be taught in all state schools. It is significant that the egalitarian goal of creating a meritocracy through equality of educational opportunity had largely disappeared from the political agenda. A further point noted by Ball (1990a) is that the Conservatives wanted to re-introduce Greek and Latin to the curriculum, and opposed the teaching of what they saw as 'critical' subjects such as the social sciences.

The vision of a state system of education organized along the lines of a market, with parental choice and devolved management, has been advocated by New Right supporters such as Caldwell and Spinks (1992). While they recognise that there are alternative ways of organising the school system, they argue that pressure from parents and local communities will see the emergence of their preferred system, where state intervention is kept to a minimum and a true free market in education develops, in which a 'culture of service' predominates. However, this has been criticised by Hartley (1994), among others, for not telling the whole story of a 'free market' in education. Hartley argues that local control of schools is accompanied by the apparently contradictory process of central strategic control, through the introduction of the national curriculum and quality control mechanisms via government inspection. According to Hartley, the reason for these parallel developments is that, in a postmodern economy, the administration (central government) can no longer administer on its own, but needs the co-operation of those administered – that is, the clients – to accomplish control. Thus in the social order in schools, and in general, compliance and the transfer of skills from one generation to the next is carried out by 'co-production' – where the state and the subjects together administer a late capitalist society. This involves the processes of centralisation and decentralisation being conducted simultaneously. It is to these developments in the 1980s, 1990s and 2000s that we shall turn in Chapters 3 and 4.

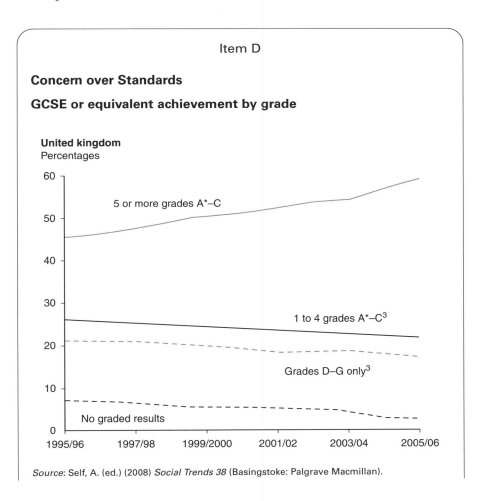

Item D

**Concern over Standards**

**GCSE or equivalent achievement by grade**

**United kingdom**
Percentages

5 or more grades A*–C

1 to 4 grades A*–C[3]

Grades D–G only[3]

No graded results

1995/96    1997/98    1999/2000    2001/02    2003/04    2005/06

*Source*: Self, A. (ed.) (2008) *Social Trends 38* (Basingstoke: Palgrave Macmillan).

Pupils reaching or exceeding expected standards through teacher assessment, by sex

| England | Percentages | | | |
|---|---|---|---|---|
| | 1997 | | 2007 | |
| | Boys | Girls | Boys | Girls |
| **Key Stage 1** | | | | |
| English | | | | |
| Reading | 75 | 85 | 80 | 88 |
| Writing | 72 | 83 | 75 | 86 |
| Mathematics | 82 | 86 | 88 | 91 |
| Science | 84 | 86 | 87 | 90 |
| **Key Stage 2** | | | | |
| English | 57 | 70 | 73 | 83 |
| Mathematics | 63 | 65 | 78 | 78 |
| Science | 68 | 70 | 84 | 85 |
| **Key Stage 3** | | | | |
| English | 52 | 70 | 68 | 81 |
| Mathematics | 62 | 65 | 78 | 80 |
| Science | 60 | 63 | 73 | 76 |

*Source*: Self, A. (ed.) (2008) *Social Trends 38* (Basingstoke: Palgrave Macmillan).

Achievement of 2 or more A levels or equivalent

**England**
Percentages[2]

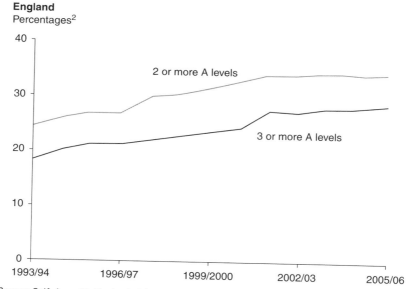

*Source*: Self, A. and L. Zealey (eds) (2007) *Social Trends 37* (Basingstoke: Palgrave Macmillan).

### Item E

Every year, in the summer, when examination results are published, there is a flurry of media stories about whether educational standards are falling. This has been going on since at least the late 1990s, as results at both GCSE and Advanced Level have shown a fairly steady increase. The speculation is that standards of the examination must be falling if such a continuous improvement is to be explained. One of the reasons why this is an important political issue is that the results of educational assessments are used to compare the situation of Great Britain to the rest of the world. The achievements of 16-year-olds in maths, science and the national language in Great Britain have traditionally been below those of the country's nearest industrial competitors such as France, Germany and Japan. In addition, standards of literacy and numeracy among school-leavers has also lagged behind those of other countries'. However, increases in the pass rates at all key stages of the national curriculum and at A level should mean that Britain is 'catching up'. Rather than this being a cause for celebration, though, many commentators argue that the increases are merely the result of 'grade inflation'; that is, an increase in passes, not because we are getting better, but because the exams are getting easier. The government has carried out numerous studies, both generally and in specific subjects, to check what is happening and to explain the increases. The evidence is complicated because examinations do change over time. For example, the change from O Levels to GCSEs included a change from norm-referencing to criterion-referencing grades. This meant that, rather than each grade only being achieved by a pre-determined proportion of candidates, any candidate could achieve any grade as long as she or he matched the description of the grade. Also, the skills that students may show change over time, so that in English, students may be less adept at spelling (relying on the spellchecker over much) but may be more creative in their writing.

## Exercise 2.10

(E)  1. Working with another sociology student, identify two arguments for and two arguments against education directly serving the needs of industry. (If you get stuck on this task, return to it after you have read Chapters 7 and 8.)

(D)(E)  2. Study Items D and E. Identify two arguments for and two arguments against the claim that educational standards are falling. You may be able to collect examination statistics from the past few years from your own school or college to provide some evidence.

Ⓘ 3. You should try to keep yourself up-to-date with the debate on educational standards. It would be a good idea for you to collect recent exam statistics to supplement those we have provided. You could do this nationally by referring to newspapers and periodicals such as *Social Trends,* which is available online, and locally by looking in your school's annual prospectus.

Ⓐ 4. Find out from teachers/lecturers at your school/college what Simon (1988) means when he says that the reforms:

   (a) depoliticise the curriculum;
   (b) widen parental choice and control;
   (c) instil market forces into education; and
   (d) enhance 'the powers of central government and individual schools in the control of education'.

ⒶⒺ 5. Can you suggest any contradictions in the New Right educational aims that Simon identifies?

### Raising standards

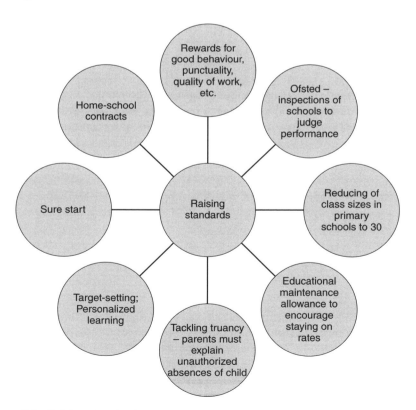

**Figure 2.1**  Raising standards

Social policies continued to be introduced throughout the late 1990s and into the 2000s that were directly related to raising standards. Figure 2.1 gives several examples of these policies that were directly linked to the day-to-day activities of schools. A fuller outline of some of these will be provided in the next chapter.

| Important concepts |
| --- |
| meritocracy • equality of opportunity • parity of esteem • tripartite system • specialist schools • comprehensivization • Fordism • Taylorism |

| Critical thinking |
| --- |
| • Consider how the concerns raised in the Great Education Debate may conflict with a broader view of education which sees individual development, expression and progress as the central point of schooling rather than training for work and measuring standards.<br>• Think of two examples of your experiences at school, college or university that could be said to have nothing to do with the world of work or passing exams.<br>• Give two examples of how the education system cannot be described as a meritocracy. |

*Chapter 3*

# Changes in Curriculum and Assessment in Britain in the 1980s, 1990s and 2000s

By the end of this chapter you should:

- understand the reasons for changes to the curriculum and assessment in the 1980s, 1990s and 2000s, and the competing views expressed about the changes
- have a critical understanding of the new vocationalism
- appreciate conflicting debates surrounding the 1988 Education Act
- recognize the implications of the Dearing Report

## INTRODUCTION

Under the influence of New Right ideas, Conservative governments in the 1980s and 1990s attempted, and to some extent achieved, a change to the educational climate and discourse in Britain. By emphasising vocationalism, standards, parental choice and teacher accountability, they aimed to achieve a more 'entrepreneurial' education system. The broad thrust of Conservative policy has been continued with the Labour governments of the 1990s and 2000s, with its emphasis on choice and diversity. To this end, three broad categories of change can be identified in education and training policy since the 1980s:

1. Changes in traditional examinations and assessment.
2. New vocationalism and new qualifications.
3. The 1988 Education Reform Act and constant assessment.

## CHANGES IN TRADITIONAL EXAMINATIONS AND ASSESSMENT

Four major changes have occurred with regard to examinations and assessment since the mid 1980s: GCSE; AS courses; vocational qualifications; and coursework.

### GCSE

The General Certificate of Education (GCE O Level) and the Certificate of Secondary Education (CSE) were replaced by the General Certificate of Secondary Education (GCSE) in 1987. The aim of the GCSE was to unify the examination system at the age of 16, to avoid the old O Level/CSE hierarchy. The GCSE was therefore aimed at the top 60 per cent of the ability range, though in practice about 80 per cent of students sit GCSE examinations. The GCSE was also designed to test what candidates 'know, understand and can do', rather than just examine the facts they have learnt for the examination. Since the introduction of the GCSE, the proportion of candidates gaining the equivalent of a pass in the old O Level has been rising steadily. As indicated earlier, this has provoked a controversy over the standards of the GCSE. Some New Right commentators have expressed a concern that the GCSE was less demanding than the O Level, and deduced therefore that 'standards are falling'. The examination boards argue that they have maintained the standards of the old O Level, while introducing new forms of assessment that allow more students to demonstrate to markers what they can do. By 2007, the School's Minister, Jim Knight, was congratulating students and teachers on achieving the best-ever English and maths GCSE results, which had shown a sustained improvement during the previous decade (but see Exercise 3.1 below). Knight hailed these results as evidence of improving standards in education resulting from investment in resources and teaching, as well as the introduction of policies designed to raise achievement (Department for Children, Schools and Families (DCSF) website press release, June 2008). In addition, vocational GCSEs, which have a work-related focus and incorporate work experience, were introduced in 2002 and are equivalent to two traditional GCSEs. These courses are preparation for post-16 vocational courses.

## Item A

### One million pupils 'failed by Labour exam policy'

According to the right-wing think tank, the Bow Group, by 2007 nearly a million young people had failed to achieve even the lowest G grade in GCSE since the Labour Party came to power in 1997. Despite the improvement to the numbers achieving five grade A–C GCSEs, there are growing numbers 'at the bottom of the pile', according to the report *The Failed Generation: The Real Cost of Education under Labour* published by the Bow Group in 2008. According to Chris Skidmore, chairman of the Bow Group, employers have warned young people that failing to get five grade A–C GCSEs will result in a high risk of not getting a job. The National Confederation of Parent Teacher Associations had also queried the use of the GCSE qualification for those who have little chance of passing. The group argues that more vocational education would be of benefit lifelong for many pupils, and give them a better chance of getting a job as well as being a better use of taxpayers' money.

The Department for Children, Schools and Families claim that, when Labour came to power, half of all secondary schools were failing to get 30 per cent of their pupils to the benchmark of five good GCSEs, whereas this figure is now down to a fifth of schools. Also, schools at the lowest levels are receiving intensive support to improve standards and attainment rates.

*Source*: Adapted from an article by Anushka Asthana, *The Observer*, 20 April 2008.

## Exercise 3.1

1. With reference to Item A, above, how many pupils did not achieve at least five basic G grades when they left school?
2. According to Skidmore, what have employers warned about the lack of achievement of at least five GCSEs in relation to getting jobs?
3. As Item A indicates, there is criticism of the GCSE system, which seems to be failing so many young people. With reference to other sociological material, explain the reasons why, according to the Bow Group, there is a relatively low pass rate for GCSEs.

## AS courses

Advanced Supplementary (AS) courses, roughly 'half an A Level', were introduced to run alongside Advanced (A) Levels. Their introduction was a response to concern about the narrowness of the post-16 curriculum. Unlike many of Britain's industrial competitors, students specialize in particular subjects at the relatively early age of 16. This specialization, it is argued, is bad for Britain's economic performance, as it discourages students from pursuing scientific subjects beyond the age of 16. However, as Conservative governments during the 1980s and 1990s consistently defended A levels as the 'gold standard' of the education system, the opportunities to change the post-16 curriculum have been limited by the insistence on maintaining these A levels. Therefore AS courses were introduced as an attempt to broaden the experiences of post-16 students without affecting A level provision. The original intention was to allow those specialising in arts or sciences to study subjects beyond those of their immediate interest by following a complementary AS course. However the take up of AS nationally was relatively small, with only the social science subjects having any significant entry. General National Vocational Qualifications (GNVQs) were introduced in the 1990s as an alternative to A Levels, and once they had become more manageable to deliver after the Capey Review ( NCVQ 1995), established themselves 'as a niche' in the 16–19 curriculum (Hodgson and Spours 2007). Part I GNVQs began to be introduced into the 14–16 curriculum, to provide an alternative qualification for younger pupils who had been 'alienated' by the traditional curriculum.

In 2000, a new A Level regime was introduced, with a first-year Advanced Subsidiary (A/S) course and an A2 second year. The AS and A2 became standalone qualifications. Students were expected to take more subjects to broaden their general post-16 education. Alongside this, the Advanced Certificate in Vocational Education (AVCE) was introduced to address criticisms that had emerged about the standards of GNVQs. AVCEs turned out to be closer to A Levels, more academic, less vocational and therefore were not taken up in large numbers, and were sometimes replaced by Business and Technology Education Council (BTEC) National Diplomas in further education (FE) colleges. See below for a more detailed account of these changes.

## Vocational qualifications

Two new qualifications aimed at bridging the academic and vocational divide were created. First, there is the job-specific National Vocational Qualification (NVQ). NVQs are industry-specific qualifications that are designed to test the competence of those taking them. That is, NVQs test not just knowledge, but also skills and understanding. These competences are tested in application, rather than just in examinations, so that NVQ candidates have to demonstrate their competence in work (or simulated work) situations. It is thus the *performance* of candidates, rather than merely their knowledge, that is the basis of NVQ assessment.

Moreover, NVQs allow prior learning to be accredited and they adopt a modular approach, so that students can build up their qualification through a planned process rather than leaving everything to the final examination. Another important dimension of NVQs is that students are empowered through being encouraged to take more responsibility for their own learning. This is achieved, according to Stanton (1990), largely through the action planning process, where students, in consultation with their tutors, chart their own way through the course.

Second, the broad vocational General National Vocational Qualification (GNVQ) was developed by various examination boards, under the umbrella of the National Council for Vocational Qualifications (NCVQ). These courses were not job-specific, but were designed to meet the vocational needs of related groups of occupations, such as health and social care. They were developed using the model of NVQs, and incorporated much of the practice associated with the more specific qualifications. For example, there was an emphasis on core skill modules, such as numeracy and information technology, later to become Key Skills, which also included literacy. The GNVQ was related explicitly to A levels, in that the courses were described in A level-equivalent terms. Thus an Advanced GNVQ was the equivalent of two A Levels. GNVQs operated across the 14–19 curriculum to offer an alternative route to jobs and higher education for older students. Intermediate GNVQs were also introduced, which were vocational equivalents to four GCSEs.

These developments have been generally welcomed, not least by many students for whom they offer a non-academic alternative. This can be seen in the increasing post-16 stay-on rates. Moreover, they have been welcomed by many educationalists as an alternative to the A Level route to higher education for those students who have found the traditional Advanced Levels inappropriate. One of the criticisms of traditional A Levels has been the low completion and high failure rate associated with them. For example, a significant minority of students had followed an A Level course for two years, but emerged from it with no qualifications. Many others drop out from A Levels as they experienced difficulty with the highly academic and abstract nature of some courses.

Concern was expressed about the standard of GNVQs, most notably by Smithers (1993), who argued that they were not the equivalent of A Levels or GCSEs and represented a downgrading of the important theoretical aspects of vocational training adhered to by our industrial competitors. Others, such as

Jones (1993), argue that GNVQs were just as rigorous as A Levels but in a different way, and identify more clearly than A Levels the capability of an individual. Another criticism was that GNVQs are no more likely than A levels to ensure that those who begin the course will emerge with the full qualification at the end. For example, a survey of twelve GNVQ colleges (FEU, 1994) showed that the completion rate for the intermediate GNVQ science course was just 60 per cent across the twelve colleges, compared with 90 per cent who completed the first year of their A Level course. To address some of the issues and criticisms concerning standards, after the Capey review the GNVQ was reinvented in 2000 to become the AVCE (Advanced Vocational Certificate of Education), which aligned the course more closely with academic qualifications. However, according to Hodgson and Spours (2007), this did little to improve their popularity or take-up and, in FE colleges, their lack of vocational content and more demanding assessment requirements led to a reversion to BTEC National Diplomas. AVCEs are now referred to as Applied A Levels (see below).

## Exercise 3.2

The following activities will help you to explore the differences between academic and vocational subjects, as perceived by those who are involved with them.

1. Interview two teachers who have taught both A Level and vocational subjects. Devise five questions (use open-ended and closed questions; also think about prompts you could use) that will enable you to understand the differences in the two areas. One of your questions could be about their personal preference and reasons for this. An example of a question is provided here for guidance:

    What would you say are the main differences in the assessment of A Levels and vocational subjects?

2. Interview two students who have taken a mix of academic and vocational courses in Years 12 and 13. Devise five questions to find out about their experiences of taking the two qualifications. You could relate questions to the ones you devised for the teachers in order to do a comparison. Again, there is a question here to get you started:

    Could you describe the differences in teaching between your A Level subject and vocational one?

A more fundamental criticism of the development of these courses, with their credit accumulation and continuous assessment, has come from the postmodernists. Usher and Edwards (1994) do not accept the argument that continuous assessment is in some way 'better' than end-of-course examination. They argue that continuous assessment is a more stressful form of assessment, and ties the student into a huge web of bureaucratic documentation; and that independent thought is squeezed out by every action and piece of work being open to assessment and codification as a 'competence'. They see the development of this type of education as an example of the increased surveillance associated with postmodern societies, as outlined by Michel Foucault (see, for example, Foucault, 1982). The concept of surveillance is used by postmodernists to describe the processes of social control in postmodern societies. Premodern societies depended on physical force to control the population. Social control in societies characterized by modernity is more likely to be achieved through the rule of law. In postmodern societies, individuals tend to 'police' themselves through ways of thinking and behaving (discourses) that define what is seen as 'normal' or 'abnormal' in society. Surveillance in this sense does not include the direct gaze of the teacher. Rather, it consists of the competences that have to be demonstrated in order to gain the qualification. In effect, Usher and Edwards argue that students become the qualification, as their public identity is defined by their progress towards achieving the competences. They exercise surveillance of themselves as they chart their own progress through their course, carrying out appropriate behaviours for the stage they have reached.

## Coursework

Coursework was introduced as part of the assessment for examination courses followed by 14–18-year-olds. Coursework is where the student offers material prepared by him or her for assessment outside the main examination. This may take the form of projects or classroom activities of various types. It was pioneered within the GCSE programme, but has also been adopted in many A level courses. The emphasis on coursework has been boosted by the emergence of GNVQs, where students have to build up a 'portfolio of evidence' based on a variety of activities. However, there has been government opposition to coursework in academic examinations, and as a consequence the percentage of coursework in most academic examinations has been restricted to 20 per cent. Concern about coursework has centred on the opportunities for candidates to cheat and to obtain help from others, notably parents. While Scott (1990) found that there was some input from parents in terms of providing opportunities and resources for their children, it was not widespread. Coursework seems to be a popular option with students as it provides them with opportunities to gain marks outside the examination room.

The introduction of coursework became part of a wider movement in education towards experiential learning. Experiential methods of teaching do not rely on the 'teacher-expert' teaching students an accepted body of knowledge. Rather, it is a way of teaching that relies on students exploring for themselves issues of interest, and thus gaining knowledge of something through their own experience of it. While experiential learning has been welcomed by many types of educationalist, postmodernists such as Usher and Edwards (1994) argue that experiential learning fits well with the postmodern culture in which we live. Postmodernists argue that all knowledge is relative, and that there is no such thing as the absolute truth. Instead, there are only multiple and partial realities based on the perspectives of individuals and groups in society. Postmodern societies are characterized by a shift away from book learning to an emphasis on images and experience as sources of knowledge. There can be, in postmodern societies, no right or wrong pieces of knowledge, because what we know depends on where we stand in social formations, such as what groups we belong to or identify with, and the sense and understanding we bring to bear on our experience. Postmodernists describe this as the 'situatedness' of the individual in the social formation. As Baudrillard (1983) argues, when what is 'real' is no longer so certain or accepted by everybody; and there is more emphasis on lived experience as a source of knowledge. Experiential learning therefore expresses at the level of education what is being experienced in the wider society.

Usher and Edwards (1994) argue that the perceived effects of experiential learning are contradictory. Experiential learning is seen by the New Right as an important counterbalance to the influence of progressive teachers, who are believed to dominate the world of education. The assumption here is that experience of the 'real' world will lay bare the falseness of left-wing ideology. More left-wing views see experiential learning as an emancipatory technique, freeing the individual learner from the tyranny of received knowledge delivered by an authoritarian teacher. Usher and Edwards stress how this contradiction is itself a 'real' one, existing at the same time in the same situation, and never to be resolved with victory for one viewpoint or another.

With the introduction of the specialized diplomas in 2008 and beyond, coursework has been more or less abandoned. Coursework in recent times has been viewed as an unsatisfactory form of assessment, as the variations in parental and teacher input could never be properly measured or controlled. It has therefore been seen as an unfair system on which to base the assessment of a child's performance. However, advanced students should have the opportunity to complete individual 'extended projects' during their course. See below for a more detailed account of changes to the 14–19 curriculum, and you can explore the pros and cons of the changes in Exercises 3.3 and 3.4).

(A)

## Link Exercise 3.1

From your own experience, explain how any two changes to examinations and assessment fit in with new vocational thinking. (Hint: consider the ways in which the courses and assessment methods give school leavers transferable skills; that is, skills they can use in the workplace.) This exercise may best be attempted when you have read the section on new vocationalism later in this chapter.

(I)(A)(E)

## Exercise 3.3

Working with two other sociology students, hold a debate on the merits and drawbacks of the changes in examinations and assessment. One of you should act as a chair to the debate, one should argue the merits of the changes, and the other should argue their drawbacks. The chair should ensure that the two speakers have an equal amount of time to make their case and that the debate is conducted in an orderly fashion. The two debaters should prepare their arguments carefully by doing some thorough background research into the changes. Each debater should know exactly what the new courses and forms of assessment are, how they differ from their predecessors, and the merits or drawbacks of the changes. If you are feeling brave, try to hold the debate in front of an audience, perhaps your sociology class. The audience could have a vote on who made the most convincing argument.

(I)(E)

## Exercise 3.4

Keep yourself up-to-date on the issues surrounding examinations and assessment by reading the educational media. You should jot down any arguments that add to those you came across during Exercise 3.3.

## NEW VOCATIONALISM AND NEW QUALIFICATIONS

New vocationalism refers to the educational initiatives that emerged in the 1980s and 1990s and continued in the 2000s in an attempt to make educational provision more responsive to industry's needs; for example, the Technical and Vocational Education Initiative. Of course, there has always been a concern to match the educational system to the demands of industry, but new vocationalism differs from previous attempts in three important ways. Watson (1993) argues that (i) new vocationalism attempts to bridge the gap between general and vocational education, rather than seeing them as separate; (ii) new vocational qualifications are awarded after proof of acquisition of particular competences, and not by serving a particular length of time in an apprenticeship; and (iii) flexible 'transferable' skills replace the narrow job-specific skills of previous attempts at vocational education.

The seven most prominent developments in new vocationalism during this period were:

1. The Youth Training Scheme (YTS).
2. Employment Training (ET).
3. The Technical and Vocational Education Initiative (TVEI).
4. The Certificate of Pre-vocational Education (CPVE).
5. City Technology Colleges (CTCs).
6. General National Vocational Qualifications (GNVQs), Advanced Certificate in Vocational Education (AVCEs) and Applied A levels.
7. Modern Apprenticeships.

Governments in power when these policies have been introduced have claimed that, through such developments, employers will receive workers who have the necessary skills to make effective use of modern technology, and thereby improve the productivity and economic performance of individual firms and the country as a whole.

## The Youth Training Scheme (YTS)

This has its origins in the Youth Opportunities Programme (YOP), which ran from 1978 to 1983. From 1986, the YTS offered a two-year training programme for 16-year-old school leavers who were unemployed after leaving school. The scheme consisted of structured, work-based training, with a minimum of twenty weeks' on-the-job training over the two-year period. By 1988, all 16–17-year-olds were guaranteed a place on a YTS programme if they wanted one. However, they lost their entitlement to income support at the same time.

In 1990, the YTS was replaced by Youth Training (YT) (see Exercise 3.5 to consider the arguments for and against Youth Training). In 1991, responsibility for Youth Training provision passed from the nationally organized Manpower Services Commission (MSC) to local Training and Enterprise Councils (TECs) in England and Wales, and Local Enterprise Companies (LECs) in Scotland. The key difference between YTS and YT is that trainees were offered a programme that varies in length according to the needs and development of the person being trained. Youth trainees are also now able to work towards National Vocational Qualifications (NVQs).

Moore and Hickox (1994) see the introduction of YTS and its successors as part of the New Right agenda, which, while leaving existing educational arrangements alone, has provided an alternative agency (eventually the Training Agency) offering courses that might prove attractive to those young people (and adults under the ET scheme) who are not keen to follow a traditional educational route to qualifications. Moreover, the providers of YTS courses were able to intervene directly in the further education sector, which undermined the principle of educational autonomy from the state.

## Employment Training (ET)

Employment Training (ET) was introduced in 1988 in order to meet the individual training needs of unemployed adults. This programme merged with Employment Action (EA) in 1993 and now bears the title 'Training for Work'. As with YT, Training for Work operates under the auspices of the TECs/LECs. The aim is to provide the unemployed, especially the long-term unemployed, with skills and attitudes that will be attractive to employers. However, the merged Training for Work programme has been criticized because it represents a reduction in the training entitlement of the unemployed from twenty-six to twenty weeks. Moreover there is no mandatory training element to the work experience offered under Training for Work, and the take-up of places has therefore been slow and the drop-out rate high (see Kirby, 1993).

## The Technical and Vocational Education Initiative (TVEI)

Known as the Technical and Vocational Extension (TVE), the TVEI was not a course. It was a way of organising and managing the education of 14–18-year-olds across the whole ability range. Its central purpose was to widen and enrich the curriculum so that young adults were prepared in a practical and relevant way for the world of work. Notable developments within the original TVEI framework included work experience placements with local employers, records of achievement, and providing or widening the provision of information technology in schools and colleges. The TVEI was seen as a way in which schools could provide access to the 'enterprise culture', whereby young people would be exposed to the 'entrepreneurial spirit'. The TVEI was financed through the Manpower Services Commission and designed to challenge existing practices in schools. This was achieved, according to Weiner (1990), through a 'carrot-dangling' process, in which extra funds were made available to schools pursuing certain types of vocational activity. But she also argues, along with Finn (1985), that such initiatives, rather than being committed to equal opportunity, signalled the end of any commitment to the principle that had been central to educational policy since the Second World War.

## The Certificate of Pre-vocational Education (CPVE)

The CPVE was a one-year, full-time course for post-16-year-old students in schools and colleges. The course consisted of three components:

1. The core, which included areas such as applied numeracy, science, technology and information technology.
2. Vocational studies, which included modules such as business and administrative services, and distribution.
3. Additional studies: these were not compulsory, and included GCSEs and leisure studies.

In addition to these three components, students undertook a work experience programme for a minimum of fifteen days.

The main successes of the CPVE and other foundation vocational courses were increased motivation and attendance (Spours and Young, 1988), thereby showing that vocational courses did have a constituency among young people. However, while the CPVE was seen as meeting the needs of some underachieving students, it was also criticized for introducing new social divisions, as those graduating from the CPVE found it difficult to access more academic courses, such as the GCSE.

The CPVE was replaced in 1992 by the Diploma in Vocational Education (DVE). This course was open to a wider age range (14–19 years) and had three levels: foundation, intermediate and national. It signalled the emergence of a national system of vocational qualifications, which were equated directly with traditional academic qualifications through the GNVQ system.

## City Technology Colleges (CTCs)

A limited number of CTCs were set up for 11–19-year-olds in large towns and inner city areas. They are independent of local authority control and were established in part with the aid of industrial sponsorship. While conforming to the requirements of the national curriculum, emphasis is given to science, mathematics and technology. For example, 60 per cent of the timetable for 14–16-year-olds is devoted to these subjects. CTCs have fostered close links with industry and offer work experience at an early age. They are modelled on the 'magnet schools' in the USA, where schools are allowed to offer specialisms to attract particular types of student.

Criticism of the CTCs has concentrated on the lack of industrial support for their establishment, with the result that the government has had to inject large amounts of cash (Ball, 1990a). The consequence of this has been, according to critics, to skew local markets in schools in such a way as to make the job of local education authorities more difficult. Moreover CTCs have been established as much in middle-class suburbs as in inner city areas, thus reducing their 'revitalisation role'. OFSTED inspectors of some CTCs have at times been critical of the education provided in these colleges.

### GNVQs, AVCEs, Applied A levels

We have already looked at the development of General National Vocational Qualifications (GNVQs) and the more recently introduced Advanced Vocational Certificate of Education (AVCE) in the section on 'Changes in Examinations and Assessment'. GNVQs and AVCEs were important elements of new vocationalism, as they were an attempt to produce examination qualifications that equal those obtained through the academic route of GCSE, A levels and traditional university degrees. They were also qualifications that were supposedly work-related in their focus, and provided students with skills ready for employment. Applied A levels is the term now applied more commonly to vocational qualifications, and these are a different educational route taken by a proportion of pre- and post-16 students.

### Modern Apprenticeships

In 2004, the government introduced a range of industry-related apprenticeships, which combined key skills with an NVQ qualification and a technical Certificate through BTEC or City and Guilds. An apprenticeship is a structured programme of on-the-job training working with an employer to build up knowledge and transferable skills in a vocational area. Apprentices earned a wage of between £70 and £80 per week in 2008. Although the take-up of these apprenticeships has been disappointing, the Learning and Skills Council, which funds the scheme, is determined to improve the popularity and marketing of more than 2,000 apprenticeships available. There are five tiers of apprenticeship, starting with a young apprenticeship for 14–16-year-olds; a pre-apprenticeship at level 1; an apprenticeship at level 2 (equivalent to GCSE); an advanced apprenticeship at level 3 (equivalent to A level); and an adult apprenticeship for those over the age of 25.

## Exercise 3.5

1. The chart below gives two arguments for and two arguments against YT. Copy out and then complete the chart by identifying four other arguments for and against YT. When considering the arguments for YT, you will find it useful to consult the literature on YT in your local careers library.

| Arguments for YT | Arguments against YT |
| --- | --- |
| 1. You get paid a wage or allowance while you learn. | 1. YT is a way of disguising the 'true' rate of youth unemployment. |
| 2. You can gain vocational qualifications while working. | 2. YT lacks status and many school-leavers feel stigmatized by joining a YT programme. |

2. Try to contact two people who have undertaken or are currently undertaking a YT programme. Show them your list of arguments for and against YT. Do they agree with the arguments you have identified? Try to get them to back up their views with their actual experiences. Overall, are they in favour of YT or not? Can they add to the list of arguments for and against YT? Share and discuss your findings with another sociology student.

3. In no more than 100 words, write your conclusions about the desirability of YT. (Hint: it is important that you state which of the two views of YT you find most plausible, and why.)

4. Take any new vocational initiative other than YT and investigate the arguments for and against its introduction. Which viewpoint do you find most convincing, and why? You may find it useful to look at past copies of *The Times Educational Supplement* or the education features in 'quality' newspapers. Making use of relevant CD ROMs will prove helpful. Teachers in your school or college could also be a valuable source of information.

---

### Exam Focus

You should now be familiar with new vocationalism of the 1980 and 1990s which placed an emphasis on *training* as opposed to education and the various viewpoints expressed about it. The question and answer exercise that follows is based loosely on areas that you are expected to know and understand for exam questions. It should help you to clarify your understanding of the debates surrounding new vocationalism and give you an insight into what constitutes good and bad practice when writing answers to examination questions. It will also provide you with more detailed knowledge about this important area.

## (Continued)

Before you begin this exercise you must read the following carefully:

- Item B and the question.
- The student responses.
- Comments on the responses.

Once you have completed the reading, mark the remaining two student responses. You should gauge the standard from the previously marked responses and comments. You should award each response a whole mark between 0 and 8. Make sure you justify your marking with comments, as in the other three student responses.

### Item B

Marxist sociologists believe that it was no coincidence that the new vocationalism arrived at a time of high youth unemployment. Writers such as Finn are of the view that youth training schemes and the new vocationalism generally provided cheap labour for employers, or put trainees in 'pretend jobs' with no prospect of real employment. Similarly, Bates and Riseborough argue the key features of the new vocationalism were that the training route was aimed at black and working-class students to keep them out of trouble and off the streets, as a form of social control, at the same time as lowering youth unemployment statistics. Furthermore, some employers were given subsidies for the young people they took on to 'train', thus lowering their wage costs. Feminists were also critical of the ways in which there was a gender divide in the vocational areas on offer, with girls being encouraged into the traditional areas of hairdressing, social care and nursing.

*Source*: Adapted from Livesey and Lawson 2005.

### Question

Item B suggests that the aim of the new vocationalism was an attempt to control young people by introducing 'training and skills' to the curriculum at a time of high youth unemployment, rather than to align the education system more closely to the needs of industry and the economy, as argued by the government. Discuss how some sociologists have explained these alternative aims. Using information from Item B and elsewhere, evaluate sociological accounts of the new vocationalism. (*8 marks*)

## Student answers

### CANDIDATE A

Durkheim has highlighted his views and argues that the various education systems, including vocational courses, exist to provide the workforce with the various skills required. Before industrialization, these skills were provided by parents in certain trades (for example, blacksmiths), but then the division of labour became too specialized and a scheme was needed. Many sociologists (especially Marxists) believe that education is not needed, and that on-the-job training is sufficient because education over-educates the workforce and allows the capitalist economy to control the workers. Durkheim also believes that the vocational system transmits the norms and values of society so that people do not deviate from mainstream culture.

Bowles and Gintis, however, argue that the system creates a set of myths, which in turn create a submissive, passive worker ready to do a lot of work for very little recognition. They believe that a meritocracy has developed, and this has led people to believe that their success is dependent on their educational achievement, and that those who work the hardest will reach the top. But this is not always true. Marxists believe that privilege breeds privilege, and that no matter what education people receive, the middle class will always reach the top as they have the means to get there. Marxists believe that the system is for the working class, yet it teaches them how to cope with their low place in society, not how to improve themselves.

## Mark and comments

*2 marks.* This answer is an attempt to apply the ideas of Durkheim, and Bowles and Gintis, to the issue of vocationalism. However, the answer does not focus precisely enough on the issue of vocationalism and much irrelevant material is included. In passing, the answer suggests that vocational schemes were needed to provide the workforce with skills that parents could no longer give their children (a positive view), and that the system is intended to produce a particular attitude in workers (a negative view). Though other bits of the material could have been made relevant, they were not applied to the question set. Nor did the answer interpret Item B effectively, or attempt to assess the two positions that were suggested.

### CANDIDATE B

Marxists would disagree that the aim of the new vocationalism is to create a better skilled and trained workforce. They believe that the creation of the YTS by the MSC and other training schemes have been introduced by the capitalists, who use their power and control of the state as a way of gaining a pool of cheap labour to further their profits. The young are easily exploited, have little public voice and are unlikely to be unionized. Westergaard and Resler claim

## (Continued)

that these attitudes were actually capitalist ones that reinforced capitalist ideology and domination. They encouraged workers to accept the status quo and the belief that the situation was their own fault because of their educational 'failure'. This could be used to distract attention from the inequalities of the capitalist system.

Other sociologists see these schemes as a way in which the government disguises unemployment figures, and so directs attention away from the failings of policies. Functionalists see the policies of the government on new vocationalism as an extension of the meritocratic educational system, whereby everybody has the same chance to achieve success.

These work schemes would further collective goals and benefit the interests of society as a whole, and ensure and maintain stability, not conflict, among those who, because of unemployment, may become marginal in society.

I think that, on balance, sociological accounts have tended to be more critical of vocational schemes than supportive.

### Mark and comments

*5 marks.* This answer is a more successful attempt to apply Marxist and functionalist positions to the issue of new vocationalism. There is also a suggestion of a third position concerning unemployment figures. The use of Marxist and functionalist ideas here is more focused on the schemes, and the answer also includes appropriate evidence. In addition, it employs information from Item B as a starting point for a discussion of the Marxist position. The answer displays appropriate knowledge, accurately reproduced. An attempt at evaluation, though limited, does emerge from the main body of the answer, where the bulk of the evidence supports a criticism of the schemes. To score more, this would have to be extended somewhat, for example by looking at the ideological positions of the supporters and critics of the schemes.

### CANDIDATE C

Some sociologists, for example, Paul Thompson, a Marxist, believe that schemes such as 'YT' produce a pool of workers who are prepared to do low-skilled, low-paid jobs. This is echoed by many who believe that vocational schemes are slave labour. The Marxists especially criticize them, saying that they support capitalism. This is because they provide cheap labour, which is done by youths who are relatively fit and healthy. Other sociologists believe that vocationalism does not succeed because there are no jobs for trainees to go to once they have finished the course. They criticize the government because YT trainees cannot claim benefit and thus have to rely on the often meagre earnings that employers pay them. They also claim that the government can keep down unemployment figures, since those on a vocational scheme are not registered as unemployed.

Sociologists have argued that young people become bored and feel dejected if they have to do basic jobs such as sweeping floors. They also believe that employers would rather have workers with academic skills and therefore few employ Youth Training students. On the other hand YT can be useful in such industries as engineering, where practical skills are acquired by experience.

In conclusion, on the basis of the evidence presented one is inclined to favour the sociologists' view that YT is not the answer. The government seems resistant to putting money into a scheme to help create jobs. Until it does, vocational training will continue to be unsuccessful.

## Mark and comments

*4 marks.* Again, this answer reveals some knowledge of the schemes offered under new vocationalism. However it offers a very one-sided, negative view of the schemes. While evidence is supplied to support this negative position, such as the work of Paul Thompson, the only positive view of the schemes is an interpretation of Item B. It is therefore unsurprising that, by depending mainly on sociological accounts, the writer has chosen to support the critics of vocational schemes. This answer is therefore an unbalanced, albeit straightforward, account of the issue under consideration and can only attract a limited number of marks.

## CANDIDATE D

New vocationalism has its foundations in the 1988 Act. It has advantages, such as training young people in the skills needed for jobs and the workforce. The government has introduced MSC, YT and ET, which are all beneficial to society. Functionalists would say youth training skills are important for industry. Conservative sociologists would agree with Item A and say that the new vocationalism provides specific skills rather than the general education that is typical of schools. Criticism of the new vocationalism is that sociologists who are liberal and social democratic would completely disagree. They say that vocationalism exploits young people. Industry is using the young and the government is just disguising the unemployment statistics.

## Mark and comments

To be completed by you.

## CANDIDATE E

Item A suggests that 'new vocationalism' is aimed at training people, teaching them skills and better attitudes to work, and providing a skilled workforce. Dan Finn claims that a document was leaked to *Time Out* showing the government's real aims were to reduce unemployment statistics, provide cheap labour, lower wages and ensure social control over the young to prevent

---

**(Continued)**

crime. He says that the government's claim that training school leavers will reduce youth unemployment is false and a cover-up, since training cannot create more new jobs. He also believes that such training schemes indoctrinate the young into being an obedient, docile and highly conformist workforce that will not threaten the status quo. Stan Cohen argues they actually de-skill the workforce and Paul Willis *et al.* argue that they keep youth in 'suspended animation' before getting a job.

Others have argued that new vocationalism has created a two-tiered system, in which schools such as CTCs and those which have opted out have better resources, better teachers, 'enrichment programmes' and can be selective, thus attracting only the best pupils. Therefore new vocationalism has reduced equality of opportunity in schools and parity of esteem, turning the clock back to the tripartite system and its inequalities. It is also argued that the long-term plan of the 'New Right' is to privatize education, which would be setting the clock back further and creating a great deal of inequality. Many criticize the new schemes for not addressing the issues of gender and race, nor the issue of cultural definitions of knowledge that reduce equality of opportunity by enforcing the white, male, middle-class view of what constitute valuable skills and knowledge.

The views of Marxists such as Finn and Willis are perhaps questioned because they are influenced by Marxist ideology and have a vested interest in showing how new vocationalism is exploitative. They also claim that new vocationalism supports their theory that the function of education is to fulfil the needs of capitalists and the economy, since it has put the needs of industry before the development of the individual's capabilities; and through vocationalism the government has been able to gain greater control over what is taught and how it is taught, outlawing subjects such as peace studies and methods such as progressive teaching that oppose their political beliefs.

**Mark and comments**

To be completed by you.

(**Note**: Student answers D and E above obtained 3 and 6 marks, respectively.)

---

**Vocationalism**

Vocationalists (those who promote the vocational element in education) are not a new phenomenon and can be found in every post-Second World War period. Moore and Hickox (1994) suggest that the importance of vocationalist strands in education is associated with the perceived need to increase the skill levels of British society in order to improve economic performance in an increasingly competitive world. The expansion of vocational education and training in the 1980s and 1990s is therefore associated with the need to increase the number staying on in education beyond the age of 16, by providing new types of courses, new ways of delivering content to students and new ways of assessing students. Vocationalists therefore claim that vocational courses are more 'relevant' than traditional courses, because they correspond closely to the 'real' needs of students and the 'real' needs of the economy.

However, Moore and Hickox also argue that vocationalism in the 1980s and 1990s had become detached from its usual 'liberal' proponents and become attached to the New Right agenda of changing the culture of British institutions, such as the education system. The aim of New Right theorists is to promote an 'enterprise' culture in education, rather than the 'liberal' and 'radical' culture of the 1960s, with its emphasis on individual fulfilment and the empowerment and upward social mobility of disadvantaged groups, such as the working class and ethnic minorities (see, for example, DES 1974). Some New Right vocationalists are therefore critical of the traditional academic curriculum, because they see it as elitist and irrelevant to the real world of work. Finn (1987) identifies this New Right critique as also being hostile to the vocational programmes of the 1970s, with their emphasis on trade union membership and workers' rights.

The concern of New Right vocationalists is therefore to use central control of the curriculum to promote an education system that encourages an entrepreneurial spirit in schoolchildren, and in which the content of the curriculum is related much more directly to the skills requirements of industry, through an emphasis on the acquisition of competencies rather than abstract knowledge. The New Right vocationalists therefore look to the German model of education, as described by Barnett (1986), as a way of ensuring that Britain produces a workforce with the high levels of skill required for a post-Fordist economy.

This approach, with its emphasis on central control, has been criticized for going against the central belief of the New Right: that the market should decide the content and outcomes of the education system. The New Right vocationalists argue that education is too important a resource to be left to market forces, where existing views on what constitutes useful education could crowd out the newer vocational approaches. The New Right vocationalists are also in conflict with other New Right strands, such as that of Scruton (1984), where the emphasis is on a traditional, subject-based curriculum, combined with respect for traditional authority.

The whole vocational approach has also come under criticism from some sociologists, such as Moore and Hickox (1994). They argue that it is impossible to forecast with any degree of certainty what the future needs of industry might be, and it is therefore impossible to create a vocational education system that is responsive to those needs. Moreover, Jones and Moore (1993) argue that the notion of competence employed by the New Right is a very narrow one and does not include the deeper intellectual competencies that are necessary to develop the flexible workforce needed in a post-Fordist economy.

## THE 1988 EDUCATION REFORM ACT AND CONSTANT ASSESSMENT

The 1988 Education Reform Act was arguably the most wide-ranging piece of educational legislation since the 1944 Education Act. The two most significant aspects of the Act pertaining to the curriculum and assessment are outlined below. We shall look at three other changes brought by the Act when we look in Chapter 4 at structural changes in education from the 1980s.

### The national curriculum

This was implemented in an attempt to create a broad and balanced, standardized, formal curriculum. By formal curriculum we mean the subjects that are offered to students for study in school. The introduction of the national curriculum was significant because it shifted the balance of power over the school curriculum. No longer were a diverse set of interest groups (local education authorities, teachers, exam boards, university academics) controlling the curriculum, but the national government. Ball (1990a) argues that the introduction of the national curriculum was made possible by the 'discourse of derision' established by New Right thinkers, which laid the blame for perceived educational failure at the door of those who had traditionally controlled the curriculum. Educational 'experts' were attacked by the New Right as being responsible for the mismatch between the needs of the economy and the skills that children learned in schools.

Table 3.1 explains how the original national curriculum was constructed, with the addition of Citizenship in 2003.

The national curriculum is essentially academic and traditional. In some ways this conflicts with the vocational emphasis of initiatives such as TVEI, CPVE, YT, GNVQ/AVCE/Applied A levels, and vocational GCSEs. What was created was a stratified system of 'core', 'foundation' and 'optional' subjects for children educated under the state sector to follow. The important changes made to the national curriculum (and national assessment) following the 1994 Dearing Report will be introduced in Exercise 3.6 below. The introduction of the national curriculum was an important landmark in the history of state

**Table 3.1** The national curriculum, 1988

**Core subjects: 30–40 per cent of the timetable**
English
Mathematics
Science

**Non-core subjects: 50 per cent of the timetable**
Art
Geography
History
Languages (modern foreign languages)
Music
PE (physical education)
Technology

**Optional subjects 10–20 per cent of the timetable**
Religious education

**Other requirements**
Sex education
A broadly Christian act of daily worship
Citizenship (2003)

education in Britain as it represented, for the first time, an attempt to control the content of education nationally. However, the establishment of a national curriculum was opposed by some members of the New Right. The libertarian right wing, which wanted a minimum of state control in social as well as economic affairs, argued against the creation of a centrally controlled curriculum. However, the temptation to concentrate power in central government's hands as a step towards destroying local authority control over education was too great (see Chitty 1993). Despite the involvement of many educationalists and teachers in the formation of the national curriculum, it has been heavily criticized by teachers for being over-prescriptive (trying to control too much of what is actually taught), bureaucratic (involving a huge increase in paperwork), increasing the burden of assessment for pupils and teachers, and responsible for squeezing other worthwhile educational experiences out of the curriculum – for example, GCSE sociology.

Moreover, there have been many disagreements over the content of national curriculum subjects. For example, there has been a long-running dispute over what aspects of history should be included. Successive government ministers have intervened to put forward a particular view of history, stressing traditional approaches. Sylvester (1994) points out that this ignores elements of history (for example, women's history) that are important in a multicultural society such as Britain. Ball (1995) argued that the attempt to establish a traditional curriculum based upon subjects such as maths, science and English, and the learning of facts was a 'curriculum of the dead' as it was focused entirely in the distant past. Postmodernists would also argue that, given the fragmented and diverse nature of postmodern societies, in which individuals have many conflicting educational needs, the attempt to impose a common curriculum on everyone is unlikely to meet those needs (Donald, 1992). For example, sociology is not part of the national curriculum, and this has had the effect of decimating the number of students taking GCSE sociology. Therefore, the national curriculum does not meet the needs of students with an interest in the social.

More recently, issues concerned with the ways in which individual pupils and students learn have received considerable attention in the educational world. The notion of learning styles (Kolb 1984) and multiple intelligences (Gardner 1983), developed in the 1980s, have been updated and taken seriously by some schools. Internet versions of tests are available, which claim to be able to identify the dominant characteristics of particular learning styles of pupils. A number of terms are used to describe a particular 'style' – visual, auditory, kinaesthetic, convergers, divergers, verbalizers, imagers, and so on. The idea is that once learning styles are identified, learning activities can be devised that cater for the learning needs of all individuals in a classroom. These ideas provide yet more criticism of a 'national curriculum', which purports to be in the interests of all children. Critics would argue that it is merely a 'one-size-fits-all' curriculum that cannot meet the needs of all children, and hence explains why so many children fail to meet the standards and targets expected of them. Coffield *et al.* (2004) however, has argued that many of the popular 'test-your-own-learning-style' kits available have not been adequately researched. Of the thirteen Coffield looked at, only two could be recommended for post-16 or higher education. An additional criticism well known to sociology students is that teachers may well label (albeit inadvertently) students in particular ways and have expectations (Rosenthal and Jacobson 1968) of their progress if they are aware of the student's learning style. Also, as sociologists, we may want to argue that categorising people in this way really only limits our understanding of how we learn, as there can be no meaningful typology of people. Consider the categorisation systems of the past based on 'race', for example, and how such systems can be used to discriminate against and disadvantage particular social groups.

An American psychologist, Kathleen Butler (2000) (see below for useful websites) has developed her own methods of gauging what she calls 'learning preferences' based on research for her PhD. She uses a system she devised to work with teachers to identify how their learning preferences may influence their teaching methods. However, Butler cautions her audience to be aware that these are 'preferences' and the key to improving learning is to work on those areas considered to be 'weak' preferences. Hence learning styles or preferences are not rigid, unchangeable or non-adaptable ways of learning, but fluid, adaptable and flexible. Learning styles may be the result of an educational movement that is in danger of becoming a 'fashion'.

Further useful information can be found on these websites:

www.lsrc.ac.uk
www.learnersdimension.com/KAB.html
www.learningfromexperience.com

However there is a much more fundamental criticism of the national curriculum, and this needs to be addressed here. Postmodernists have argued against the existence of any fundamental truths in society that can be translated into a national curriculum. For example, one of the main elements of the national curriculum is science, which the postmodernists would describe as a 'metanarrative' – a 'story' or myth, not a collection of truths, that attempts to explain the whole of existence.

In contrast, the postmodernist Baudrillard (1983) argues that it is not possible to penetrate the appearance or surface of things to see what is 'really there'. To Baudrillard, the only reality is the surface reality of the images of the media age – the 'signs' we absorb from the media, which form a new type of reality: the 'hyperreality'. Therefore, according to Baudrillard, our 'knowledge' of the world is not gained from experience itself, but from our experience of media images. What we 'know' about the USA, Israel or South Africa is drawn from our experiences of visual media such as TV or film about them. Similarly, what we 'know' about science is drawn from the hyperreal and not from learning the 'truth' about the world in schools.

There is, in the postmodern view, a collapse of the 'economy of truth' (Hebdige 1989) in the contemporary world; that is, the notion that there is any verifiable truth is both irrelevant and misleading. Therefore, to present a national curriculum that is supposed to encompass everything a child in Britain should know is an enterprise doomed to failure. All information, according to the postmodernists, is shifting and precarious. What is today's 'knowledge' will be tomorrow's 'falsehood'. But postmodernists go further than this, arguing that any attempt to find out what is 'really going on' is pointless, and therefore the idea of identifying what is 'science' or 'history' – as the national curriculum attempts to do – is useless. What the national curriculum therefore represents is not knowledge but a type of ideology; a 'discourse' (see Foucault 1979) or perspective that is not true, but is powerful. The national curriculum is powerful because it is a way of organizing information, so that the world is seen as being organized in one particular way as opposed to another.

Critics of this view argue that science is more than just a 'metanarrative' – it is a distinct way of producing 'truth' that transcends, or goes beyond, individual or cultural experiences. What this means is that scientists in different societies and from different ideologies can agree that some things have been proved to be 'true' about the underlying reality of the universe. Scientists do not just examine surface realities, but can verify knowledge through their methodologies. There is thus a body of knowledge called science that can be presented to children as the 'truth' of things.

## National assessment and national strategies

This involves standardized assessment tests (SATs) in certain subjects at the ages of 7, 11, 14 and 16. These tests were introduced as a way of monitoring standards in schools and keeping parents informed of their children's progress. National testing has proved to be one of most controversial aspects of the national curriculum arrangements, with teachers boycotting them in 1993 and 1994. Au (2007) argues that the existence of high-stakes, standardized testing in both the USA and in Great Britain has had the effect of defining what is seen as legitimate education through what he calls 'pedagogic discourse'. There are two features of the testing arrangements to which many teachers object. First, they argue that the testing arrangements force them to 'teach to the test'. They spend so much time preparing their students for the SATs that there is little time for any other form of education, and so subjects such as art, social studies and even science get squeezed out of the curriculum (see Renter *et al.* 2006). Not only does this affect what is taught, but also *how* it is taught, as teachers turn to teacher-centred strategies to ensure the transmission of the facts that are needed to pass the tests. Independent learning strategies and field trips are downgraded to meet the demands of the testing regime (see Taylor *et al.* 2001).

Second, the results of the tests are compiled into 'league tables' of schools, giving parents information about how a school is performing. Critics of league tables argue that they are a very crude measure of a school's effectiveness. A school may appear to be doing very badly in the league table, but it in fact provides an effective learning environment for lower-ability pupils. Some pupils might have done better than if they had gone to another school that concentrates less on low-ability students, yet this second school's test scores may be better because it attracts more able students in the first place. A more sophisticated measure of performance is now being used, based on the school's ability to 'add value' to the achievement of its pupils. Value-added scores take the attainment levels of the pupil on entry to the school and then measure how much the school has been able to help that pupil improve his/her levels of attainment. This is argued to be a more objective way to compare school performance, by looking at the progress of the pupil rather than just examining the crude exam results measure. Value-added scores are intended to allow comparisons between schools with different socio-economic profiles. For example, pupils attending school A with a higher socio-economic intake may achieve results in Key Stage 2 (KS2) tests above the expected national level, while pupils at school B, with a lower socio-economic profile, may have made more progress than other pupils relative to their Key Stage 1 (KS1) starting point, and therefore have a higher value-added 'measure'. The value-added score is therefore a more accurate measure of the school's performance.

A number of National Strategies for areas such as Literacy, Numeracy, Science, Foundation Subjects, Key Stage 3 and school improvement began to appear from the late 1990s onwards, and each set out targets for improvement through a number of teaching and learning initiatives, as well as school strategies. Learning targets were set for all age groups, with expected standards to be achieved by each cohort, such as 80 per cent of 11-year-olds to achieve the expected standard for the age group, or the achievement of five grade A*/A–C GCSEs by 50 per cent of 16-year-olds.

Marion Fitzgerald (2005) has argued that, in order to measure educational performance relative to social factors, it is better to trace development through the whole period of formal education. Hence she has used official statistics from the Department for Children, Schools and Families (DCFS) (formerly the Department for Education and Skills – DfES) at all of the key stages to show performance related to gender, ethnicity and social class. These sorts of measures of performance and league tables are being used to conduct, albeit critically, research into trends and patterns that are emerging over time.

The notion of control by central government was taken a step further in 1998, when daily literacy and numeracy hours were introduced into primary schools. Described by the National Literacy Trust as an 'unprecedented intervention in classroom strategies', it set out how the daily hour for each skill should be spent in the primary school classroom. During the literacy hour, the first thirty minutes would be spent working as a whole class, developing spelling, punctuation, vocabulary and grammar in literacy, and in the second half of the lesson working in groups or individually, with the teacher focusing on one group at a time. In the numeracy hour, time would be spent developing mental arithmetic and problem-solving skills. The National

Strategies published in 1999/2000 refined the guidance about teaching during these hours to include notions of lively, stimulating and effective teaching, both with the whole class and with pupils working in groups on collaborative activities.

By 2008, according to Christine Gilbert, the chief inspector of schools, as many as 20 per cent of children were functionally illiterate when leaving school (Gilbert, 2008). In 2009 test scores for 11-year-olds had got worse.

(An)(E)
## Exercise 3.6

Drawing on the material you have read so far, think about the difference between a national curriculum and pedagogy (ways of teaching and learning) compared with the needs of the individual pupil (learning styles), and write down some reasons why, despite all the initiatives that have taken place since the 1980s, a substantial proportion of children still 'fail to make the grade'.

Useful website: www.dcsf.gov.uk.

## Exercise 3.7

In the 1970s, Young (1971) wrote about the social construction of educational knowledge. He claimed that powerful groups in society ensured that the formal curriculum taught in schools was stratified into high- and low-status subjects. Some might argue that Young's ideas can be applied to the national curriculum, as established in 1988. This is because there is a clear distinction between core and foundation subjects.

(I)(A)(E)  1. Your task is to find out what were the core (possibly high-status) and foundation (possibly low-status) subjects. When you have done this, copy out and complete the table below. You should also write a short evaluative paragraph that reflects the extent to which the core subjects can be deemed high-status and the foundation subjects low-status.

The national curriculum – status of subjects

| Core or high-status subjects | Foundation or low-status subjects |
| --- | --- |
| | History |
| | Music |

(I)(E)  2. Below is a number of statements relating to the curriculum and assessment aspects of the 1988 Education Reform Act. Your task is to identify which are the arguments in favour of the Act, and which are against it. When you have made your choices, record your answers in a table that clearly separates the arguments for the 1988 Education Act from the arguments against it. Rewrite the statements in your own words rather than simply copying them out.

3. When you have completed the task, do some further research into the 1988 Education Reform Act (this could be an ongoing research programme). You could begin by seeking the opinion of teachers in your school or college about the national curriculum, and by keeping a close eye on the educational press. Add to the list of arguments you have written down so far. You should aim to end up with at least three arguments for and against each curriculum aspect of the 1988 Education Reform Act.

## Arguments for and against the 1988 Education Reform Act and its curriculum and assessment provisions

1. It is too Eurocentric. It allows few opportunities for ethnic minority students to explore and draw on their own cultural roots.
2. The government has omitted those subjects to which they are politically opposed; that is, environmental science, sociology and politics.
3. Testing will provide parents with vital information on their children's educational progress and will help them to support their future educational needs.
4. Testing can put undue stress on students. Schools may set students tests to help them cope with tiered examinations at ages 11 and 14. Evidence suggests that setting such tests can have a detrimental effect on the educational achievement of lower-band students.
5. If all students have to follow a core curriculum it may help to prevent the division between girls' subjects and boys' subjects, and thus reduce stereotyping.
6. Testing is not useful unless a great deal of money is provided to support those children who are 'failing'.
7. It will ensure that there is some consistency in what is taught in schools across Britain. Repetition and lack of continuity between primary and secondary schools will be avoided. Students who have to move from one part of the country to another will find the transition less disruptive to their education.
8. Standardized national testing provides a reliable means by which society can evaluate the success of individual schools and the education system as a whole.

## CHANGES TO THE NATIONAL CURRICULUM AND ASSESSMENT – THE DEARING REPORT 1997

In response to the many criticisms of the national curriculum and the standardized assessment tests (including those highlighted in Exercise 3.6) the government performed a political somersault in accepting Sir Ron Dearing's recommendations to slim down the highly prescriptive national curriculum and simplify the burdensome testing procedures at various key stages. Dearing also laid the foundations of the subsequent reforms of the 14–19 curriculum (see Exercise 3.8). Dearing also recommended the introduction of tuition fees for students in higher education (see later).

---

### Item C

**The Changing National Curriculum**

The introduction of a National Curriculum did not solve all the problems of the curriculum and assessment in schools. Indeed, it immediately came under criticism for being opaque and hard for parents to understand, without over-simplifying the statistics of achievement. For example, a school that has relatively low Key Stage 4 results could actually be doing better than a high-scoring school. It all depends on the intake. If the intake to a school are high achievers and at the end of their schooling they achieve roughly at the same high level that might have been expected of them, then that school might not be adding anything to the intake's attainment. A school with low achiever entry that pushes those students to achieve more than might have been expected is adding value to that intake's educational achievement.

In 1994, there was a major review of the national curriculum as the government attempted to respond to the concerns of parents and teachers that the testing regime was too rigid to adequately measure real attainment. Teachers had in the previous year been boycotting national tests as a protest over the sheer intensity of testing that left teachers being compelled to 'teach to the test' as they tried to improve their league table position. The key element of the reform was to reduce national testing significantly. Instead of assessing all subjects at all key stages, only English, Maths and Science would be tested at 7, 11 and 14.

In addition, there was some freeing up of the 14–16 curriculum to create space for more vocational subjects to be taken by students, though GCSEs would be the main testing regime at Key Stage 4. Further down the school, compulsory content in non-core subjects would be reduced. In Key Stages 1–3 reports at the end of Key Stage tests would remain on a 10-point scale so that an individual student's progression in any subject throughout school could be tracked.

In 2007, further alterations were made to the national curriculum, such as allowing 14–16-year-olds not to do a foreign language as part of their suite of GCSEs. Skills such as enterprise and the ability to take control over one's own learning were also highlighted. A key new development was the introduction of a compulsory Citizenship element into the curriculum. From 2009, Key Stage 3 tests were no longer compulsory in schools and could be replaced by teacher assessments

## Exercise 3.8

Read Item C and complete the following tasks.

1. Explain what changes have been made to the national curriculum and national assessment since its introduction.
2. Draw up a two-column table and make a list of the positive and negative aspects of the changes.

It would be a good idea to do some further research to help you complete these tasks in greater detail. Useful government websites are: www.dscf.gov.uk and www.qca.org.uk.

## Item D

## THE PRIVATIZATION OF EDUCATION

UK spending on education as a proportion of gross national product

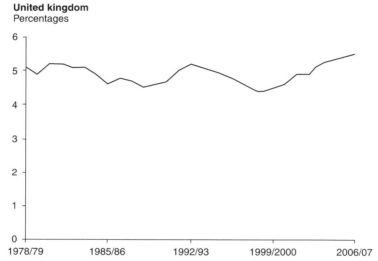

**United kingdom**
Percentages

*Source*: Self, A. (ed.) (2008) *Social Trends 38* (Basingstoke: Palgrave Macmillan).

School pupils by types of school

|  | Thousands | | | | |
|---|---|---|---|---|---|
| **United Kingdom** | **1970/71** | **1980/81** | **1990/91** | **2000/01** | **20006/07** |
| **Public sector schools** | | | | | |
| Nursery | 50 | 89 | 105 | 152 | 157 |
| Primary | 5,902 | 5,171 | 4,955 | 5,298 | 4,922 |
| Secondary | | | | | |
| Comprehensive | 1,313 | 3,730 | 2,925 | 3,340 | 3,407 |
| Grammar | 673 | 149 | 156 | 205 | 219 |
| Modern | 1,164 | 233 | 94 | 112 | 103 |
| Other | 403 | 434 | 298 | 260 | 212 |
| All public sector schools | 9,507 | 9,806 | 8,533 | 9,367 | 9,021 |
| **Non-maintained schools** | 621 | 619 | 613 | 626 | 671 |
| **All special schools** | 103 | 148 | 114 | 113 | 106 |
| **Pupil referral units** | | | | 10 | 16 |
| **All schools** | 10,230 | 10,572 | 9,260 | 10,116 | 9,813 |

*Source*: Self, A. (ed.) (2008) *Social Trends 38* (Basingstoke: Palgrave Macmillan).

## 1992 WHITE PAPER

Following on from the 1998 Education Reform Act, the then Conservative government watched developments in schools very carefully. Their overall aim was to reduce the power of local authorities and increase the operation of market forces within the education system. For a section of the New Right, the wholesale privatization of education was the dream. For more pragmatic Conservatives, various voucher schemes were examined, but always rejected on the grounds of complexity and cost. However, progress in one of the main planks of the 1998 Act, the ability of schools to opt out of local authority control was painfully slow. By 1992, only 219 had chosen to do so and there was no rush among the others to join them.

This led to new proposals from the government in Choice and Diversity: a new framework for schools in 1992. The legislation that followed was designed to speed up the process of opting out and giving greater incentives to schools to do so. The Funding Agency for Schools was established to give money to opted-out schools and reduce the responsibilities for local authorities to carry out statutory duties such as the provision of school transport. In addition, schools were to be encouraged to specialize in particular subjects, and this was interpreted by many opposed to the reform as a signal to schools that they could select by the back door, recruiting those who had an aptitude for their specialist subject.

While the effects of these new provisions were not massive, the broad thrust of the policy has been continued by subsequent Labour governments. So, more and more schools have become Specialist Schools (sometimes doubly specialist) with the more favourable financial position that this includes. The Academy programme of the Labour governments in the early 2000s is a further diminution of local authority control. Labour continues to repeat the mantra of choice and diversity in its educational policy.

### The 1992 Education White Paper

- Opting out made easier for schools.
- New Funding Agency for Schools to take over responsibility for channelling funds to opted-out schools.
- All schools can specialize in one or more subjects in addition to teaching all national curriculum subjects.
- A new School Curriculum and Assessment Authority (SCAA) was created.
- A new Education Association can take over responsibility for running schools which inspectors judge to be failing.
- Rights of parents of special needs students to be strengthened, and special schools may be able to opt out of local authority control.

## Exercise 3.9

This exercise will help you to develop the skills of interpretation, application, analysis and evaluation, as well as furthering your knowledge and understanding of the issues raised so far.

Read Item D and answer the questions and sentences below. Make sure that you write out the questions and statements as headings for your answers.

(I) 1. What proportion of GNP was devoted to education in 1992/3?

(I)(A) 2. Match the amount of spending on education against which party formed the government in the relevant years. Is there any correlation between party and spending on education?

(I) 3. How many students were educated in the private sector in 2006/7?

(I) 4. What is the trend in private education numbers over the period shown in the table?

(A) 5. Suggest two reasons for any trend you have identified?

(A) 6. Why do you think the Conservative party is favourable towards private schooling?

(A) 7. Why do you think the Labour Party has continued to undermine the role of local authorities in education?

(E) 8. Construct two arguments for and two arguments against Specialist schools.

(E) 9. Assess the view that the main reason for the Academy programme of schools is to increase central control of education.

## MARKET FORCES AND DIVERSITY

Since the 1990s, there has been considerable debate about the effects of educational policies on the education system. The rationale behind many of the policies introduced by Conservative governments that we have discussed above, such as open enrolment, school performance tables and grant maintained schools, was that, if schools are under pressure they will become more innovative and diversify to make their school distinctive and thereby attract pupils. The belief was that the education system would begin to adopt characteristics of the 'market'; this has since become known in sociology as marketisation. However, work by Whitty (1993) on city technology colleges, and later by Fitz *et al.* (1997) on grant-maintained schools revealed that they had not reinvented themselves but had 're-badged' themselves in the form of the established academic curriculum. Davies *et al.* (2003) point to the increasing polarisation of schools, with market forces bringing about changes in schools on the basis of size and resources. What they describe as 'large, expanding over-subscribed schools' seem to have the freedom to develop and/or maintain a particular curriculum even against parental pressure, and this curriculum is usually traditionally academic. By comparison, small, declining schools were increasingly limited or pragmatic in their offered curriculum, with the key emphasis of needing to bolster sixth form numbers. Similarly, the two types of schools described by Davies *et al.* attract different types of pupils, with the difference closely aligned to the old grammar/secondary modern divide. Indeed, some of the smaller, declining schools in their study had previously been secondary moderns.

## Important concepts

New Right • New Left • postmodernism • new vocationalism • surveillance • national curriculum

## Critical thinking

- Consider how and why the changes in educational policy since the 1988 Education Reform Act have brought about conflicting perspectives on the nature and role of education.
- Which types of qualifications and assessment were in existence when you were at school? What, in your experience, were the divisions and differences between the qualifications and the pupils/students taking them?
- Do you think central control of the curriculum and examinations is good for the education of young people? What alternatives could you put forward?

*Chapter 4*

# Changes in Policy and Structure in Britain in the 1980s, 1990s and 2000s

By the end of this chapter you should:

- be sensitive to changes in education and training for 16–19-year-olds and higher education
- understand the reasons for the changes and the conflicting views expressed about the changes
- be familiar with the privatization process taking place in schools
- understand the developments in the 14–19 curriculum and Every Child Matters

## INTRODUCTION

The 1988 Education Reform Act did not just bring about fundamental change in the curriculum and assessment in schools. As we have seen, the aims of the Conservative government at that time was to change the whole culture of schooling to bring it more in line with what it saw as the dynamic business sector. Because the Conservative Party was ideologically attached to the idea of competition and the greater efficiency of the private sector compared to the public sector, it tried to introduce these aspects into schooling in 1988. There were three main changes in policy and structure brought in by the Act: open enrolment; local management of schools (LMS); and grant maintained schools (GMS).

## Open enrolment

This places an obligation on schools to enrol all comers to their full capacity and provides parents with a wider choice in the type of state school to which they can send their children. Moreover, it exposes schools to internal market forces as they seek to compete for pupils. The creation of a market in education has been one of the main policies of successive Conservative governments since 1979. The aim of the New Right theorists who have influenced the government was to introduce into the state sector as many features of the private sector as possible. The New Right wishes to introduce the idea of consumers (parents and children) exercising choice in a system characterized by diversification (that is, the introduction of many different types of school), which would offer consumers real choices. Through open enrolment and the league-tabling of examination results, parents will be able to identify 'star' schools, and these will become popular. Conversely 'sink' schools will be forced to change their practices for the better or they will suffer a decline in their fortunes, which logically could lead to closure.

The New Right argued that this would encourage the spread of good practice throughout the school system. Critics of open enrolment have argued that, in reality, oversubscribed schools can choose whom they accept or reject, so that there is only limited parental choice in the system. Given that popular schools can choose their pupils, these critics argue that selection is being introduced through the back door. This has the effect of recreating the inequalities and hierarchies in schools that existed before the reforms of the 1960s (Elliott and MacLennan 1994).

## Local management of schools (LMS)

This increases the financial responsibilities of head teachers and governors as they are given direct control of 90 per cent of their school budget. The budget is largely determined by the size of the school roll, and therefore one of the effects of LMS is to encourage competition between schools for pupils. LMS has had a number of consequences, but head teachers and governors have been enthusiastically in favour of the devolution of decision-making into their hands (Simkins 1994) as it can increase staff commitment. Conversely, as Ball (1990b) notes, staff may be faced with unfamiliar demands on their time to undertake marketing and finance-raising activities, which they may resent or be ill-prepared for. New Right theorists argue that giving autonomy to schools in this way will increase diversity and choice in the education system, as schools will seek to specialize in different areas. However Moore (1990) notes that schools in Chicago, when given autonomy, have tended to emphasize traditional academic criteria rather than new specialisms. Thus autonomy may lead to a new uniformity rather than increased diversity.

## Grant maintained schools (GMS)

This part of the Act allowed head teachers and governors to 'opt out' of local authority control, provided the majority of parents whose sons/daughters attend the school voted for it. Unlike LEA schools, GM schools received their budgets from central government through the Funding Agency for Schools. This quango (a non-elected, government-appointed organization) offered GM schools increased autonomy, as they would have full control over their budgets and a complete say in how their schools were run and organized. GM schools that 'opted out' of LEA control so far were influenced by one of two factors: they had either been under threat of closure by the LEA; or had wished to offer a fairly traditional curriculum.

Rather than promoting choice and diversity, as postmodernists would suggest, GM schools were largely a type of reconstructed grammar school, with a heavily academic emphasis. Moreover, the autonomy of GM schools was circumscribed by central government control. Like LEA schools, under LMS they had been given operational control (that is, day-to-day control) over their budgets. However, the government retained allocative control (that is, the government decided the total funds to be allocated) in terms of the overall education budget, which necessarily curtails what GMs would have liked to achieve.

Ball *et al.* (1994) concludes that many of the changes introduced by the Conservatives, such as open enrolment, the publication of league tables and most of the policies associated with the 'marketization' of the education system, have led to a decline in equality of opportunity. Children who were already at a disadvantage at school were further disadvantaged; that is, they became the losers in a system that has become increasingly divided. One example of this is that those parents who can afford to move house often do so to make sure their children attend a 'good' school – a school with good exam results. Estate agents often advertize houses as being in the catchment area of a particular school, and house prices reflect this. Parents who do not have the material and economic resources to move house are confined to a geographical area that becomes increasingly disadvantaged as the more affluent move out, and the local school will similarly be affected by these changes, struggling for pupil numbers and a wide ability range.

According to Denscombe (2004), in 2004 housing in the 'catchment' areas of better schools – those identified as having excellent exam results in performance tables – cost more money. The National Association of Estate Agents estimated that up to 65,000 families pay prices for houses that are much higher than their actual value to ensure that their children get a place at a 'good' school. Those who can afford to move to secure a place at a good state school will often do so, while those that cannot afford to move have less of a choice about the school their children will go to. This has been defined as 'selection by mortgage'.

## Exercise 4.1

Complete the grid below to evaluate the 1988 policy reforms. There are some statements below the grid that can be slotted into the appropriate cells to start you off. You have to decide to which aspect of policy each statement belongs, and then whether it is an advantage or a disadvantage.

|  | Advantages | Problems |
| --- | --- | --- |
| Open enrolment |  |  |
| Local management of schools |  |  |
| Grant-maintained schools |  |  |

1. Head teachers can spend their budget as they see fit. Money that used to be held back by the local authority for administration can now be spent on books, equipment and employing more teachers.
2. Schools will be forced into a competitive market place. Schools will raise standards and offer an improved service in the hope of attracting students from nearby educational institutions. The quality of the whole education service will improve as a consequence.
3. It may lead to a fall in educational standards if experienced (costly) teachers are replaced by inexperienced (cheaper) ones.
4. It will prove more difficult for local authorities to co-ordinate resources and services for all schools in the area.
5. Competition between schools is likely to create a climate of hostility and suspicion between educational institutions, rather than mutual support and co-operation.
6. There is a great danger that a two-tier education system will emerge as some schools opt out. Well-funded opted-out schools will attract more students than under-funded local authority schools.
7. Over-subscribed schools will have to turn away some students, and schools will be tempted to select their students on the basis of ability.

## THE EXPANSION OF EDUCATION AND TRAINING FOR 16–19-YEAR-OLDS

Educationalists have pointed out that one of the main problems with the education system, in relation to the industrial performance of the British economy, has been the low staying-on rate in post-compulsory schooling. Raffe (1993) suggests that there are four main reasons why this has traditionally been the case. He argues that national culture, and especially working-class culture, has held schooling in low esteem, and that many 16-year-old students have perceived themselves as being designated as 'failures' by the system. Also, while A Levels have borne a high risk of failure, vocational qualifications have not yet achieved parity of esteem, and therefore the lure of the labour market has persuaded many 16-year-olds to choose to go into employment. However, as jobs became scarcer during the 1980s, these factors began to be less important in dissuading young people from staying on at school.

Moreover, the further education sector, as a major provider of vocational education, was criticized during the 1980s for failing to respond quickly enough to the needs of a changing economy, and for ignoring individual needs in the courses they offered (see Theodossin 1986). The colleges were also seen as providing expensive courses, which potential customers were not particularly keen on.

Hence a major objective of government educational policy since the mid-1980s has been to increase the provision and quality of education and training for 16–19-year-olds. The substantial increase in staying-on rates is illustrated in Item A.

### Item A

**Table 4.1** Participation rates (percentages) in education and training at age 17, selected OECD countries, 2004

| | |
|---|---|
| Belgium | 100 |
| Japan | 96 |
| France | 92 |
| Germany | 92 |
| Republic of Ireland | 86 |
| USA | 85 |
| UK | 83 |
| Portugal | 75 |
| Greece | 70 |

*Source*: Department for Education and Science (DFES) (2006) *The Five-Year Strategy for Children and Learners*, September.

**Table 4.2** Participation rates (percentages) in full-time UK education at age 16, selected years

| | |
|---|---|
| 1985 | 48 |
| 1990 | 60 |
| 1995 | 71 |
| 2000 | 71 |
| 2005 | 76 |

*Source*: Department for Education and Science (DFES) (2006) *The Five-Year Strategy for Children and Learners*, September.

## Exercise 4.2

1. Study Table 4.1 of Item A. Which OECD countries have:
   (a) the lowest participation rates in education and training at the age of 17?
   (b) the highest participation rates in education and training at the age of 17?
2. What is the percentage increase in participation rates in full-time education in the UK at age 16 between 1985 and 2005, according to Table 4.2?

## REASONS FOR THE INCREASE IN PARTICIPATION RATES IN POST-COMPULSORY EDUCATION

Maguire *et al.* (1993) offer five reasons to account for the huge increase in participation in post-compulsory education:

1. The increased number of well-qualified students following improvements in GCSE results.
2. The fall in the number of employment opportunities available to young people as a result of the recession of the late 1980s and early 1990s, and the 'credit crunch' of 2008 onwards.

3. The decline in the number of training places available because of cutbacks in YT funding.
4. Changes to social security arrangements, whereby 16–17-year-olds lost their entitlement to income support.
5. The wider provision of courses and places in further and higher education.

Additionally, the government has introduced means-tested Educational Maintenance Allowances (EMAs) for those who maintain a good level of attendance on post-16 courses, to encourage more students from poorer backgrounds to stay on at school or college.

The increases in the number of students following courses in the 16–19 sector would seem at first sight to be desirable. It is argued that this increase will open up opportunities to study at the higher education level and provide industry with better-educated and skilled workers. However, there are also problems with such a rapid expansion. The Audit Commission and the Office for Standards in Education (OFSTED, 1993) has pointed out that 30 per cent of those following post-16 studies do not complete or are unsuccessful in their courses. Maguire *et al.* (1993) shows particular concern for those students who extend their education for one year only. She maintains that one-year students are unlikely to improve their employment prospects significantly by undertaking an extra year. Indeed, she suggests that they may be disadvantaged because they have to compete with younger and cheaper 16-year-olds in an increasingly competitive employment market.

As well as expanding, in the 1980s the further education sector became subject to the 'marketization' that has been a key policy of successive Conservative governments. Post-16 colleges' connections with local government authorities were severed and they were centrally funded through the government-appointed Further Education Funding Council (FEFC) and then the LSC (Learning and Skills Council), which retains allocative control over the sector. This extended the relative control over budgets that local authority schools were given through the Local Management of Schools initiative, so that colleges directly control the bulk of the money they receive. The aim of freeing the 16–19 sector from local authority control was to introduce greater competition into the sector, so that quality education could be offered and a greater number of students could be persuaded to continue their education after reaching the age of 16.

The day-to-day or operational control of the further education sector was handed over to revamped governing bodies, in which local authority representatives were displaced by local business personnel, who would ensure that the colleges were more responsive to the local labour market. As Sieminski (1993) argues, these local markets were shaped increasingly by a change from Fordist methods of production towards neo-or post-Fordist methods, in which there is a need for a highly skilled and flexible labour force to produce the quality goods required in a highly differentiated market. The role of the further education sector was to provide a flexible labour force.

In order to ensure that competition between further education colleges increased the quality of provision, the finance a college received was tied (a) to the number and type of students it attracted; and (b) to the expansion of student numbers over a number of years. Therefore, different types of student were worth different amounts to a college. The aim of this was to ensure that recruitment concentrated on those types of students the government defined as desirable.

There was also a commitment to increasing the quality of the education the students received (DES 1991) by linking the outcomes of the colleges (in terms of the qualifications students gained) with the cost of delivering the curriculum. For example Muller and Funnell (1991) argue that post-16 colleges can adapt the workings of industry and operate a total quality management (TQM) system, which would place the learner at the heart of the procedures of the college and 'give ownership' of learning to the learners themselves. This would provide a 'value added' dimension to the education the students received, so that the service performed by the colleges would not just be measured in terms of the qualifications gained, but also by the quality of the educational experiences that students had received.

However, critics of this approach have argued that the development of a new curriculum in the further education sector, through the introduction of NVQs, GNVQs, and more recently AVCEs, alongside the more traditional BTEC qualifications may not be as empowering to the students as New Right advocates suggest. Supporters of vocational education argue that there are benefits for students in the 'competence' approach to education. Here, students are encouraged to acquire 'transferable skills' through gaining specific competences during the course of their studies (see Guy 1991), and are rewarded for their practical achievements and not just their academic knowledge. Critics argue that the potential for personal development in such teaching style innovations as action planning and project-based work have been restricted by the narrow focus of vocational courses on 'competence' (see Raggatt 1991). Thus the creativity supposedly developed by the new vocational courses is argued by Cathcart and Esland (1990) to be an illusion, as pre-packaged material is substituted for individually generated projects. It may be – according to Edwards (1991), among others – that a core of workers will be trained to be flexible for steady, full-time work, while the periphery of workers are trained to be flexible in a different way; that is, to move in and out of employment as the local labour market expands and contracts.

The introduction of the specialized diplomas that started in 2008 has once again transformed the educational landscape, with the notion of a 16–19 phase of education becoming 14–19 instead. Although the numbers of students taking the first diploma was expected to be only around 20,000, with numbers increasing as schools and colleges felt they were well enough prepared to deliver the new courses (actual starting numbers were lower than this). Schools and colleges that had been collaborating in some areas, such as in providing programmes for excluded pupils, are now given funding to work together to develop the new diplomas in specific geographical regions. This initiative is not without its problems, not least of which has been the different culture and ethos of schools and colleges, as well as the differences in expertise and qualifications of teaching staff in the different institutions.

## THE EXPANSION OF HIGHER EDUCATION

The growth of higher education (HE) in Britain has occurred in two waves. The first wave followed the Robbins Report (1963) and led to the expansion of the 'old' universities and the creation of new 'red brick' universities and polytechnics (do Exercise 4.3 below to further explore the differences between these types of university). The second wave was more recent and reflected the government's concern to increase the participation rate of young adults and adult returners in higher education. The rate of increase in the number of students taking degree and equivalent courses, though rising to over 1.5 million, has therefore not been constant, but has been shaped by economic factors (such as a fall in student numbers after the financial cuts of 1981) and government policy towards the higher education sector.

Moreover, this growth in student numbers has increased the diversity of students taking up degree work. The introduction of the Open University and the re-designation of polytechnics as universities following the 1993 Education Act have allowed a shift away from the traditional university course, which was originally designed as a three-year residential experience, provided mainly for young, middle-class males (see Halsey 1993).

While the expansion of the higher education sector has created greater equality of opportunity for women, this is not so for working-class individuals: the *number* of students of working-class origin may have grown as the system has expanded, but the *proportion* of these receiving higher education has remained fairly static despite varying greatly from university to university, with Cambridge having the lowest percentage of undergraduates from 'skilled manual and unskilled backgrounds' at 9 per cent, and Wolverhampton having the highest at 45 per cent. The overall percentage for all higher education institutions is 26 per cent. According to the Institute of Employment Studies (2008) there has been little change in the 'social mix' over the previous five years, despite attempts to widen access to HE. Although the numbers of students from social classes 111M, 1V and V has increased in line with total numbers, the proportion entering HE has not increased. Research has also shown that, once at university working class students continue to experience disadvantage and are more likely to leave their courses early. Furlong and Forsyth (2003) found that lack of funds and fear of debt, alongside the cultural isolation and unfamiliarity of the higher education system, were the main factors that led to working-class students experiencing problems. The expansion of the HE sector has therefore led to increased opportunities for middle- and upper-class children, relative to their numbers in the population.

Women now outnumber men as undergraduates. According to Universities & Colleges Admissions Service (UCAS) data, there has been a steady 'feminisation' of higher education since girls began to outperform boys at school in their GCSE and A level results. (See Chapter 7 – 'Bringing It Together' – for a more detailed discussion of the interplay between gender, ethnicity and social class in educational performance.) This is not unique to Britain, as the same trend is evident in Europe and North America.

For further useful material which also gives trends over time, see: www.ucas.ac.uk; www.hesa.ac.uk; and www.hefce.ac.uk.

## Exercise 4.3

With a small group of your fellow students, look at the websites for the universities of Cambridge, Durham, Warwick, Wolverhampton, East London and Salford. For each one, say what impression the website gives overall. What key words appear most often? Does the university pride itself on 'world class research' renowned courses, position in league tables, teaching and learning, its famous previous undergraduates, or honorary graduates/professors?

From your own perspective, what might draw you to a particular university? Are there aspects of the sites that might appear 'unfamiliar' to students who are the first in their families to have the opportunity to go into higher education?

The higher education sector has, like all other sectors of education, been subject to increasing marketization of its services. The pressure to change the curriculum and teaching methods is related to the development of what are called post-Fordist production techniques in the economy as a whole, and the consequent need for 'flexible' and 'multi-skilled' workers by industry. The term Fordism is used to describe the method of manufacturing that was dominant from the beginning of the twentieth century until the 1950s and 1960s. Fordism was characterized by the mass production of standardized goods for a mass market, in which consumer demand was undifferentiated. Workers under Fordism were required to perform under the control of Taylorist principles, whereby they required little skill and their every move was directed towards greater production of a standard product. Taylorism was developed by F. W. Taylor as an organisational structure, in which tasks were broken down into the simplest of operations, so that less skilled workers could be employed on fragments of production rather than highly skilled workers producing an entire product individually. Fordist organizations were therefore characterized by hierarchical bureaucracies, in which management's main task was the integration and co-ordination of the actions of many highly specialized, but unskilled, workers.

Post-Fordism is a move towards a different kind of economy, in which services such as leisure facilities, retailing and finance are just as important as the manufacturing of goods. Moreover, in a post-Fordist economy, markets are no longer 'mass' and undifferentiated. Rather, there are multiple markets with specialized needs and demands. These demands are being met by both manufacturing and service industries through the development of new computer technologies, which, for example, allow the high-speed transfer of information or the development of 'just-in-time' production, so that industry can respond quickly to constant changes in demand by the consumer. Therefore, because post-Fordist organizations have to be responsive and flexible, innovating constantly to maximize profits, they need, for their core activities, flexible and multi-skilled workers who are not resistant to changes in working practices. It should be noted that the ideas of post-Fordism have been challenged by sociologists such as O'Reilly (1992), who argues that the extent of post-Fordist practices and multi-skilling in society is in fact limited, and that those that do exist are not creating a new type of postmodern society, but are only extensions of long-standing worker exploitation.

The supposed role of education in this shift from Fordist to post-Fordist methods of production is to produce the flexible and multi-skilled workers that the new arrangements need. As the core workers in post-Fordist organizations have to be highly skilled, the role of the HE sector is crucial for developing a workforce with the requisite skills and attitudes to make post-Fordist organization successful and profitable. The problem facing educational institutions is that knowledge is no longer certain for success. Therefore, the key skill that

HE ought to be developing, it is argued, is the capacity for learning itself. The creation of the 'lifelong learner' is seen as a key development if a society is going to compete successfully in a global economy (see Ahier *et al.* 2003).

Indeed, Edwards (1993) argues that the institutions of post-compulsory education are themselves subject to post-Fordist changes in working practices as the government requires them to be more 'productive' and 'efficient', taking more students through their courses at a lower cost. Traditional roles in higher education are therefore breaking down as lecturers are required to take on new roles, such as marketing, counselling, budgeting, and so on. This is combined with the loss of security of employment and the increased use of part-time and temporary staff (the casualization of the workforce) that is associated with post-Fordist organizations.

The search for greater flexibility in higher education led to a number of developments, such as the creation of distance learning and the modularization (or unitisation) of degrees during the 1980s and 1990s. However some of the 'new' universities in the early years of twenty-first century reverted to the traditional system of terms rather than semesters and a year-long delivery of courses. The arguments levelled against modularization, such as the lack of continuity or progression of learning and the difficulty of achieving an appropriate depth of learning seem to have been accepted by these universities. The ending of the 'binary' division of universities and polytechnics meant increased competition between higher education institutions. Moreover, the government expects the unified university sector to attract a greater proportion of its income from private sources, thus making state support for the system less important. Postmodernists argue that one characteristic of the HE sector that is symptomatic of the development of a postmodern society is the dissolving of the boundaries of time and space that are traditionally associated with a university education.

In general terms, postmodernists suggest that 'modern' societies are typified by rigid 'temporal and spatial' boundaries. For example, a 'modern' curriculum in the universities would have very distinct boundaries between subjects, which would be studied in separate locations (university departments) and at separate and distinct times (for example, a person would 'go' to a physics lecture and then 'go' to a chemistry lecture). Education in a modern society would therefore be a closed and bounded system, forming a distinct segment of an individual's life. In a postmodernist society these boundaries dissolve and melt into each other, so that distinctions of time and space become less important. For example, the differences between traditional academic subjects begin to disappear, as these subjects contribute to developments with each other. Spatial and temporal rigidities also dissolve. The traditional university course lasted for three years at an identifiable university site. The development of distance learning and the success of the Open University suggest that this is no longer necessarily the case, as university degrees can be obtained over differing numbers of years and without the necessity of residing in a university situation. Rustin (1994) argues that it is the ideology of 'flexibility', held and promoted by the administrators in the university sector, that is the cutting edge of this dissolving of traditional boundaries.

In the marketization process, students themselves have been subject to privatising forces, as the government has allowed the value of the student grant to decline as a proportion of income and introduced a system of student loans, to be paid back when the student gains employment. Healey (1989) argues that the case for student loans is usually couched in terms of the benefits for both higher education and student motivation, and rarely in terms of savings to public expenditure, which, he suggests, constitutes the underlying reason for their introduction. But, as Jarvis (1990) has suggested, the real impact of student loans may be that 'future indebtedness' acts as a disincentive to working-class students when considering higher education.

The Teaching and Higher Education Act (1998) extended marketization for students. Through this law, grants were abolished and replaced by a new system of loans and tuition fees. The maximum fees for 2008/9 are £3,145. These would be paid back directly from salaries when students graduated and began earning a predetermined yearly amount. There was considerable criticism of the new funding system in that it was said to discourage and disadvantage poorer students. This was ironic, as the government had set a target of 50 per cent of under-30-year-olds to 'gain an experience of higher education' by 2010, targeting those groups that were under-represented in higher education; that is, the working class and some minority ethnic groups. The government has introduced funding to universities to provide means-tested bursaries and grants for students to meet its agenda of widening participation to recruit students from poorer backgrounds through the Aimhigher initiative. For further useful information, see www.aimhigher.ac.uk.

Another consequence of the changes to higher education in the 1980s has been the onset of 'credential inflation' in Britain (Collins, 1981). This concept emerges from the idea developed by Dore (1976) of a 'diploma disease' – the overproduction of educated personnel in developing countries, which were unable to absorb the numbers of highly skilled graduates emerging from the HE sector (see Exercise 4.4 below for the counter-arguments). This led to high levels of graduate unemployment/under-employment and social discontent among the most educated section of society. The process in the USA and Britain has led to many students going on to follow postgraduate courses in order to increase their employment chances in a labour market characterized by an oversupply of highly educated workers.

---

### Item B

## GRADUATE OVERSUPPLY IS A MEDIA MYTH, STUDY SHOWS

According to a study undertaken by sociologist Dr Kate Purcell at the University of the West of England and Professor Peter Elias at the University of Warwick based on a longitudinal survey of 1995 graduates surveyed in 1997/8 and again 2002/3 seven years after graduation, whether from a long established 'elite' university or one of the newest universities 'nearly all . . . were working in jobs appropriate to their qualifications'. Furthermore, there were high levels of satisfaction expressed both with current employment and career development. The research seems to support the expansionist policies of UK governments who have aimed to encourage greater access to HE. The expansion from a third towards a half of young people plus mature students studying at university seems to be of long-term personal and occupational benefit. The evidence of an oversupply of graduates seems to be the result of research of first postgraduate jobs which is often temporary, short-term, stop-gap employment. Hence first destinations data may be unreliable. According to Purcell and Elias, many graduates do take some years to achieve a job appropriate to their qualifications and aspirations. Their findings, however, show that graduates' earnings are at a premium and closely related to holding a degree, and employers still value higher education highly in their recruitment.

*Source*: Adapted from Elias and Purcell 2004

---

### Exercise 4.4

1. According to Item B, in what year did the students in the study graduate?
2. What is a longitudinal study?
3. What are two problems connected with using longitudinal research?
4. According to Item B, why might the UK government's policy to encourage access to HE be supported by the research?
5. Write a short paragraph to put forward the arguments for accessing higher education.

## THE PRIVATIZATION OF STATE SCHOOLS

Government policy in the 1980s and 1990s was geared towards raising standards, increasing parental choice and making education responsive to industry's needs (Burgess, 1994). However, a number of sociologists claim that they are, in effect, policies of privatization. For example, Green (1994) argues that the American postmodernist Rorty (1982) supports the views of the New Right, with their emphasis on the free workings of the market and their assumption that the private sector is always superior to state provision. American New Right sociologists Chubb and Moe (1990) claim that bureaucratic state control inhibits effective performance by schools, and that the solution to dissatisfaction by 'consumers' is to open up the school system to the market. They argue that, by introducing the financial disciplines of the marketplace to schools and freeing them from unresponsive bureaucratic control, standards will be raised as schools will be forced to respond to the demands of the consumer. Chubb and Moe argue that the private sector in schools has a strong motive to please parents, and therefore opening up the state sector to these same incentives would make schools more responsive to what parents want, or they would simply close. The work of Chubb and Moe has been criticized for its methodology, where the statistical connection between effective state schools and low levels of bureaucratic control is very weak. For example, Green (1994) argues that Chubb and Moe do not deal with the fact that the most effective school systems, such as Japan's, have high levels of centralized control.

In Britain, the New Right has supported the development of the grant maintained sector ('opting out') and the city technology colleges, which, though still under the financial control of central government, have created a semi-independent sector. The driving force behind this privatization is open enrolment, or what is called the 'marketisation of education' (carry out Exercise 4.5 below to develop your understanding of this argument). Edwards and Whitty (1992) argue that the introduction of market mechanisms, through parental choice, will lead to children from less advantaged backgrounds being concentrated in certain schools, while 'better' schools will be filled with the children of the middle class. As popular schools become crowded they will begin to select their entrants, usually on the basis of ability, so that different schools will increasingly be differentiated according to ability – a new selective system. What has become called 'selection by mortgage' (Denscombe 2004) describes how gaining access to the better schools has had the effect of increasing the value of houses in the catchment area, and more affluent parents will often pay a premium to move into the catchment area of a good school.

Use Item C and other sources (possibly newspaper articles and the paragraph above) to support the claim that state schooling is being privatized.

---

### Item C

There have been various attempts to link the private and state sectors of schooling, both informally through exchange visits and more formally through programmes like the Assisted Places Scheme. Established by a Conservative government in the 1980s and abolished by Labour in the 1990s, the scheme was to promote the attendance of young, able, working-class students in the private-school sector, who would otherwise not be able to afford to attend them. The scheme was highly controversial, hence its abolition, as was seen to be a state subsidy for private schools, while seeming to insult the maintained sector by implying that comprehensive schools were not good enough for bright students. The key principle in support of the scheme was that it was extending parental choice, so that poor parents could also have the opportunity of a private education for their children. This clash of principle has been characterized as the tension between 'the academic costs associated with comprehensive education and the social costs associated with academic selection'. Despite its abolition of the Assisted Places Scheme, the Labour government of 1997 remained keen to promote parental choice and collaboration between the private and the public sectors of education.

### Item D

A Marxist approach to the sociology of education casts teachers as agents of the ideological state apparatus, whose role is to ensure that working-class children get working-class jobs – a process known as cultural reproduction. To ensure that teachers fulfil this task, they have to be carefully controlled by the state, which rules in the interests of the dominant class in society. This control, however, is not a crude coercive control, but is achieved by subtle ideological pressure by the state.

A key element in this control was achieved by the Education Reform Act of 1988 that established the national curriculum (NC). The NC was presented as a common-sense solution to the problems of education, ensuring that all children had an equal opportunity to receive a similar education. In reality, Marxists argue, the NC is an ideological device that seeks to control the knowledge that is provided to young people, and restrict what they come to know through a highly structured educational experience. The concentration in the NC on maths, science and English is not arbitrary, but constitutes the core knowledge that modern capitalism needs in it workers. By defining these as the core curriculum, the NC effectively squeezes out other forms of knowledge.

In particular, the content of the NC does not include any subjects that might lead to a questioning of contemporary society by its potential workers. Subjects such as politics, economics and sociology are deliberately excluded, while Citizenship is reduced to 'doing good works'. Large issues that impinge on the rights of the democratic citizen, such as global warming or the credit crunch, are dealt with, if at all, in corners of the humanities curriculum or some often vague cross-curricular provision.

## Exam focus

It is important that you now assess your understanding of the debates covered in Chapters 2 and 3. Using material from Items C and D above, and material from other parts of the chapter, attempt the questions below.

Before attempting to answer the questions, observe our advice on tackling them. When you have completed your answers, hand them in to your sociology teacher/lecturer for marking.

### Questions

1. What does Item D mean by the phrase 'economics, politics and sociology are deliberately excluded' from the national curriculum? (*2 marks*)

   The question is one of interpretation and application. As two marks are available, you should work out where the two marks lie. You should conclude that you have to discuss the ideological dimension and suggest why this was deliberate.

2. Identify two 'academic costs associated with comprehensive education' and two 'social costs associated with academic selection' (Item C). (*6 marks*)

   Again, interpretation and application is the skill dimension of the question. Be careful to offer the appropriate number of reasons in each section. Refer back to Item C and the context of the phrases to help you work out what they mean.

3. With reference to information in Item C and elsewhere, assess sociological explanations of the role of private education in Britain. (*12 marks*)

   The wording of the question requires you to refer to Item C (interpretation and analysis) and other sources (knowledge and understanding) and then assess (evaluation). Note also that the question requires you to evaluate 'explanations' showing skills of analysis, so you need to address more than one. Make sure that you look at the strengths and weaknesses of those you choose. Only by so doing will you come to a balanced conclusion.

4. Apart from the national curriculum (Item D) and the Assisted Places Scheme (Item C), discuss the importance of any one other educational change since 1980. (*20 marks*)

   Note that there are two educational changes you cannot use (interpretation and application), but apart from these you have a free choice. Make sure that you keep within the time constraint. Choose the educational change you are most familiar with, and when discussing its importance, refer to its advantages and its problems (evaluation). If possible, make reference to any sociological studies that support the points being made (application).

5. Critically assess recent developments in post-16 education and training (*20 marks*).

   You have to use your skills of evaluation in this question, drawing on the knowledge you have gained about recent developments towards the end of this chapter. As there have been only some limited sociological critiques of the most recent developments, this is a good chance to develop some evaluation skills of your own, by applying principles to each of the developments identified.

6. Using ideas from Item D and elsewhere, outline and evaluate the Marxist approach to the sociology of education. (*8 marks*)

   You should be able to work out for yourself the skills required here. While the question assumes that there is only one Marxist approach, you will be rewarded if you challenge this in your discussion. It is important to make your evaluation through a balanced consideration of the insights the Marxists have provided and the limitations they have.

## EDUCATION REFORMS SINCE 1997

After its election in 1997, the Labour government, influenced by new leaders such as Tony Blair, began to address the emerging concerns of the educational system discussed in Chapters 3 and 4, such as the 'appropriateness' of the national curriculum, how to increase the numbers staying on into post-16 education, vocational education and assessment, and testing. Inevitably, the policy changes introduced by the Labour governments of the late twentieth and early twenty-first centuries had an impact on both the structure of education and the curriculum and assessment issues explored in Chapter 3. In this section we shall examine how changes brought in by the Labour government have affected the education system as a whole.

The desire to have British education perform more favourably in international league tables was a major driver in both Labour and Conservative policy development. Huddlestone and Oh (2004) argued that this preoccupation or 'causal connection' between education and the performance of the economy is not new. They trace debates back to the mid-nineteenth century and the report by the Samuelson Committee in 1884 that had concerns about the nation's lack of competitiveness in Europe.

However, by 1997, schools were already 'disapplying' the national curriculum; that is, not teaching the whole of the national curriculum but introducing other forms of learning they felt would be of greater benefit to their pupils and students. The achievement of five grade A–C GCSEs remained stubbornly stuck at below 50 per cent of 16-year-olds, and some individual subjects such as mathematics had even lower achievement rates. (See government websites such as www.dcsf.gov.org.uk for trends/patterns of results.) Another major issue had also emerged – about 10 per cent of 16-year-olds were not in education, employment or training (NEETs) at all and were 'lost' in terms of records and information about where they were. The Bow Group – a right-of-centre think tank – produced a report entitled, *The Failed Generation: The Real Cost of Education under Labour*, in 2008 which estimated that nearly 60 per cent of pupils 'had not gained five C grades at GCSE' in the period 1997–2007 (reported by Anushka Asthana in *The Observer*, 20 April 2008).

Hence, many of these issues provided the impetus for the curriculum reforms that came out of the Dearing Report and later the Tomlinson Report and beyond.

## CURRICULUM 2000

The introduction of new modularised A Level specifications in 2000 (C2K) was an attempt to reduce the burden of the content covered in the old qualifications, broaden and increase the flexibility of the post-16 curriculum, and introduce a Key Skills qualification. Advanced Levels had increasingly come under criticism for their narrow academic nature and their elitism in only meeting the needs of those learners (Hodgson and Spours 1997).The C2K two-year course was divided into an Advanced Subsidiary (AS) first year and a second Advanced year known as A2. Post-16 qualifications were streamlined to consist of three, six or twelve units (modules) of work. Typically, an AS was three units, a full A Level six units and a two-year Advanced Certificate in

Vocational Education (AVCE) – formerly known as GNVQs – in total a twelve-unit qualification equivalent to two A Levels. The students generally took an examination at the end of each unit, so that the full A Level would consist of the successful passing of six examinations, or five exams and a piece of coursework. Students were expected to take four or five subjects, and there was the possibility to mix and match vocational and academic qualifications. The flexibility of the new A Levels was expected to improve the rates of staying on into the sixth form. GCSEs and Intermediate GNVQs were retained. The replacement of GNVQs with AVCEs aimed to improve the parity of esteem between the two types of qualifications, because historically vocational qualifications had been seen by many teachers, parents, universities and students as inferior to academic qualifications. However, in the move to align AVCEs more closely with A Levels there was a marked lack of popularity and take-up, especially in further education colleges, according to Hodgson and Spours (2003). A particular weakness of vocational qualifications was the lack of 'recognition' by higher education (Hodgson and Spours 2007). An attempt was also made by the Higher Education Funding Council for England (HEFCE) to improve the knowledge and understanding of university admissions tutors when considering applicants to higher education who had successfully completed GNVQs or AVCEs.

There has been an improvement in staying-on rates into sixth forms and FE colleges since 2000, but it has been suggested that this may be more to do with the introduction of educational maintenance allowances (EMAs) – means-tested payments to 16–18-year-olds of £30 per week if they attend a post-16 course – than with the changes in examinations (Livesey and Lawson 2005). The C2K qualifications have been criticized by leading universities and some sections of the media for 'dumbing down' A levels because of their reduced subject content and an assessment regime that was perceived to be easier than that of the previous A levels. Teachers felt there was never enough time to complete the teaching of the new specifications because the courses ended earlier in order to fit in all the new examinations. A further criticism was that the burden of assessment had become too great, with both students and teachers focusing on preparation for exams rather than on the learning/teaching of the subject.

## THE 14–19 CURRICULUM, 2000–8

There were supporters and critics of Curriculum 2000, but a general view emerged in government and educational circles during the early part of the twenty-first century that the sphere of qualifications should be broadened to encompass the whole 14–19 cohort. The idea that qualifications should be routeways or 'lines of learning' through the educational system, starting at the age of fourteen, was a key feature of the post-Curriculum 2000 debate under the leadership of the then Education Minister, Charles Clarke. The government decided that the whole framework of post-14 qualifications needed to be reviewed, and appointed Mike Tomlinson, a former chief inspector of schools, to head a review committee on all post-14 and post-16 qualifications and propose a new curriculum relevant to the skills needs of the economy in the twenty-first century that would be appropriate for all learners. A further rationale was to create qualifications that would encourage 14–19-year-olds to aspire to higher levels of achievement, whatever their starting point. One of the main criticisms of GCSEs was that they were poor preparation for advanced level study or employment at the age of 16, and that the 14–16 phase needed to be better linked to the 16–18 sector.

## The Tomlinson Report

When Tomlinson was about to present the report from the committee to the government in 2004 there was a change of minister, and Ruth Kelly took over from Charles Clarke. Initially, it appeared that Kelly had rejected the main content of the report and said publicly that A Levels would be retained as the 'gold standard', whereas Tomlinson's report had advocated a variety of new qualifications rolled into an all-encompassing Diploma that could incorporate GCSEs, A Levels and other post-14 qualifications. Tomlinson envisaged that both GCSEs and A levels would eventually be abolished 'by evolution rather than revolution' (DfES 2004, p. 14). Between the publication of the Tomlinson Report and the introduction of the Diplomas, discussion and planning had taken place between employers, examining boards and educationalists to prepare the content and assessment of the Diplomas that were to be offered. By 2008, the new-style Diplomas (see below for a detailed summary of the structure of the diplomas) had been launched by the newly named Department for Children, Schools and Families (DCSF formerly the DfES). In 2007, Ed Balls was in charge of the Department of Education and Gordon Brown had taken over from Tony Blair as prime minister. Balls was a strong proponent of the new diplomas and said 'The Diploma will be crucial in addressing the long standing gaps in our educational system and bridging the pernicious academic and vocational divide. It has already captured the imagination of top employers, universities and colleges' (Polly Curtis reported in the *Guardian*, 25 March 2008; see http://www.guardian.co.uk/education/2005/jun/01/schools.uk).

The new Diplomas were developed in partnership with employers and universities to combine theoretical and practical learning which would engage a wider range of young people, rather than alienate many, as GCSEs were claimed to have done. A leaflet published for the HE sector by the DCSF in 2009 stated that the ten-year reform programme of the education system was 'designed to encourage more young people to continue learning for longer and gain the qualifications they need to progress to further and higher education or skilled employment' (DCSF 2009). However according to Hodgson and Spours, the Specialized Diplomas were in danger of becoming a 'middle-track' qualification between the academic track and apprenticeships 'which will inhibit the Specialized Diplomas from becoming highly regarded and popular qualifications' (Hodgson and Spours 2007).

## THE 14–19 EDUCATIONAL REFORMS, 2008–12

The first five Diploma subjects: Construction and the Built Environment; Creative and Media; Engineering; Information Technology; and Society, Health and Development were introduced in September 2008. Other Diplomas will be introduced up to 2011: in 2009, Environment and Land-based Studies; Hair and Beauty; Business, Administration and Finance; Hospitality; and Manufacturing and Product Design. Public Service; Sport and Leisure; Retail; and Travel and Tourism will appear in 2010, and Science; Languages; and Humanities in 2011.

The Diplomas have three levels; Foundation level, equivalent to five GCSEs at grades D–G; Higher level, equivalent to seven GCSEs at grade A*–C; and Advanced level, equivalent to 3.5 A levels.

The structure of the Diplomas is different from previous qualifications and encompasses six elements:

- *Principal learning* – the skills and knowledge related to a particular group of industries.
- *Functional skills* – the application of English, maths and ICT skills to relevant situations in further education, work and life.
- *Personal learning and thinking skills* – demonstration of the acquisition of skills such as teamwork, creative thinking and self-management.
- *Additional or specialist learning* – enables students to take an additional qualification to deepen and broaden their study.
- *An extended project* – student can explore a topic of interest to themselves, in agreement with their teachers, to demonstrate higher-level skills and autonomous working.
- *Work experience*.

## GCSEs

Vocational GCSEs were introduced in 2002 and are the equivalent in weighting to two traditional GCSEs and the same size as the Part One GNVQs. There are eight subject/work-related areas each consisting of two internally assessed units and one unit that is externally examined. The areas initially offered were Applied Art and Design; Business; ICT; Engineering; Health and Social Care; Leisure and Tourism; and Manufacturing. Most coursework options for GCSE have been abolished.

## A Levels from 2008 onwards

In addition to these changes, in 2008, A levels were reduced from six assessment units to four, to encourage time for learning rather than encouraging a focus solely on assessment. Coursework options in most Advanced level subjects have been abolished. The incorporation of 'Stretch and challenge' to the A2 part of the programme requires more open-ended questions in examinations, synoptic assessment and the development of more holistic understanding of the subject in order to develop higher-order thinking and skills such as critical analysis and evaluation. The notion behind stretch and challenge is to make sure those students deemed to be academically talented are sufficiently engaged with their work and given the scope to display their abilities at the highest level.

## Apprenticeships

Apprenticeships which brought about structured on-the-job training were introduced in 2004 with funding from the Learning and Skills Council. There are five tiers of apprenticeship starting with one designed for 14-year-olds and continuing in stages to an adult level. The courses combine Key Skills with NVQ and promote transferable skills in an occupational area. To help to improve the status of apprenticeships, UCAS published tariff scores for some apprenticeships in 2007, and the government wanted to see more progression from Advanced Apprenticeships to higher education as part of the reforms.

## Evaluation of the 14–19 changes

The specialized diplomas have been strongly supported by the government as a means of inspiring young people to continue their education and improve their attainment rates. There has been recognition in the design of the Diplomas that young people have different learning needs that should be appropriately 'tailored' to them. However, as Hodgson and Spours (2007) have argued these new 'lines of learning' are likely to be directed at a wide range of young people – disaffected learners, those who wish to gain entry to higher education or employment, and those who have not gained at least five A\*–C grade GCSEs by the age of 16. Recent history, they argue, shows that to meet this wide range of needs is likely to involve compromising the aims of the qualifications. Multi-purpose qualifications have several inherent tensions when trying to serve the needs of different groups, with a wide variety of characteristics.

The importance of collaboration between schools, colleges and employers is seen as the cornerstone of the success of these changes. Both the National Commission on Education in 1993 and the Working Group on 14–19 Reform in 2004 argued that the segregation of educational institutions, and hence divisions in academic and vocational qualifications, have exacerbated the problems of low participation and performance. This focus on collaboration has replaced the more competitive marketization ethos of the education system that took place in the 1990s under Margaret Thatcher's Conservative government, which included open enrolment, the creation of school performance tables and parental choice. However, as the first Diplomas came on stream in 2008, collaboration was far from complete, with schools being expected to play the major role in delivering the Diplomas, but without the resources, expertise or facilities to offer more than a small number of them.

## Criticisms of the 14–19 curriculum

1. The retention of GCSEs and A Levels as separate from the Specialized Diplomas will mean that they are still perceived to be superior and more prestigious academic qualifications taken by more 'able' and predominantly middle-class learners. Hence the old divisions of social class will remain in the education system, with working class students being assigned the practical, work-related curriculum, and those from the middle class following the academic stream into higher education (see Exercise 4.6 below).

2. The Specialized Diploma will be a 'middle track' qualification, sitting between the traditional academic qualifications and apprenticeships. Hence the Diplomas will fail to become embedded as popular and high-status qualifications, and the same tensions between academic and work-related learning will continue to exist in the minds of students, parents and wider society. 'Academic drift' – 'the process whereby vocational qualifications may take on the feature of academic counterparts' (Hodgson

and Spours 2007) – may occur, as happened with the introduction of AVCEs, if the status of the Diplomas is not consolidated.

3. The rushed implementation of the Diplomas, with most on stream by 2010 rather than 2013 as originally planned, may cause problems in trying to establish their position in the 'qualifications landscape'. Without 'radical whole-system reform' absorbing GCSEs and A levels into the Diplomas, work-related or vocational learning will still struggle with issues of prestige.

4. The government has presented the Specialized Diplomas as a positive addition to the qualifications framework, but also as an 'alternative' to academic study. Once again, the division between vocational and academic study is highlighted as different in character and, by implication, status.

5. The Specialized Diplomas and the practical, work-related learning associated with them could been seen as preparing young people for their place in the workforce, as a means of socialising them into capitalist work values, habits and attitudes. Hence the real purpose of curriculum change is to create a docile, passive workforce for the benefit of employers.

6. The content of the Specialized Diplomas could exacerbate gender divisions in the choice of subject taken during the pre-14 phase. Whereas previously students had limited choices in their GCSEs not making, gendered subject choices until the post-16 phase.

## Exercise 4.6

Read again the first point made in the last section on' Emerging Criticisms of the 14–19 Curriculum', about the class-divided nature of the education system. List as many other examples of educational policy and practice that could be given as evidence that there has always been a two-tier education system in the UK based on social class. Also identify sociological studies where appropriate. Use the information given below as your first example.

## EVERY CHILD MATTERS (ECM)

The government has developed a new approach to childhood well-being since the death of Victoria Climbié, who was murdered in February 2000 while in the care of her aunt. Now, all organisations such as schools, welfare agencies, Sure Start, the police and health care providers that provide services to children are beginning to work together and share information to protect children from harm and to enable them to achieve their aspirations.

ECM is an approach to childhood from birth to the age of 19, and aims to make sure children are healthy and safe, are able to enjoy and achieve, make positive contributions and achieve economic well-being. Useful websites are: www.dcsf.gov.uk/publications/childrensplan andwww.ecm.gov.uk.

| Important concepts |
| --- |
| marketization • widening participation • privatization of education |

| Critical thinking |
| --- |
| • Should the needs of the economy drive an education system to the extent that schools should mirror the practices of industry?<br>• Do teachers have any influence over educational policy? Should they?<br>• In your opinion, has the attempt to improve staying-on rates at school and widening participation rates for under-represented groups in higher education been successful? |

*Chapter 5*

# Explaining Class Differences in Educational Achievement

By the end of this chapter you should:

- be able to describe class differences in educational achievement
- be able to assess different explanations of class differences in educational achievement
- appreciate the way government educational policies can affect the educational achievements of different social classes
- have given critical thought to the concept of social class in postmodern societies
- have reflected on student answers to exam questions
- have practised structured exam questions yourself

## INTRODUCTION

Despite, or perhaps because of, the educational changes since the late 1940s, class inequalities in educational achievement remain as firmly entrenched as ever. In this chapter we shall consider the disparities in attainment by class, and then offer a set of explanations to account for such differential educational performance. 'Class' here refers to socio-economic inequality: that is, differences in income and wealth that characterize capitalist economic systems such as that in the United Kingdom. Four types of explanation will be advanced: (i) genetic explanations, focusing on innate differences in intelligence; (ii) outside school explanations (non-genetic), which find their answers in terms of the home backgrounds of the different social classes; (iii) inside school explanations, which look at systems of organization and social processes inside schools; and (iv) a structuration approach, which combines elements of the outside school and inside school explanations.

At the end of Chapter 7, 'Bringing it all together', there is some recent sociological material about the interplay between class, gender and ethnic difference in relation to educational achievement.

## EVIDENCE OF CLASS DIFFERENCES IN EDUCATIONAL ACHIEVEMENT

Sociological evidence suggests that working-class pupils underachieve in the education system compared with middle-class pupils, and have done so for a long time. Though it is sometimes difficult to measure these differences, because the government does not always collect statistics in a form that is useful for class analysis, there has been long-standing evidence that a social-class attainment gap exists in the British education system. The failure of successive governments to tackle the issue of the social-class attainment gap has meant that unequal outcomes are the destiny of many working-class students (Reay 2006). Items A and B below provide some evidence of the disparities that exist, and Exercise 5.1 will help you to explore them.

### Item A

**Table 5.1** Standardized scores for KS2 (age 11) and KS4 (age 16), by social class background of pupils, 2006

| Social class | KS2 | KS4 |
|---|---|---|
| Higher managerial and professional | 0.63 | 0.59 |
| Lower managerial | 0.35 | 0.30 |

**Table 5.1**   (Continued)

| Social class | KS2 | KS4 |
|---|---|---|
| Intermediate | 0.13 | 0.05 |
| Small employers | 0.01 | 0.03 |
| Lower supervisory and technical | −0.10 | −0.17 |
| Semi-routine | −0.23 | −0.29 |
| Routine | −0.34 | −0.48 |
| Long-term unemployed | −0.62 | −0.73 |
| **Gap (top versus bottom)** | **1.26** | **1.32** |

*Note*: Average for all pupils standardised at 0. Figures indicate deviation from the average by social class groupings. A positive number indicates that the class achieves higher than the average. A negative number indicates that a class achieves lower than the average.
*Source*: Adapted from Strand, S. (2008) *Minority Ethnic Pupils in the Longitudinal Study of Young People in England*, University of Warwick.

## Item B

**Table 5.2**   Standardized scores for KS2 (age 11) and KS4 (age 16) children, by mothers' highest educational qualification, 2006

| Mothers' highest educational qualification | KS2 | KS4 |
|---|---|---|
| Degree or equivalent | 0.80 | 0.80 |
| HE below degree | 0.34 | 0.32 |
| A Level or equivalent | 0.22 | 0.20 |
| GCSE grades A*–C or equivalent | 0.02 | −0.03 |
| Other qualifications | −0.26 | −0.28 |
| None | −0.46 | −0.34 |
| **Gap (top versus bottom)** | **1.26** | **1.14** |

*Note*: Average for all pupils standardised at 0. Figures indicate deviation from the average by mothers' highest educational qualification. A positive number indicates that the class achieves higher than the average. A negative number indicates that a class achieves lower than the average.
*Source*: Adapted from Strand, S. (2008) *Minority Ethnic Pupils in the Longitudinal Study of Young People in England*, University of Warwick.

## Item C

**Table 5.3** Social class background of students gaining five or more grades A*–C GCSEs, England and Wales, 2002 (percentages)

| Social class | Percentage |
| --- | --- |
| Higher professional | 77 |
| Lower professional | 64 |
| Intermediate | 52 |
| Lower supervisory | 35 |
| Routine | 32 |

*Source*: Department for Education and Skills (2002) *Youth Cohort Study*.

## Exercise 5.1

1. According to Item A, what pattern emerges from the data concerning attainment at Key Stage 2 and Key Stage 4 in relation to occupational categories?
2. Using the information in Items A and B, write a paragraph supporting the claim that differential educational achievement exists by social class.
3. With reference to Item B, what is the impact of a mother's educational background on the attainment of her children?
4. What might be the advantages of using the mother's educational qualifications rather than the father's to understand and explain the achievement of children?
5. Suggest one explanation for the differences in performance by social class shown in the Items.
6. Sociologists could level the criticism that terms such as 'professional' and 'routine', as used in Items A and C, are too broad. Suggest a way in which the 'routine' category could usefully be subdivided.

## Exercise 5.2

Official statistics can go out of date quickly. Try to update the statistics we have presented on class inequalities in educational attainment. You could start this search by referring to the most recent edition of *Social Trends*, which is available on the internet. If your search is successful, repeat questions 1 and 2 in Exercise 5.1. There are some excellent websites with easy-to-access statistical information, which will allow you to compare these figures with more up-to-date versions: www.nationalstatistics.gov.uk; www.statistics.gov.uk; www.neigbourhood.statistics.gov.uk; www.ons.gov.uk; and www.dcsf.gov.uk.

It is not only governments that collect information on social class inequality in education. Charities such as the Joseph Rowntree Foundation, who are concerned with child poverty, focus on educational under-achievement as a main cause of such poverty. Hirsch (2006) argued that the differences between social classes in terms of educational qualification are much greater in the UK than in other similar countries. Other measures of educational disadvantage can also be taken into account. The proportion of working-class students who enter university is about a third, while three-quarters of their middle-class counterparts do so. Munn and Lloyd (2005) showed that working-class pupils were more likely to be excluded from school than middle-class pupils. Where working-class students *do* obtain qualifications, they lead to less social mobility than middle-class students with equivalent attainment (Marshall 2002).

## EXPLANATIONS OF CLASS DIFFERENCES IN EDUCATIONAL ACHIEVEMENT

Now that you have some appreciation of the extent of class inequalities in educational performance, we shall move on to address what have become established explanations for such inequalities. Four explanations will be considered.

1. Genetic explanations.
2. Outside school explanations.
3. Inside school explanations.
4. A structuration explanation.

### Genetic explanations

Genetic accounts of class differences in educational attainment are suggested by some psychologists. Four main points are put forward in this explanation.

1. Intelligence is fixed at birth and can be measured in a scientific way using intelligence quotient (IQ) tests (see Exercise 5.3 to try some IQ test questions for yourself).

2. Objective IQ tests have shown that working-class students are less intelligent than middle-class students.
3. 'Measured' differences in 'natural' intelligence account for class inequalities in educational achievement.
4. Class inequalities in educational performance continue over time because intelligence is largely genetically inherited – the inequalities are in effect passed down from one generation to the next.

## Exercise 5.3

1. Below are five questions taken from an IQ test. Try to answer the questions yourself for fun!

   (a) Underline the odd-man-out.
      Byron   Shelley   Keats   Chamberlain   Chaucer
   (b) Underline the phrase which completes the sequence.
      Alfred had his cakes; Bruce had his spider; Canute had his waves.
      Which comes next:
      Charles with his Nell; John with his barons; Keats with his poetry; Henry with his wives; or Richard with his hunchback?
   (c) Underline which two of these six drawings do not make a pair.

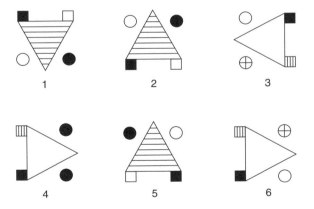

   (d) Underline which of these is not a film star.

      BALEG
      RAYLOT
      OROPEC
      PALSREM
      DABTOR

(e) Underline which of these is not a girl's name.

SAYDI
BLISY
SHOLT
TEEMILCNEN

*Source*: H. J. Eysenck, *Know Your Own IQ* (Harmondsworth, Penguin) 1962.

Ⓘ Ⓔ 2. A number of sociologists have questioned the methodological basis of genetic explanations. It is argued that the IQ tests are culturally loaded in favour of middle-class children and are therefore not objective. Justify this claim in the light of the IQ questions you have just attempted.

Ⓘ Ⓔ 3. Give two other criticisms sociologists have made against genetic explanations of class differences in educational achievement.

It is important to note that it is not just psychologists who put forward genetic explanations, but also sociologists. Peter Saunders (1994) argues that there is a strong body of evidence to support a link between intelligence and social class. However, Saunders does not rely on intelligence testing on its own, but argues that, in a truly meritocratic society, we should expect to find some connection between social class and occupational success. He argues that, as the middle class has expanded through occupational changes, the proportion of working-class children who make it into the middle class are much the same as might be predicted if intelligence was the key factor influencing class membership. His conclusion is that Britain is a society largely based on talent. However, his work has been criticized for denying the importance of IQ testing, while at the same time using the concept of IQ in his calculations of the intelligence of different classes. It is also important to note that Saunders is critical of the conclusions reached by Herrnstein and Murray (1994) concerning race and intelligence. He suggests that class is socially selected and therefore subject to a 'sorting out' process, where, over generations, the less intelligent filter to the bottom of the class system, whereas race is fixed at birth and therefore is not subject to this same sifting process (see Chapter 6).

Gillborn and Youdell (2001) have argued that, while the term 'intelligence' is seldom used in British education, it has been replaced by what they call a 'proxy' term – 'ability' (see Exercise 5.4 below to explore this concept). In their research they found that teachers commonly used the term to describe their students and see it as a fixed, objective term that had the effect of determining a pupil's achievement and performance. Gillborn and Youdell also make the case that the term 'ability' is used in systematic ways to disadvantage particular groups, such working-class children and those of a black, African-Caribbean heritage.

## Exercise 5.4

Use the table below to write down, from your own experience, ways in which teachers and/or schools use the term 'ability' in day-to-day teaching and interaction with pupils. One example is given to get you started.

| Example of use of term 'ability' in school | Explanation and elaboration of the action associated with the application of the term |
| --- | --- |
| Banding/streaming/setting | Pupils in primary and secondary schools are tested and ranked by their ability then put into groups based on that ability. In primary schools, children are commonly put together at a table for different subjects – they may be moved during the literacy/numeracy hour, for example. In secondary schools, pupils may be streamed by subject or as a whole class. |

### Outside school explanations

Sociologists reject the notion of innate ability or intelligence, because both terms are socially constructed. We have given meaning to behaviour and attached a label to it. In Western society, 'intelligence' is usually related to academic ability, for example, and we tend not to consider other 'intelligences', such as emotional intelligence (Gardner 1983), as having a similar status. See Chapter 2 for a discussion of these issues. Within a more sociological framework, the effects of home background have been a key focus of research and sociological investigation over many years. Three distinct social (as opposed to genetic) explanations have emerged from the 'outside school' approach. These all adopt a macro approach, looking at the structures of society to examine educational underachievement:

- Material deprivation theory
- Cultural deprivation theory
- Cultural difference theory

*Material deprivation theory*

This explanation focuses on income inequality and the material social problems that go with it (see Exercise 5.5 below). It is argued that working-class households have lower incomes than their middle-class counterparts, and as a consequence experience material deprivations such as an unhealthy diet and unsatisfactory housing conditions. These deprivations in turn are said to hinder the children's chances of success at school (as judged by test and examination results). Douglas (1964) in *The Home and the School,* a longitudinal study that followed children born in a particular week in March 1958, offers partial support for the materialistic approach. For example, he demonstrates that unsatisfactory housing conditions did in fact depress school test performances at the time of the study. In a more recent example of perceived inequalities arising out of material deprivation, government ministers were considering giving free computers to the million poorest families in England in order to ensure that all children can benefit from the new technologies.

One implication of the material deprivation theory is that, as the material conditions of the working class improve, then differential educational achievement can be eliminated. However, improvements in social conditions since the 1960s have not brought about a decrease in the gap between working-class and middle-class educational achievement. Yet the statistical link between material deprivation and educational underachievement still remains, with schools drawing their pupils from the most deprived areas of cities performing less well than those in more affluent suburbs.

Ⓐ

## Exercise 5.5

A spider diagram has been started for you (Figure 5.1), to show the way in which material deprivation depresses the school performance of working-class students. Copy out and complete the diagram yourself by indicating three other ways in which a lack of income may contribute to working-class underachievement in schools.

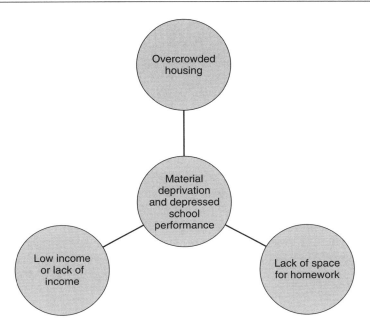

**Figure 5.1**   Material deprivation and depressed school performance

### Cultural deprivation theory

Cultural deprivation theory locates class differences primarily in educational attainment in terms of the varying attitudes towards education that emerge from different class cultures. It is claimed that working-class attitudes and values are in some way 'inferior' or less beneficial for education than the middle classes' value systems, and as a consequence the working-class home acts as a 'deficit system'. This idea is based on the assumption that most working-class parents share a value system that encourages their children to drop out of school early, and devalues what they learn there. However, this is to assign to the working class as a whole features that may only pertain to a part of it. It ignores, for example, the long tradition of educational self-help of other sections of the working class.

A number of studies, including Douglas (1964) and the Plowden Report (1967), have pointed out that working-class parents offer less encouragement and support towards their children's education than do middle-class parents do, and that this helps to explain in some part the differences in educational performance between the social classes (do Exercise 5.6 below to explore this further). However, others, such as Tizard *et al.* (1981), argue that the apparent lack of interest by working-class parents in their children's education may mask their lack of confidence or knowledge in dealing with schools, rather than an indifference to their children's fate. Research, conducted by Feinstein (2003) using more recent statistics, supported Douglas's findings about the correlation between parents' lack of interest in their children's education and poor achievement. Masud Hoghughi, Professor of Parenting and Child Development at Northumbria University, argues that parental attitudes to schooling are the most potent factors in children's achievement. Low-achieving pupils typically come from backgrounds in which parents suffer low self-esteem and have low expectations in terms of educational attainment (Hoghughi, reported in *The Times Educational Supplement*, 12 February, 1999). The DfES (now DCFS) also found that parental attitudes to education were 'significant' in shaping the achievement of children throughout their schooling, especially in relation to aspirations and staying-on rate after the age of 16 (Desforges and Abouchaar, 2003).

Reay (2001) suggested more recently that middle-class mothers invest emotional labour in their children's education, which develops a sense of value in education itself, whereas working-class mothers do not place particular value in their children getting a good education. This is manifested in working-class children leaving school as early as possible, and middle-class children staying on and going to university. Reay points out that middle-class mothers will encourage their children, help with homework and schoolwork generally, as well as engaging with the school to improve their children's performance. (For a general review of parental involvement issues, see Desforges and Aboucharr 2003.)

New Right theorists, such as Charles Murray, point to the formation of an underclass which, because of material and cultural factors, is largely outside the system. This group have become know as NEETs – young people who are 'not in education, employment or training'– on the margins of society. They are the stereotypical 'school refusers' – those who have played truant, not taken any exams, perhaps with poor literacy and numeracy skills, been difficult at school, causing disruption, and had periods of being excluded from school.

Ⓐ
## Exercise 5.6

Working with another sociology student, identify four possible examples of 'deficient' parental attitudes or values that might contribute to working-class under-achievement in schools. The following example should help to get you started.

1. Working-class parents are less likely to attend parent evenings.
2. Some parents may collude in their children's truancy.

*Compensatory educational policies*

During the 1960s, one solution to cultural deprivation was attempted, with compensatory education programmes. These were an attempt to provide additional educational provision for the 'culturally deprived', to try to offset those attitudes and behaviours that were said to restrict educational achievement. In the USA, the government's compensatory package was named 'Operation Head Start', and in Britain the government established 'educational priority areas'. It should be noted that these programmes were genuine attempts to promote equality of opportunity and had the effect of channelling funds into areas of deprivation. Central to the operation of these schemes was the belief that, if it was possible to encourage positive attitudes towards schooling early enough, then the negative effects of working-class culture could be countered.

The Sure Start scheme (2003/4) was introduced in Britain by the government to try to improve parenting skills, prepare children from deprived backgrounds for entry to school and provide free child care. Its aim was to bring together education, health, child care and family support in neighbourhood Children's Centres as service hubs for children aged under five. The target is that every community should have a Sure Start Children's Centre with an integrated service by 2010. The impetus for the development of Sure Start was the continuing evidence that children from particular backgrounds entered school already disadvantaged because of material and cultural deprivation. For example, according to DfES research into differences in performance, 73 per cent is related to a child's level of achievement on starting secondary school (see www.dfes.gov.uk/research/data/uploadfiles/SSU_SF_2004_02.pdf). For useful information refer to: http://www.surestart.gov.uk/.

Another recent manifestation of compensatory education in Britain has been the widening participation programme, which provided government funding to universities to develop projects to encourage children from families with no previous experience of higher education to go to university. This programme operates through the Aimhigher Agency and typically works with 13–19-year-olds from the most deprived areas, whose parents' occupations are generally in the less skilled sector. Its purpose is to raise the aspirations, motivation and self-esteem of these pupils in order to raise levels of attainment at Key Stages 3 and 4, and to encourage progression to higher education.

The history of these schemes suggests that the effects of such interventions are varied and depend on a number of factors, including how 'success' is actually measured. They are also subject to changes in political attitudes. While the postwar social democratic consensus held sway, the schemes were seen as an appropriate way of encouraging meritocracy. However left-wing critics argued that the schemes were based on middle-class professionals' misconceptions of working-class culture, rather than on any real research. Right-wing opponents disliked the increased state intervention that the schemes involved, seeing them as overly bureaucratic and a drain on taxpayers' money.

ⒾⒺ

## Exercise 5.7

This exercise is designed to broaden your understanding of compensatory education. Search the Internet for any information that covers 'Operation Headstart' and 'educational priority areas', making brief notes on them by jotting down the different aspects of the policies and the criticisms that have been made of them. For example, you might look at the Institute for Employment Studies' website: www.employment-studies.co.uk, for information about the effects of debt on students from poorer backgrounds, and the implications for their progression through higher education.

### Material and cultural deprivation theories – an evaluation

The strengths of the theories are as follows:

1. They are an improvement on earlier genetic-based theories, because they recognise the importance of social (as opposed to biological) causes of class inequalities in educational attainment.
2. The explanations have served to generate a great deal of further sociological research into class inequalities in educational performance.
3. Most of the empirical support for the two theories is of a quantitative nature and is therefore high in reliability.

ⒾⒶⒺ

## Exercise 5.8

Below are a number of partly completed statements relating to the weaknesses of the material and cultural deprivation approaches. Your task is to complete these statements by selecting the appropriate end to each sentence from the three alternatives provided.

1. The explanations have only looked at factors outside the school . . . . . .
2. The explanations are to some extent deterministic because . . . . . .
3. Cultural deprivation theory implies that the working-class child is in some way deficient . . . . . . .

Matching sentence endings:

(a) they see the child's performance as being determined by external social forces.
(b) but it could be that they are simply different. Many argue that it is the education system that is deficient because it is not prepared for the working-class child.
(c) they have ignored the influence of social processes operating inside schools – for example, the effects of streaming.

---

Ⓐ Ⓔ

## Exercise 5.9

One further criticism that can be made of the material and cultural deprivation approaches is that there is no attempt to link the cultural with the material. This is a major weakness, because it is necessary in order to understand the way in which material factors shape cultural behaviours. The 'flow' diagram below illustrates one of the possible links. Your task for this exercise is draw two other 'flow' diagrams that further illustrate the material and cultural connection.

The necessity to work night shifts (material constraint)

↓

Non-attendance at parent evenings (cultural behaviour)

---

As Keddie (1971) argued, focusing on the deficiencies of children and their families directs attention away from the issues connected to the school.

### Cultural difference theory

This theory focuses on the mismatch between working-class culture and the middle-class culture of schools. Historically, it is associated with Bernstein's (1975) language codes theory and Bourdieu's (1973) and Bourdieu's and

Passeron's (1977) cultural capital theory. As an explanation for class differences in educational attainment, it can be considered to be more sophisticated than the cultural deprivation theory. This is because the theory draws on the notion of cultural difference rather than cultural deprivation (deprivation almost implies inferiority), and the fact that its theorists recognise that the education system is in some way responsible for the underachievement of working-class pupils.

Bernstein's examination of the relationship between social class, mode of cognitive expression and educational attainment can at times be complex (see, for example, Bernstein, 1975). What follows is a simplified version of some of his earlier thoughts on this subject, developed in the 1960s and 1970s.

First, people's position in the class structure determines the mode of cognitive expression (language code) they are socialised into.

Second, working-class children are generally socialized into a restricted language code, characterized by:

1. A limited vocabulary.
2. Context-bound speech – that is, particular to the context in which it is spoken.
3. Grammatically simple.
4. Short and descriptive sentences.

A typical sentence might be: 'Me ma learnt me to read.'

Third, middle-class children are generally socialised into an elaborated language code (though they too have access to the restricted code). This form of language is largely confined to the middle classes and includes the following characteristics:

1. An extensive vocabulary.
2. Context-free speech – that is, independent of the context in which it is spoken.
3. Grammatically complex.
4. Long and analytical sentences.

A typical sentence might be: 'My mother taught me how to read.'

Fourth, the different language patterns people adopt affects their educability (their potential to be educated). This is because the formal teaching of schools and externally set examinations are undertaken in the elaborated language code.

Fifth, middle-class children are more likely to succeed at school because they are able to draw on the elaborated language code, which is essential for educational success. For example, they will be able to write essays that demonstrate abstract analysis.

Finally, working-class children are more likely to under-perform at school because the language code they adopt clashes with the speech patterns used in schools – it is in effect inappropriate for educational success. For example, they may write essays that are overly descriptive and lacking in analysis.

## Exercise 5.10

Using the account of Bernstein's thoughts in this chapter, write a short paragraph (no more than sixty words) that summarizes his language code theory of differential educational performance. You could start your paragraph in the following way:
'Working-class students underperform educationally in comparison with middle-class students because...'.

### The work of Labov

Labov (1973) conducted research that challenged the notion that working-class speech was somehow 'deficient'. In his work with young, black American children he found the linguistic variation or deprivation was the result of the way in which research had been conducted. He found that certain interviewing techniques produced particular results. When children were put at ease they would open up and show their rich language skills. Furthermore, when their supposed 'deficient' language skills were interpreted by someone from the same background, the meanings behind the language were clear and appropriate for the world in which they lived. Hence, consciously or unconsciously, interviewer and cultural bias has been apparent in studies such as Bernstein's, whereby language codes had been interpreted from a middle-class, white perspective.

Bourdieu's work, like that of Bernstein, is complex, and we offer only a simplified version of his ideas, which were developed in the 1970s (see Bourdieu 1973; Bourdieu and Passeron 1977).

First, social groups with control over economic capital (wealth) can ensure that their sons/daughters also pick up cultural capital (knowledge, demeanour, language, tastes, lifestyle).

Second, the possession of cultural capital is essential if educational capital (qualifications) is to be obtained. This is because schools are essentially middle-class institutions that assess pupils in terms of their grasp of 'high' (middle-class) culture. See our earlier point on page 98 about the effect of middle-class mothers' investment in emotional labour to ensure the educational success of their children (Reay 2001).

Third, working-class students underachieve in the education system because they do not have the same access to cultural capital; for example, trips to the cinema, the theatre and museums. Working-class culture is in effect too distant from the 'academic' culture embedded in schooling to allow for educational success.

Thus a major function of schools is to pass on privilege from one generation to another. Given the ideological importance of the concept of meritocracy in justifying social arrangements, schools ensure that the children of the working class will remain in the working class because they are handicapped in the acquisition of cultural capital by their home background.

Critics of cultural approaches to working-class under-achievement argue that the cultural differences between working-class children and middle-class schools are not as important as the material disadvantages suffered by working-class children. While being aware that real cultural differences do exist, Lynch and O'Neill (1994) argue that it is poverty that often lies behind this tension. They give the example of school rules concerning shoes, which were resented by working-class parents, not because of shape or colour, but because they could not afford separate shoes for home and school. Hence the major problem facing working-class children is that their parents have insufficient material resources to take advantage of the opportunities that schools provide. See our earlier point regarding lack of access to information and communication technologies (ICT) among deprived households.

Moreover, we should be careful not to stereotype social class groupings into automatic 'successes' or 'failures'. Aggleton (1987) shows how some middle-class children with cultural capital resist schooling in ways similar to working-class children, and come out of school with poor qualifications. Aggleton argues that there is a conflict between the culture of the home backgrounds of these middle-class resisters, which stresses personal fulfilment and creativity, and the stifling regimentation of most school life. The major difference between these middle-class resisters and their working-class counterparts is that, in the labour market, the middle class do not seem to be impaired in the same way as the working class, so that their cultural capital pays off, despite their lack of formal qualifications.

*An evaluation of cultural difference theories (Bernstein and Bourdieu)*

**Strengths:**

1. They recognize that the working-class child is culturally different rather than deficient.
2. They appreciate that the education system is in some way at fault because it is not responsive to a range of cultural backgrounds – it is too middle-class.

**Weaknesses:**

1. They both lack empirical support.
2. They are both deterministic. They assume that working-class culture is inevitably passed on. They do not acknowledge that some working-class students do break away from their culture, have a high level of cultural capital and adopt elaborated language codes.

### Inside school explanations

These explanations adopt a micro sociological framework, turning inwards to look at the internal workings of schools and the role of teachers. Two areas of the schooling process have been paid particular attention by interactionist sociologists interested in explaining class differences in educational attainment:

- Streaming (banding or setting).
- Teachers' expectations.

Both these areas constitute part of what is called the hidden curriculum. This is all the unofficial or informal learning that takes place inside schools and in the classroom. Sociologists argue that, through the hidden curriculum of streaming and teacher expectations, educational success and failure are socially constructed. What is meant by this is that failure or success in schools is not a natural phenomenon, linked to genetic ability alone. Rather, the experiences that children have in schools shape and influence the qualifications they emerge with at the end of their schooling.

While it is obvious that the formal curriculum (timetabled subjects such as history, biology and so on) has an important effect on what is learnt in schools, sociologists have argued that factors such as the structure of the school or the way teachers deal with different types of pupil also have important effects on educational outcomes. Marxist sociologists in particular have suggested that this hidden curriculum is the most important part of schooling, because it legitimises inequality through the application of the label 'failure' to those from a working-class background. Those so labelled end up in working-class occupations, believing that their low position in the social hierarchy is a result of their own inadequacy.

## Exercise 5.11

This exercise has been designed to get you to think about the way in which streaming and teacher expectations affect educational outcomes. The fictitious characters are deliberately stereotyped so that the effects of the hidden curriculum are immediately visible to you.

Read the case studies and then answer the questions that follow. You should initially do this on your own, but compare and discuss your responses with at least two other sociology students when you have finished.

### Fictitious background

Each student is enrolled at Leicester City Comprehensive School (11–18), and all are 14 years of age. They are streamed into three sets for maths, English and foreign languages, and are taught in mixed ability groupings for all their other subjects. School uniform is worn between the ages of 11 and 16.

### Student A

- Mother lives off state benefits as a single parent.
- Smells.
- Comes to school in 'tatty' clothes and has been sent home twice this year for 'inappropriate dress'.
- Very quiet in class.
- Rarely works in class and is frequently seen 'doodling' and daydreaming.
- Sits on her own and is not liked by the other students.
- Her English and design teachers have described her as 'lazy' and 'thick'.
- In the lowest sets for maths, English and foreign languages.

### Student B

- Mum is a school nurse and a school governor. Dad is an accountant.
- Well dressed.
- Works reasonably quietly.
- Homework is often late but always handed in.
- Very popular with the 'bright' pupils.
- Described at her last school as an 'underperforming' student.
- Had three detentions this year for smoking in the toilets.
- Predicted GCSE results: two Es, five Ds, one C, one B.
- In the middle band for maths, English and foreign languages.

*Student C*

- Mum works in a pub. Dad is a paint sprayer.
- Often fails to wear the school uniform. Three letters have already been sent home this year.
- A noisy and disruptive pupil.
- Has handed in three pieces of homework since starting school.
- Plays truant and feels that school is a laugh.
- Very popular with the 'lower ability' students.
- Described by his geography teacher as a 'good for nothing'.
- In the lowest sets for maths, English and foreign languages.
- Hates teachers.

*Student D*

- Dad is a primary school head. Mum is the owner of a local bookshop.
- Has a new school uniform each year.
- A very quiet worker.
- Homework is always handed in on time.
- Very popular with the 'bright' students.
- Quick to ask questions in class.
- In the top sets for maths, English and foreign languages. Obtained a B grade in GCSE maths at the age of 13.
- Sits on the school council.

*Student E*

- Mum is a single parent and works as a childminder.
- Often fails to wear a school uniform. Mum was called in by the head last week to make her conform.
- Very 'noisy' in class.
- Homework is handed in late.
- Popular with all the students in her year.
- Described in her last report as an arrogant student.
- In the top set for English and bottom sets for maths and foreign languages.
- Hates all her teachers other than her tutor.

1. Which social class is each student from?
2. How are the teachers in the school likely to respond to each student?
3. What will be each student's reaction to schooling?
4. What are the likely educational qualifications and jobs each student will obtain?

*Streaming*

The issue of streaming in schools is an important one, both sociologically and politically. Streaming according to ability (as defined by testing) has usually been associated with traditional modes of teaching. 'Progressive' teaching is more associated with mixed ability classes. The arguments in favour of mixed ability teaching are (i) it is less divisive than streaming; and (ii) it allows the less able to be helped by the more able, so that educational standards will be improved. Theorists of the New Right argue that the effect of mixed ability teaching is to lower standards, as 'bright' students are held back by the slowness of the less able. On the other hand, streaming allows the appropriate pitching of lessons for both bright and less able pupils.

There has been a trend for primary schools to set pupils by ability. However, according to research, this is leading to children being grouped largely by their social class, resulting in significant differences in the way children are taught and different outcomes in terms of educational achievement (Lupton *et al.* 2006). Thus critics of streaming and setting argue that they institutionalise failure and, in so far as children are selected according to their social class background, these processes contribute to the educational underachievement of working-class children. In lower sets, mainly occupied by working-class children, the pupils experience lowered expectations and a loss of self-esteem (Hallam and Ireson 2006). In this way, streaming and setting might be regarded as the formal process of labelling children as successes or failures.

Differentiation has become a more recent focus, particularly in relation to Ofsted inspections of schools, when teachers are observed in their classrooms and judgements made about their standard of teaching. Differentiated teaching is supposed to take into account the different levels of ability, different learning styles or preferences, the pace each child can work at, and to ensure that all can achieve their potential. Teachers are expected to plan their lessons with differentiated teaching methods and assessment strategies if they are to be judged good teachers. (See Chapter 2 for a discussion on learning styles.) Differentiation is intended to overcome the variation in 'ability' and allow children to work at their own pace to achieve similar results.

Exercise 5.12

The eight paragraphs below summarize the main findings of a series of studies carried out on the effects of streaming in secondary schools. These studies include the work of Hargreaves (1967) and Lacey (1970). Bearing in mind what you have learnt from Exercise 5.10, complete the missing gaps by selecting appropriate words from the list provided below.

1. Streaming is based on ....... High-ability students are placed in high ...... and low-ability students are placed in low streams.
2. While streaming is supposed to be based on ability there is a strong correlation with social class. ....... -class students are found in the high sets and ...... -class students are found in the low sets.
3. There is little movement between streams.
4. Before streaming, most students (both working-class and middle-class) were committed to the school's ....... For example, hard work and good behaviour.
5. Since the introduction of streaming, the high streamers have developed a ....... Emphasis is given to hard work, punctuality, good behaviour and so on. However, the low streamers have developed an ....... This oppositional culture rejects the norms and values of the school (and the pro-school culture) and replaces them with an alternative set of deviant norms and values. A high value is placed on .......
6. The anti-school subculture is a group response to being ...... by the school as .......
7. The anti-school subculture offers a form of ....... Status and respect can be earned from other group members by following the deviant norms and values of the subculture. For example, .......
8. In summary, working-class students under-perform in the education system because they are placed in low sets, they see themselves as failures, and form anti-school subcultures that reject the value of educational success.

**Missing text to be inserted above:**

(a) working
(b) copying, lateness, cheeking the teacher, toughness, truanting
(c) 'failures'
(d) who can get to the lesson the latest!
(e) ability
(f) norms and values
(g) pro-school culture
(h) status recovery
(i) Middle
(j) labelled
(k) streams
(l) anti-school subculture

---

*Teachers' expectations*

Teachers' expectations of children's performance depend on a whole range of factors, such as gender, ethnicity and social class. It is argued that these expectations are important because they provide the framework within which individual pupils perform and within which they are classified as a success or failure. Thus it is suggested that powerful stereotypes operate in the classroom, and in the school generally, that affect the performance of those subject to the stereotypes. Thus a labelling process operates in schools, which, in changing the behaviour of those labelled, results in a self-fulfilling prophecy (see Exercise 5.13 below). A self-fulfilling prophecy occurs when individuals live up to a label that has been placed on them. Both Rosenthal and Jacobson (1968) and Becker (1952) conducted research which showed teachers employing stereotypes and labelling in their day-to-day interaction with pupils that informed their expectations of the children, and treated them according to these labels. In particular, Becker found that pupils were labelled in accordance with social class stereotypes. Cordingly (1993) argues that class stereotypes have 'dropped off the educational agenda', with the result that, while gender and racial stereotypes are combated within schools, the discrimination that white, working-class boys experience through teacher stereotyping is ignored. This is especially important when one considers that white, working-class boys are one of the lowest-achieving groups in the education system. Nor do teacher training courses prepare teachers adequately to examine social equity issues as they pertain to social class (Gazeley and Dunne 2007). Partly as a result of this invisibility of the issue, Smith (2003) found that teachers did not make a distinction between low attainment and under-achievement when analysing previous attainment data on their pupils. As a result, they often underestimated the potential of working-class students by assuming that their under-achievement was just low attainment. Dunne and Gazeley (2008) found that teachers tended to define middle-class and working-class under-achievement differently and locate the reason for working-class under-achievement in factors that were outside their control, such as the home life of such students.

ⒾⒶ
## Exercise 5.13

Figure 5.2 offers a summary of the self-fulfilling prophecy effect that teachers' expectations have on pupils. Some of the research studies in this area include Cicourel and Kitsuse (1963), Rist (1970), Nash (1973) and Dunne and Gazeley (2008).

Using the diagram, write a brief paragraph (no more than 60 words) explaining how teachers' expectations contribute to class differences in educational attainment.

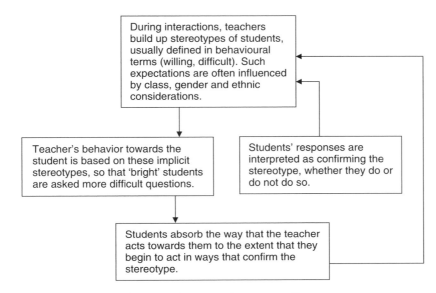

**Figure 5.2**   The effect of teachers' expectations on pupils

## Control of the school

New Right theorists in the 1980s and 1990s argued that the major reason for the under-achievement of the working class was the deadening hand of the state in controlling what went on in schools (see Brown and Lauder 1991). Brown and Lauder began from the idea that fundamental human nature consists of rational self-interest, and therefore, in a world where credentials are a clear route to success, everyone is interested in gaining the maximum qualifications possible. They therefore suggest that a free market in schools, where parents can exercise their choice rationally, will of itself get rid of educational inequality. Freeing schools from state bureaucratic control and empowering parents to make realistic choices about which school their children should attend, Brown and Lauder suggest, will eliminate working-class parental apathy about schooling and increase their interest in education. Another aspect of this 'parentocracy' would be to shift power away from middle-class producers (the teachers) and towards working-class consumers (the parents) and thus break down the middle-class monopoly on cultural capital.

One criticism of this approach is that it is difficult to see how a one-off decision about choice of school, even if it is a real choice, could, on its own, eliminate inequality. Moreover, New Right theorists assume that all parents are free and equal in this educational market place (see Ranson 1990), while in fact knowledge, skills and access to material resources are unevenly distributed among parents.

### Type of school

What has become clear in the years since, first, Conservative and then Labour policies in the 1990s and 2000s began to have an impact on the development of schools, is that there are differences in the status of schools even within the state sector. As Gewirtz (1998) found, inner city schools containing largely working-class pupils and with a high proportion receiving free school meals (FSM) have difficulty in recruiting and retaining teachers, and encouraging the involvement of parents. Day-to-day issues such as dealing with poor behaviour subsume any time that might be available to strategically improve the quality of education for the pupils. On the other hand, 'beacon' or 'leading edge' schools attracting a largely middle-class intake and maintaining a strong performance in league tables can focus on issues related to learning and teaching to improve their quality of education. These are schools in which teachers 'want' to work, and parents actively organize where they live to secure places for their children in what has become known as 'selection by mortgage'. Ruth Lupton (2003) concluded that neighbourhood poverty and poor schooling go hand-in-hand. However, the question is, which comes first? Are schools poor because of their intake, or vice versa?

### Inside/outside school – the interplay between them

In reality there is considerable overlap between inside/outside school factors that affect a child's performance in relation to his/her social class background. Peer group influence is one example whereby children may know each other on their estates and form friendship groups in which status can be gained by being 'anti-school'. The attitudes and values developed in the community are then transferred into school, resulting in poor behaviour, punctuality and attendance; treating teachers impolitely or disrespectfully; not doing homework; wearing incorrect uniform; and generally gaining respect from peers for this approach. The opposite can be true for pro-school subcultures. As Paul Connolly (2006) has pointed out treating boys as an homogeneous groups is dangerous in that boys from more middle-class backgrounds are markedly more successful educationally than working-class boys and this success is shaped by a home background that largely values education. In his research he found middle-class boys developed their sense of masculinity by displaying 'specialist knowledge and technical skills' (Connolly 2006) and competing to show their knowledge of computer games, books and films with their peers. Furthermore, when asked about career intentions, middle-class boys mentioned typically high-status occupations involving lengthy education and training – such as doctor, lawyer or pilot – while working-class boys typically listed lower-status jobs – such as mechanic, builder or carpet fitter as their examples.

*Inside school explanations – an evaluation*

## Exercise 5.14

Listed below are a number of evaluation points of the 'inside school' explanations. Identify which are the strengths and which the weaknesses. Record your answers in a two-column table that clearly separates the strengths from the weaknesses. When you record your answers, rank them in order of importance, then justify your ranking to another sociology student.

1. They fail to explain the expectations of teachers. The question has to be asked: why do teachers label working-class students as being less able?
2. The division between pro-school and anti-school cultures in streaming studies is too crude. Woods (1983) identifies eight modes of adaptation to schooling, ranging from complete compliance to outright rebellion.
3. The explanations have highlighted important implications for the way teachers should be trained.
4. The interactionist-based explanations offer a fresh counter-balance to positivistic explanations. In particular, they provide a useful insight into the social construction of educational success and failure.
5. The explanations are somewhat deterministic. They assume too readily that a self-fulfilling prophecy occurs after negative labelling, yet some students succeed in casting aside their negative labels and do well educationally. It is as if the label acts as a spur to work even harder, so they can prove their teachers wrong.
6. The explanations are supported by a number of empirical studies of high validity.

## A structuration explanation – Willis (1977)

Willis's work is influenced in its structure by the theories of the French sociologist Althusser (1972), who argued that education systems are primarily 'ideological state apparatuses', concerned with the cultural reproduction of capitalism. Althusser's argument is that the main function of education is to ensure that the privileges of one generation are passed on to the next, through the ideological conditioning to be found in schooling. In Althusser's theory, individual experiences are unimportant; it is the overall effect of cultural reproduction that he found fascinating about schools. Willis draws on the notion of cultural reproduction, but wishes to examine the processes in schools that contribute to the transfer of privilege and disadvantage across the generations.

Therefore, the central question Willis attempts to answer in his book *Learning to Labour* is why working-class children fail. To understand this phenomenon, he adopted an ethnographic approach, which included observation and interviews. His approach can be considered innovative because he combined structurally based outside-school explanations with action-based inside-school ones. Willis's synthesis of micro and macro perspectives is a classic example of what Giddens (1984) subsequently termed structuration theory – structural and action perspectives combined into one set of ideas. What follows is a review of Willis's findings.

First, working-class educational underachievement can be understood in terms of anti-school cultures (the action-based part of his explanation).

Second, Willis's counter-school culture has similar features to Hargreaves' (1967) and Lacey's (1970) anti-school subcultures. For example, its members avoid school work, play truant, make use of 'sharp language', and disobey teachers. Given these characteristics, the chances of succeeding in school are limited.

Third, Willis sees the counter-school culture as having very different origins from those identified by Hargreaves and Lacey. He rejects the view that counter-school culture is a product of students being labelled 'failures' at school; rather, it has its origins outside school in working-class culture (the structural part of his explanation).

Fourth, working-class culture has a number of characteristics:
1. A belief that no amount of educational qualifications will produce more jobs or improve opportunities for the working class as a whole. There is an acceptance that working-class people will do manual work.
2. A belief that non-manual jobs are 'boring', 'soft', 'desk-bound', 'cissy-work'.
3. A belief that coping mechanisms should be employed to provide diversions and alternative satisfactions for menial work. For example, taking unofficial breaks at work.

Fifth, given that working-class pupils bring this cultural background into the school, it is not surprising that they form counter-school cultures that:

1.  Have little interest in academic work or gaining qualifications.
2.  Oppose authority and reject those who are conformist (the ear'oles).
3.  Emphasise having 'a laff'. For example, by cheeking teachers, or smoking at school.

For Willis, then, the counter-school culture (and hence educational failure) is seen as being rational. Working-class children bring into school a 'shop-floor culture' and choose not to get on at school. They make this choice because they realise they have limited opportunities to succeed in middle-class terms, and see schooling as a kind of training ground to practice ways of remaining human in the alienating factory jobs they eventually expect to fill (work through Exercise 5.15 below to consolidate your understanding).

## Exercise 5.15

Create a flow diagram similar to the one mapped out for teachers' expectations (see page 11) to summarise Willis' structuration explanation of working-class underachievement in schools.

*An evaluation of Willis's structuration theory*

## Exercise 5.16

For this exercise, complete the statements below concerning the strengths and weaknesses of Willis's work. For some of these you will be able to select from the matching text provided, while others require logical completion in your own words.

### Strengths

1.  He has exposed the inadequacies of earlier explanations of class inequalities in educational achievement by recognising the need to.......
2.  ......Giddens' structuration theory.
3.  The use of a range of qualitative research methods such as participant observation and informal interviews means that his findings are high in.......

## Weaknesses

1. ......as it was based on a sample of twelve.
2. He has focused too much on counter-school cultures.......
3. As with Hargreaves and Lacey, the distinction between conformist and counter-school cultures is too crude because there are.......

## Some of the missing text

(a) and neglected the sociological significance of conformist subcultures (a charge that can be made of others, such as Lacey).
(b) combine structural and action perspectives.
(c) His research has had a major impact on sociological theory. For example, .......

One problem with Willis's work is that it was carried out at a particular time, towards the end of what postmodernists describe as the 'modern' period and at the beginning of the 'postmodern world'. In particular, since then post-Fordist factories have transformed the prospects of Willis's 'lads' in ways they might have found disturbing. The economic restructuring of the 1980s meant that the manual labour underpinning the masculine culture of the Fordist factory is disappearing, and the new production heroes are computer operators engaged in lifetime learning careers. Rather than the 'lads' of the 1990s making the transition from school to work, these individuals are more likely to experience a world of training programmes, or be reluctant post-16 students, as youth unemployment has hit hard. This transition to a 'postmodern' world has brought about what has been called a 'crisis of masculinity' in education, with the curriculum being defined as more 'girl-friendly' and leaving little scope for boys to define their identity very easily. Mac an Ghaill (1996) argued that social class remained the main indicator of the success or failure of boys in schools. Francis (2000) also argues that, within schools, concepts of masculinity have not changed, whereas changes in society have meant that girls construct their concepts of femininity to include a much wider range of options than in the past. The interplay between gender and social class is also relevant to these changes, with working-class boys being the 'underachievers.'

With boys falling behind at every level of the system, sociologists and governments have paid some attention to trying to provide explanations for this phenomenon and solutions to the problem. See 'Bringing It Together' at the end of Chapter 6.

## GOVERNMENT EDUCATIONAL POLICY AND CLASS INEQUALITIES IN EDUCATIONAL ATTAINMENT

In Chapters 2 and 3 we gave detailed consideration to the way in which educational policies have shaped the nature of educational institutions and the teaching that takes place within them. When working through this material, you may well have come to appreciate that the various policies have to a certain extent influenced (or may yet influence) the educational achievements of different social classes. We shall now ask you to apply your understanding of educational policies to the debate on class inequalities through a link exercise.

<table>
<tr><td>(A)<br>(E)</td><td>Link Exercise 5.1</td></tr>
</table>

For this exercise we ask you to assess the extent to which educational policy has affected class inequalities in educational performance. To do this you will need to draw on material from Chapters 2 and 3. It is important that you adopt a balanced approach in your assessment, thus you should reflect on policies that may or have widened or reduced class inequalities in educational achievement. Draw up a table that clearly separates the positive and negative influences of social policy in relation to their effect on social class inequalities.

(Hint: the policies that may or have reduced class inequalities in educational attainment could include the commitment to comprehensive schools; introduction of vocational education; testing at age 7, 11, 16; student loans; the post-Dearing national curriculum; the introduction of vocational GCSEs, AVCE and other vocational courses, and the new Diplomas.)

The influence of social policies on social class inequalities

| Positive influences | Negative influences |
|---|---|
|  |  |
|  |  |
|  |  |
|  |  |
|  |  |

## THE DEATH OF CLASS?

Social class differences in educational attainment have been one of the persistent themes of the sociology of education since the Second World War, yet statistics on social class performance are increasingly difficult to obtain. The lack of official interest in class differentials is partly a consequence of the ideological notion of classlessness, in which the importance of class relationships in contemporary industrial societies is played down, and the claim that such societies are meritocratic rather than class-based is dominant. This is reflected in sociology itself, where the primacy of class analysis has been replaced by concern about other social relationships and identities – for example, gender and ethnicity.

Postmodern theories have been at the forefront of the attack on class-based analysis, arguing that it is derived from the 'metanarrative' of Marxism, in which all social relationships are reduced to class relationships. By metanarrative, postmodernists are referring to social theories that seek to explain the whole of human history and society, generally by use of one central theme or idea. In seeking to explain the totality of society, Marxists have focused on class analysis as a way of laying bare the 'true' and often hidden nature of capitalist societies. Postmodernists have, in varying degrees, dismissed the search for a single explanation of society as a whole. They argue that such a search is not only futile, but also goes against the conditions of postmodernist societies, in which social groupings are fragmentary and fractured. For example, Laclau and Mouffe (1985) argue that Marxists deny the importance of a whole range of social identities – such as gender, generation, ethnicity and nationality – when they assert the primacy of class relations. Marxists, in effect, are said to 'subsume' these social characteristics within class, thus imposing a single explanation on situations that are multilayered and complex.

According to postmodernists, developments since the 1960s have intensified the social changes that produced the conditions of postmodernity, in which all the old certainties and loyalties of class have been dissolved. The growing importance of the mass media in people's lives and the fragmentation of the working class through new forms of production and technology are important features of this process. In place of class identity, new social movements (NSMs) have emerged, and these are more likely to express the interests of postmodern individuals. These NSMs are based on issues of gender, ethnicity, ecology, sexual politics and so on, and represent a fundamental shift, according to postmodernists, from the class-based certainties of modernism. In the sociology of education, the demise of class is illustrated by a switch of focus away from examining differences in class attainment to a greater interest in gender and ethnic differences in educational performance. However, recent research (see the end of Chapter 6) has shown the continued influence and effect of social background on educational achievement. The focus on gender and ethnicity has somewhat masked the continuing legacy of social class. The statistics overall show a continued and sustained improvement in official examination results, with all groups improving their performance but at different rates. However, we also know from government statistics that there is a significant proportion of 16-year-olds (11 per cent in 2007) who are not in education, employment or training (NEETs – Swale 2006) – could these be described as an 'underclass' who drift in and out of unskilled, casual employment, or resort to illegal means to earn a living? See page 242 for a fuller explanation of postmodernism and education.

More recently, there has been some attempt to reclaim the notion of social class as a central dimension of an analysis of the workings of the education system. The work of cultural analysts of class, such as Skeggs (2004), has focused on how the processes and practices of class create the 'unacknowledged normality of the middle class' in education. Class is deployed both as a resource and a form of property to further the success of children from middle-class backgrounds. For example, every new educational initiative, such as Excellence in Cities, Gifted and Talented or Widening Participation has been systematically 'co-opted by the privileged' and disproportionately advantaged the middle classes (Reay 2006). Reay argues the educational gap between rich and poor has widened and, based on evidence from the Office for National Statistics (ONS) and the Sutton Trust, concludes that 'social class injustices have never been adequately tackled in education' (Reay 2006). The failure of the working class is enshrined in processes of streaming, setting and the hidden curriculum as well as in the division of classes in the official curriculum. The higher-status academic curriculum of GCSEs and A Levels are highly prized by the middle class, with the vocational curriculum being the preserve of the working class. Furthermore, the notion that schools and teachers can in some way overcome educational disadvantage is a fallacy, since the acknowledgement of class is not part of the discourse of either schools or teacher training. Reay found little evidence that teacher training courses dealt with issues or research related to social class and educational achievement, and that, in her own research, teachers had 'ill-informed and prejudicial views about working-class parents'.

Reay points out in her short history of education that schooling has been *by* the middle class *for* the middle class. The education of the working class since the nineteenth century has been about preserving elitism and privilege –

in short, serving the interests of the middle class and creating a subservient working class. The whole system is run by and in the interests of the middle class, with the authority for management and administration of education being part of the accepted cultural capital of the middle class. Hence the working class are outsiders, marginalized, 'outcasts on the inside' (Bourdieu 1973) or 'working classes without a self' (Skeggs 2004) destined to be the 'failures' of the system in terms of types of qualifications undertaken, achievement of qualifications, leaving school early, and labelling by teachers and the system. Reay concludes that the processes that have led to the 'myth of meritocracy' (Cohen 2000) are the result of the historical underpinnings of the education system – to pacify and contain the working class. Hence the lack of attention to key issues connected with social class and educational success and failure has been bound up with this powerful myth of meritocracy, which leads us to believe that through education we can achieve social mobility, when evidence suggests that social mobility has been declining (Summerfield and Gill 2005).

Savage (2003) argues that there needs to be a new theorisation of social class, a new paradigm that can recognize the ways in which the system has become marketized, and the effects of this on individual and social class performance in schools. Furthermore, the ways in which class is mediated across gender and ethnic divisions are crucial in developing an understanding of the nature of the education system. However, the attainment gap still reflects the gap between rich and poor, according to Reay (2006), and policy initiatives have had virtually no impact on the social class divisions in the education system.

## Becoming skilled at answering examination questions

The following material will help you to develop a sound approach to writing essay and exam answers, but you must begin by breaking down the question that has been set before you begin to answer it.

First, you must 'decode' the question. What are the 'command' words that indicate which skills are being assessed? Questions often include words such as 'explain' 'suggest reasons' 'examine' 'assess' 'evaluate' or 'discuss', so you need to be absolutely sure of the meaning of these words.

Second, you must tease out the elements that are contained in the question. In the question 'Using material from the Item and elsewhere, assess sociological explanations for the educational achievement of children from different social classes' there are four elements, as shown in Table 5.1.

**Table 5.1** Elements contained in the question

| Elements | Aspects of the elements |
| --- | --- |
| Use the Item and other material | Pick out key points from the Item and elaborate further, developing a greater depth of understanding.Use additional sociological research and studies relevant to social class and achievement |
| Assess (command word) | Use arguments/evidence for and against the connection between social class and achievement. Be critical of the material related to under-achievement. |
| Social class and achievement | Use social class evidence as a basis for your essay, but also bring in other social factors such as gender and ethnicity to 'assess'. |
| Sociological explanation | What it says – do not use common-sense, biological or psychological explanations. |

Here is a question for you to try. Use the following student answers and the guidance from the marking on pages 127–8 to gauge the standard of your answer.

---

### Item D

Within the state school system, approximately 5 per cent of students achieve no passes at GCSE, and about 25 per cent achieve no passes higher than a grade D. There is also a correlation between the most disadvantaged students and the worst-performing schools. The Joseph Rowntree Foundation, in its report *Tackling Low Educational Achievement* (2007; see http://www.jrf.org.uk) found four factors associated with low achievement: eligibility for free school meals; neighbourhood unemployment rate; percentage of single-parent households; and proportion of parents with low educational qualifications. These factors indicate that the lower social classes are likely to do the least well in education because of their disadvantages before entering school, thus leading to a self-fulfilling prophecy. However, the Rowntree Foundation also found that schools can and do make a difference to students' achievements.

(I)(A)  (a) What does the term 'self-fulfilling prophecy' mean in sociology? (2 marks)

(I)(A)  (b) Suggest three ways in which 'neighbourhoods' may affect educational achievement. (6 marks)

(An)(E)  (c) Outline some of the reasons for the underachievement of children from the 'lower social classes', (12 marks)

(An)(E)  (d) Using material from Item A and elsewhere, assess the view that working-class under-achievement is more to do with teachers and schools than with home background. (20 marks)

## Item E

By 2010 the Sure Start programme should have a Children's Centre in every community. These will be a service 'hubs', which integrate the provision of health, welfare, education and parental support to help raise the achievement of the most disadvantaged children before they go to school. Free child care is provided, and parents are encouraged to look for work as well as being given guidance in parenting skills. The focus of Sure Start is the intellectual, linguistic and social development of young children, in an attempt to break the cycle of low educational attainment rates of children from unskilled working-class backgrounds. There is a considerable amount of research in sociology that points to a poor start in life having a lasting legacy for education achievement and employment status. Feinstein (2003) used secondary data for children born in a single week in March 1958 (The National Child Development Study) and the British Cohort Study using a similar group of children born in 1970 to discover factors affecting educational success. Feinstein found evidence that linked financial difficulties most strongly to low achievement among other factors such as lone motherhood, but overall it was lack of parental interest, as also found by Douglas (1964), that was the main reason for working-class children's under-achievement.

(I)(A)  (a) Explain what a sampling frame is. (2 marks)

(A)  (b) Suggest two factors that could be included in a sample of children in the Sure Start scheme.(4 marks)

(I)(An)  (c) Suggest two reasons why sociologists might use unstructured interviews. (4 marks)

(An)(E)  (d) Suggest ways in which sociologists could use observation in research into the Sure Start scheme. (20 marks)

## Exam Focus 1

Read Items F, G and H and then look at the questions on education that follow. We have provided two answers by students for you to mark, using the marking scheme provided. Pay careful attention to the marks allocated to each part. We suggest that, when looking at any answer, you first try to locate it within a mark band and then try to give it the correct mark within that band.

### Item F

In looking at perpetuating gender inequality in schools, the pivotal role is that of the teacher. The attitudes of the teachers towards the proper type of education for girls on the one hand and boys on the other will affect the way they interact with each gender. These attitudes will be influenced by wider social forces that define what is right for men and women in terms of social roles. There are several ways in which the impact of wider notions of gender can be played out in the classroom. At one level, they will influence the time that teachers give to boys in the classroom, rather than girls, so that boys will come to dominate exchanges and thus benefit from the teacher's attention. At a different level, boys can bring into the classroom ideas about the legitimacy of sexual violence against women and girls, and initiate acts of violence and harassment that have a sexual connotation against both female students and teachers.

### Item G

#### Schools make a difference

While it is clear that some working-class children succeed in school and some middle-class children do not do as well as might be expected, it is not always obvious why this should be the case. The intelligence of the children who move up and down the occupational hierarchy is one factor that is important, but there is a great deal of evidence to show that the school a child goes to also makes a difference. It is well established that good schools focus on behaviour and attendance, while the teachers in them are encouraging, well organized, and involved in wider extra-curricular activities: all of which engage the students and promote their achievement.

---

### Item H

**The self-fulfilling prophecy**

When pupils come into a school, teachers make judgements on their ability, based on many different things. These labels are, for example, 'bright', 'able', 'thick', 'less able', 'practical', 'academic' and so on. However, these labels are not neutral, nor do they describe the real possibilities of students, but are based on common-sense knowledge of which types of student are 'good' and which 'bad'. Thus it has been shown that teachers have stereotypes linked to class ('from broken homes'), gender ('she's just a girl'), race ('West Indians are noisy') and even physical attractiveness ('snotty-nosed kid'). Teachers then act towards students on the basis of such stereotypes – for example, those students who are labelled 'bright' are given more time to answer questions than those who are seen as unlikely to know the answer anyway.

---

## Questions

(I)(A) (a) How does Item F suggest male violence is legitimated in schools'? (2 marks)

(I)(A) (b) Identify three factors which Item G suggests contribute to upward mobility. (6 mark)

(An)(E) (c) The concept of the self-fulfilling prophecy described in Item E has been criticised by some sociologists. Identify some of the ways in which the concept might be criticised. (12 marks)

(An)(E) (d) Assess how far school factors, such as those contained in the Items, satisfactorily explain differential educational achievement between social classes. (20 marks)

## Student answers

CANDIDATE A

(a) Item F suggests that male violence in schools is legitimated by the wider ideals of society being brought into schools by boys.

(b) Item G suggests that both individual intelligence and going to a 'good' school with good quality teaching (such as having encouraging teachers) contribute to upward social mobility.

(c) In Item E the self-fulfilling prophecy is described as coming into force when a teacher makes judgements about a pupil based on things such as race, gender and class, and then shapes their behaviour towards that pupil accordingly. Although research shows that teachers often hold an image of the ideal student (Howard Becker) it seems that such research (often interactionist) assumes that the self-fulfilling prophecy is an automatic process and thus the concept can be criticised for being too simplistic and assuming that labelling automatically leads to the self-fulfilling prophecy that is said to be always a result of labelling. Labelling and the self-fulfilling prophecy do not necessarily go hand in hand either. Furthermore, research by Fuller showed that African-Caribbean girls actively rejected stereotypical labels and worked hard to achieve well in school and not succumb to the self-fulfilling prophecy.

The concept is also somewhat unfair to teachers and assumes that they have constructed attitudes about race, class and sex merely within the interaction of classrooms. Their ideas must have come from somewhere. Marxists say that teachers are not, as this concept suggests, instigators of unfairness, but rather victims of capitalism's 'ruling-class ideology'. By blaming teachers, we do not look at the state's influence in maintaining a stratified, sexist, racist society. Sharp and Green show that teachers are under immense pressure to comply with things like the national curriculum and cannot be blamed for working-class under-achievement.

This concept does not do justice to pupils either. They are viewed as passive and manipulated by the education system. Studies of ethnicity in education, for example, show that labelled black children were able to resist what teachers thought of them.

(d) Interpretivists again focus on the school itself in trying to explain differential achievement between social class. Ball pinpoints streaming and banding as particularly important and, as in Item E, the self-fulfilling prophecy comes into effect here. Ball's case study of a comprehensive school shows that while band one pupils were 'warmed up', band two pupils were 'cooled down'. As we can see from Items C and D, teacher attitudes are most important and, as Ball showed, middle-class pupils were more likely to be placed in band one. However, though Lacey, Hargreaves and Nell Keddie all identify this same pattern, the tendency to place middle-class students in higher bands cannot merely be explained by teacher attitudes.

Functionalists in their cultural deprivation explanation of working-class achievement see parental attitudes and socialisation experiences as being responsible for the underachievement of the working class.

Newsom, Newsom and Barnes see the ignorance of working-class parents as hindering their child's educational achievement. Bernstein shows that the speech patterns of the working class prevent them from succeeding within the system because schools, teachers, etc. use the middle-class elaborated code and not the restricted code.

Although such studies outline the need to look at environmental and home factors and stress the problem with focusing on school factors such as those in the Items, they have been heavily criticized as blaming parents and children and seeing their culture as inferior.

Keddie argues that factors within the school should change, not working-class children.

Marxists argue that if the nature of the economy were to change from capitalism to communism, then schools would no longer be ideological conditioning devices, manipulated by the ruling class, and we would have a classless society. Marxists effectively show us that it is not enough to focus on such school factors as labelling, subcultures (Willis, Lacey, Hargreaves) and self-fulfilling prophecy, as these are just effects of a wholly unequal society. What we need, they argue, is a fundamental change in the economy. We can see from things like the 1988 Education Act that those in power do control the nature of education. Sociologists such as Clyde Chitty and Mike O'Donnell show that such Acts reinforce class divisions and effectively introduce a tiered system of education.

However, such Acts would effectively change the day-to-day running of schools and so would be relevant to school factors. Assessing such school factors as those in the Items does explain the class differences that operate in schools. They are valuable in assessing how such Acts as that of 1988 directly affect schools and change teacher attitudes, and for this purpose at least they are valuable.

CANDIDATE B

(a) Item F suggests that the way in which male violence is legitimated is making this violence seem part of everyday life; that is, accept it without question.
(b) Item G suggests that individual intelligence and going to a good school are reasons contributing to upward social mobility.
(c) Self-fulfilling prophecy can be criticized on the ground that, because it is based on common-sense knowledge, it is changeable. Also, studies have indicated that pupils cannot conform to these stereotypes (Fuller) and revolt against the teacher's negative manner. Pupils have been shown (as any individual) to be non-conformist. It may be that the pupil may have outside influences that are similar to those of teachers.
(d) Explanations of the differential educational achievement between social classes include biological factors, out-of-school factors and in-school factors.

Biological differences have been rejected on the grounds that middle-class culture has been seen as higher than working-class culture. Also the IQ tests themselves have been problematic because they favour middle-class culture, and cheating was found to have taken place. It has been shown that out-of-school factors are present when it comes to educational achievement. Prosser and Weiss found that, over the country, middle-class children were performing better in schools than their working-class counterparts. Coates and Silburn agree, suggesting that, because working-class children come from poor home backgrounds, lacking in educational toys, and parents have little or no interest in school, these children are less intelligent.

More importantly, school factors such as those found in the hidden curriculum are becoming more and more influential in educational achievement. Keddie uses education itself to show this. Those pupils who come top at school with concrete education are shunned because the sort of education that is highly regarded is abstract knowledge. These pupils are thought of as bright and teachers encourage them to become more aspirational. Those with concrete education (their own personal experiences) are thought to be less intelligent. This has also fuelled labelling and self-fulfilling prophecies. Interactionists have been criticised for using too many ethnographic, detailed accounts of teachers and pupils. They rely on subjective experience and lack reliability. Other factors to be considered are cultural experience, and restricted and elaborated codes (Boudon, Bourdieu, Labov).

## Marking scheme

(a) How does Item F suggest male violence is legitimated in schools'? (2 marks). The marks will be given for ideas being brought in from wider social forces or any acceptable equivalent.
(b) Identify three factors which Item G suggests contribute to upward social mobility; 2 marks for each one – any form of words that identify individual intelligence, good teaching and a good school can score.
(c) The concept of the self-fulfilling prophecy described in Item H has been criticised by some sociologists. Identify some of the ways in which the concept might be criticised. (12 marks) Any reasonable criticisms that have been fully explained can score up to the maximum of 12 marks, with 3 or 4 marks allocated to each criticism given. The most likely could be lack of consistency in applying labels, no notion of pupil resistance, the 'automatic' nature of the process, evidence of resistance, no account of teachers who have high expectations, etc. Use of supporting studies and appropriate elaboration of the criticisms can be rewarded.
(d) Assess how far school factors, such as those contained in the Items, satisfactorily explain differential educational achievement between social classes. (20 marks)

  0: no relevant points.
1–7: answers in this band may well concentrate on reproducing the factors identified in the items in more detail, or seek to apply these factors in a minimal way to social classes. Any assessment is likely to be commonsensical.
8–15: in this band, candidates may seek to assess through juxtaposition of alternative factors. The more candidates apply these factors to an

explicit critique, the higher they are likely to appear in the band. Studies cited must be interpreted well and applied to the question in some measure.

16–20: assessment should be explicit to reach this band, with alternative factors being used effectively to provide a critique of school factors. The very best will arrive at a balanced conclusion which emerges from the debate.

## Exam Focus 2

The following questions are ones for you to do yourself. We have provided some hints and ideas after each question. Make sure that the length of your responses are appropriate to the number of marks allocated to each part question.

### Questions

(a) According to Item I, which type of pupil has benefited least from the introduction of the GCSE? (2 marks)

(Hint: the question is directing your attention to Item I, so you should be able to interpret the answer from it. Be careful not to spend too much time on this part, as there are only two marks available for a correct answer.)

(b) Using only the material in the Items, summarize in your own words the patterns of differential educational attainment in Britain. (6 marks)

(Hint: the crucial thing to notice in this question is that you are only allowed to use the material in the items. Bringing in other knowledge cannot be rewarded, because of the wording of the question. Therefore you should focus strictly on the information in the items. However, you also have to use your own words, so be sure to read the material first and then write down your understanding of it, avoiding the wording in the items.)

(c) Item I suggests that children from poorer households are less likely to achieve, and Item G indicates a class bias in GCSE attainment. Assess the extent to which home background can affect educational achievement. (12 marks)

(Hint: the focus of this question is on the effects of home background on educational achievement. While the bulk of your answer could concentrate on home factors, note that you are required to evaluate the extent to which home background is influential. You could do this through a consideration of the effects of home background compared with other factors. However, you should be critical of the effects of home background factors in their own right and not just juxtapose home and school factors. This is only an implicit assessment – you should be explicit in your evaluations.)

(d) Using material from the Items and elsewhere, assess the views that claim working class underachievement is the result of factors related to the school environment. (20 marks)

(Hint: read the question very carefully. You are asked to 'assess' 'school factors'. Make sure you balance the essay to include a number of criticisms. Include relevant studies that relate to working-class under-achievement. Make sure the material you use is elaborated and extended from the Items provided as well as other material you have learnt about. You will gain marks for explaining your material clearly and making it relevant to the question set. Show your skills of identification by selecting appropriate writers and evidence. Analysis and evaluation should be explicit in your critical discussions. Where appropriate, show your understanding of sociological perspectives. Good organisation and structure of your essay will go a long way towards ensuring a good mark.

---

### Item I

One of the declared aims of introducing the GCSE to replace the old style O levels was to offer many more students the chance to achieve a qualification at the age of 16. While the O level had been targeted at the top 20 per cent of achievers in any year group, GCSE was designed to allow the top 60 per cent to obtain a 'pass' grade. However, this still left a significant proportion of students at the lower end of the ability range not benefiting from the introduction of GCSE. It has been suggested that the home background of such students, and in particular their poverty, is a major factor in their lack of achievement. There was a further complication. The introduction of compulsory coursework in GCSEs seems to have benefited girls more than boys, presumably because this style of examination suited girls better. The result was that it was low-ability boys who did not gain much from this change in examination structure. As the GCSE developed, it has become clear that achievement has risen for most students. However, there is still a stubborn 'tail' of students who do not achieve any qualifications at the age of 16.

## Item J

**Table 5.2** GCSE or equivalent attainment by free school meal eligibility in England 2005–6 (Pupil numbers in percentages)

|  | 5 grades A*–C | 5 grades A*–C including English and Mathematics | Any passes |
|---|---|---|---|
| Free school meals | 32.6 | 19.5 | 93.7 |
| No free school meals | 60.7 | 47.5 | 197.8 |

*Source*: Summerfield and Gill (2005).

## Item K

The relationship between gender and subject choice has long been of interest to sociologists. The particular focus of attention has been on the natural sciences, such as chemistry, physics and biology, as these subjects seem to attract fewer women than men. However, this is not necessarily the case. Biology, for example, is the most popular science among women, and many biology classrooms in schools are dominated by female students. The gender imbalance is most marked in physics, where males predominate. It has been argued that the 'male atmosphere' of such classrooms deters many female students from choosing the subject at school. There is therefore an attrition rate associated with female participation in physics. As the level of physics education increases, the proportion of women engaged in it decreases, thus reinforcing the dominance of men in the area. However, it might be said that the absence of women from physics is also mirrored by the relative absence of ethnic minority and working-class students.

## Important concepts

- material deprivation • cultural deprivation • cultural difference • compensatory education • teachers' expectations • hidden curriculum • self-fulfilling prophecy • educational attainment • critical thinking

## Critical thinking

- Think about the reasons why socio-economic background has been such a persistent theme in the sociology of education since the Second World War.
- What do you consider to be the relative importance of inside- and outside-school factors in shaping educational achievement of the social classes?
- How do you think modern policies in education such as Sure Start will bring an improvement in educational attainment for the lower social classes?

# Chapter 6

# Explaining Gender Differences in Educational Achievement

By the end of this chapter you should:

- be able to describe gender differences in educational achievement and understand the interplay between gender, social class and ethnicity
- understand changes in gender inequalities that exist in the higher education sector
- be able to assess different explanations of gender differences in educational achievement and subject choice
- appreciate the way government educational policies can affect the educational achievements of males and females
- have reflected on a student's answer to an exam question
- have practised a structured exam question yourself

## INTRODUCTION

Gender was investigated as a mainstream issue relatively late in the sociology of education. Prior to the 1970s, sociological discussions focused mainly on class differences in attainment. However, with the impact of feminist scholarship during the 1970s and 1980s the educational experiences of female students increasingly came to the fore. This chapter will start by mapping out gender differences in educational attainment and subject choice. Three sets of explanations will then be put forward to account for the observed variations in educational performance and subject choice: (i) genetic explanations, which focus on biological differences in intelligence; (ii) outside school explanations (non-genetic), which emphasize childhood socialization processes based on external cultural and structural factors; and (iii) inside school explanations, which look at the sexism inherent in the hidden curriculum. We shall also examine the extent to which educational policies and initiatives have been responsible for the significant improvement in female academic achievement in recent years.

## EVIDENCE OF GENDER DIFFERENCES IN EDUCATIONAL ACHIEVEMENT

When gender first began to be investigated by sociologists of education, the focus was largely on female under-achievement at every level of the education system, and the ways in which traditional ideas about the proper role of women in society prevented them from achieving their full societal potential. However, females have improved their educational performance markedly during the 1980s, 1990s and 2000s (see Exercise 6.1), so that the contemporary situation, while not without its problems and issues for girls in schools, is one where the educational opportunities open to females have possibly never been greater. Wilkinson (1994) argues that this is part of a 'genderquake' in which a fundamental change in attitude towards women's roles in society has been achieved. Prominent among the 'transformed circumstances' of women is a more positive attitude towards education as a means of improving chances at work. However, while there are now undoubtedly more and greater opportunities for girls and women, their roles can still be quite traditional in nature and their earnings are still only about three-quarters of men's. According to the Office for National Statistics (ONS, 2001), in that year the average gross wage for men was £247 a week, compared to £119 for women.

### Summaries of examination results by gender

| Item A | | | | | | | | |
|---|---|---|---|---|---|---|---|---|
| A Level results by gender, all boards/all subject areas, selected years 1991–2007, cumulative totals (%) | | | | | | | | |
| | | **A** | **B** | **C** | **D** | **E** | **N** | **U** |
| 2007 | *M* | 24.8 | 47.9 | 70.7 | 87.5 | 96.8 | | 100 |
| | *F* | 27.2 | 52.9 | 75.9 | 90.9 | 98.0 | | 100 |
| 2003 | *M* | 19.8 | 40.6 | 63.1 | 82.2 | 94.2 | | 100 |
| | *F* | 22.5 | 46.6 | 70.0 | 87.3 | 96.3 | | 100 |
| 2000 | *M* | 17.8 | 36.2 | 56.8 | 75.5 | 88.5 | 95.3 | 100 |
| | *F* | 18.4 | 38.5 | 60.3 | 78.5 | 90.4 | 96.3 | 100 |

|      |   | A | B | C | D | E | N | U |
|------|---|------|------|------|------|------|------|-----|
| 1998 | M | 17.2 | 35.4 | 55.7 | 73.9 | 87.3 | 94.5 | 100 |
|      | F | 17.1 | 36.8 | 58.2 | 76.5 | 89.0 | 95.6 | 100 |
| 1996 | M | 16.5 | 34.1 | 53.3 | 71.4 | 85.3 | 93.2 | 100 |
|      | F | 15.9 | 34.4 | 54.6 | 73.1 | 86.6 | 94.0 | 100 |
| 1993 | M | 14.9 | 31.5 | 48.6 | 66.2 | 80.8 | 90.2 | 100 |
|      | F | 12.8 | 29.6 | 47.8 | 66.3 | 81.3 | 90.5 | 100 |
| 1991 | M | 13.3 | 29.0 | 45.4 | 62.7 | 77.7 | 88.1 | 100 |
|      | F | 10.6 | 25.8 | 43.2 | 62.0 | 78.2 | 88.8 | 100 |

*Notes*: F = female; M = male. Headings A, B, C, etc. refer to grades awarded in A level examinations.

*Source*: Inter-board statistics, 1992, 1994, 1997, 1999, 2001, 2004, 2008 (see http://www.jcq.org.uk).

## Item B

Gender differences in performance at A Level, all boards/all subject areas, selected years 1991–2007. Females outperform males by these percentages:

|     | 1991 | 1993 | 1996 | 1998 | 1999 | 2000 | 2003 | 2007 |
|-----|------|------|------|------|------|------|------|------|
| A   | −2.7 | −2.1 | −0.6 | −0.1 | −0.1 | +0.6 | +2.7 | +2.4 |
| C+  | −2.2 | −0.8 | +1.3 | +2.5 | +2.3 | +3.5 | +6.9 | +5.2 |

*Notes*: Col. 1 – A and C+ = A Level grades achieved.

*Source*: Inter-board statistics, 1991, 1993, 1996, 1998, 1999, 2000, 2003, 2007 (see http://www.jcq.org.uk).

## Item C

GCSE results by gender, all groups/all subject areas, selected years 1990–2007, cumulative totals (%)

|      |   | A* | A | B | C | D | E | F | G | U |
|------|---|-----|------|------|------|------|------|------|------|-----|
| 2007 | M | 2.7 | 10.8 | 25.5 | 45.8 | 62.7 | 76.6 | 87.0 | 94.2 | 100 |
|      | F | 5.8 | 18.3 | 37.0 | 58.4 | 73.7 | 84.7 | 92.1 | 96.7 | 100 |
| 2003 | M | 4.2 | 13.9 | 29.1 | 55.0 | 73.9 | 86.6 | 93.9 | 97.3 | 100 |
|      | F | 6.9 | 20.0 | 38.2 | 64.2 | 80.1 | 90.0 | 95.5 | 97.8 | 100 |
| 2000 | M | 3.7 | 13.1 | 28.6 | 52.0 | 71.4 | 85.3 | 93.7 | 97.6 | 100 |
|      | F | 5.6 | 18.5 | 37.0 | 61.2 | 78.6 | 89.7 | 95.7 | 98.3 | 100 |

| 1998 | M | 3.4 | 12.3 | 27.2 | 50.2 | 69.5 | 84.0 | 92.9 | 97.2 | 100 |
|------|---|-----|------|------|------|------|------|------|------|-----|
|      | F | 4.9 | 16.9 | 34.8 | 58.9 | 76.6 | 88.6 | 95.0 | 97.9 | 100 |
| 1996 | M | 2.9 | 11.7 | 28.2 | 49.9 | 69.2 | 83.9 | 93.6 | 98.3 | 100 |
|      | F | 3.9 | 15.8 | 35.4 | 58.3 | 76.1 | 88.3 | 95.7 | 98.8 | 100 |
| 1994 | M | 2.5 | 11.2 | 27.7 | 48.8 | 68.1 | 82.8 | 93.4 | 98.2 | 100 |
|      | F | 3.2 | 14.8 | 34.3 | 56.7 | 74.8 | 87.4 | 95.4 | 98.8 | 100 |
| 1992 | M |     | 10.8 | 24.7 | 46.9 | 65.7 | 81.5 | 92.7 | 98.3 | 100 |
|      | F |     | 13.8 | 30.4 | 53.9 | 72.3 | 86.0 | 94.6 | 98.5 | 100 |
| 1990 | M |     | 9.8  | 23.1 | 44.9 | 63.6 | 79.7 | 91.4 | 97.3 | 100 |
|      | F |     | 11.8 | 27.2 | 50.5 | 69.2 | 83.7 | 93.2 | 97.7 | 100 |

*Notes*: As table in Item A above.

*Source*: Inter-board Statistics 1991/1993/1995/1997/1999/2001/2004/2008 (see http://www.jcq.org.uk).

## Item D

Gender differences in performance at GCSE, all groups/all subject areas 1990–2007. Females outperform males by these percentages:

|     | 1990 | 1992 | 1994 | 1996 | 1998 | 2000 | 2003 | 2007 |
|-----|------|------|------|------|------|------|------|------|
| A+  | 2.0  | 3.0  | 3.6  | 4.1  | 4.6  | 5.4  | 6.1  | 7.5  |
| C+  | 5.6  | 7.0  | 7.9  | 8.4  | 8.7  | 9.2  | 9.2  | 12.6 |

*Source*: Inter-board statistics, 1990, 1992, 1994, 1996, 1998, 2000, 2003, 2007 (see http://www.jcq.org.uk).

## Exercise 6.1

1. Identify the patterns of educational attainment shown in Item A.
2. Examine Item B. What patterns in gender differences in educational performance at A level emerged between 1991 and 2007?
3. Which educational policies and practices in schools could account for the differences between male and female performance at GCSE as illustrated in Item C?
4. Write a paragraph in your own words to summarize the information in Items A and C regarding performance by gender at GCSE and A Level over time.

(A) 5. Study Items C and D. Females are consistently achieving a higher rate of grades A*–C in GCSEs than boys. What factors outside school could account for these differences?

Having completed Exercise 6.1, you should now have an appreciation of the extent of gender differences in educational attainment and subject choice (see below). You will have recognized that females outperform males in GCSE and A level examinations. You will also have noticed that performances at GCSE and A level vary according to the subject taken, such that females are well ahead in the arts but behind in scientific subjects (apart from biology). The relative under-achievement of females and their low take-up of scientific-based subjects at the ages of 16 and 18 is clearly significant; statistics on first entry into higher education suggest that females are less likely to choose degrees of a scientific or technical nature. The gendered nature of higher-education subject choice (see Exercise 6.2 below) is important, because the degree schemes that females opt for are of lower status and afford fewer opportunities to enter the most powerful and well-paid occupational positions.

## Exercise 6.2

Participation by gender (%) in selected subject areas at A level, 2007

|                    | Males | Females |
| ------------------ | ----- | ------- |
| Physics            | 77.8  | 22.2    |
| Mathematics        | 61.1  | 38.9    |
| Computing and IT   | 70.4  | 29.6    |
| Business Studies   | 59.0  | 41.0    |
| Home Economics     | 5.7   | 94.3    |
| Art                | 30.4  | 69.6    |
| Education/RE       | 31.7  | 68.3    |
| Social Science     | 32.0  | 68.0    |
| English Literature | 29.6  | 70.4    |
| Modern Languages   | 35.6  | 64.4    |

*Source:* Adapted from Inter-Awarding Body Statistics 2008; see www.jcq.org.uk.

Higher education – participation by gender (undergraduate and postgraduate) and subject area, 2006/7 (2000/1): all UK higher education institutions

|  | Males | % Males | Females | %Females |
|---|---|---|---|---|
| Medicine and Dentistry | 22,490 (18,300) | 41.6 (45.6) | 31,595 (21,830) | 58.4 (54.4) |
| Physical Sciences | 42,630 (38,015) | 58.4 (61.9) | 30,330 (23,380) | 41.6 (38.1) |
| Mathematical Sciences | 17,345 (11,110) | 62.8 (62.2) | 10,280 (6,750) | 37.2 (37.8) |
| Computer Science | 67,210 (72,115) | 78.3 (74.0) | 18,680 (25,315) | 21.7 (26.0) |
| Engineering and Technology | 82,790 (83,375) | 85.0 (85.4) | 14,640 (14,210) | 15.0 (14.6) |
| Sociology | 8,140 (6,995) | 27.4 (28.4) | 21,590 (17,600) | 72.6 (71.6) |
| Law | 29,165 (20,370) | 39.5 (40.5) | 44,610 (29,965) | 60.5 (59.5) |
| Business | 110,905 (93,915) | 50.3 (48.2) | 109,525 (100,815) | 49.7 (51.8) |
| Languages | 37,565 (25,000) | 32.0 (31.1) | 79,865 (55,485) | 68.0 (68.9) |
| Education | 49,840 (37,060) | 24.5 (26.8) | 153,255 (101,195) | 75.5 (73.2) |

*Source*: Higher Education Statistics Agency (2008); see http://www.hesa.ac.uk/.

All students in UK higher education by gender (000s)

|  | 1970/1 | 1980/1 | 1990/1 | 2000/1 | 2006/7 |
|---|---|---|---|---|---|
| Males | 416 | 526 | 638 | 1,009 | 1,010 |
| Females | 205 | 301 | 537 | 1,279 | 1,482 |

*Source*: Higher Education Statistics Agency (2008); see http://www.hesa.ac.uk/.

1. Write a paragraph in your own words to summarize the information given in the three tables above.
2. Look at the overall patterns shown in the statistics above. Suggest reasons why there is a division along gender lines by subject at A level, and undergraduate and postgraduate levels.
3. Use the UCAS or DCFS websites (http://www.ucas.ac.uk/ and http://www.dcsf.gov.uk, respectively) to find out about the latest statistics in relation to subject choice by gender in higher education.

## HIGHER EDUCATION

The proportion of women undergraduates has risen since the Second World War. According to UCAS statistics, by 2007, women accounted for 54 per cent of accepted applicants to higher education, though it is in the new universities that the growth is most marked. In the early 1970s men outnumbered women in higher education, but in the early twenty-first century, women outnumber men (see www.hesa.ac.uk). However, sociological research has shown that there continue to be important differences in the higher education experiences of men and women. For example, Castleman and Poole (1990) show that there is still important gender segregation in subject choice at university level, and Mickleson (1989) shows that men receive greater rewards than do women at the outcome of their education.

It is also the case that academics are generally male, and women tend to occupy the least prestigious and more temporary university posts. Middleton (1993) suggests that this is because of 'academic machismo' (Morgan, 1981), whereby female academics are marginalized by academic discourses or ways of thinking that are dominated by men. For example, Middleton argues that what counts as sociology is decided by male gatekeepers – conference organizers and journal editors – who constitute the organizing principals of the subject. If they are to progress in their chosen field, women academics have to 'bracket out' their femaleness and accept androcentric (male-centred) definitions. Female academics are also more likely to be on fixed-term, short-term, fractional contracts that make their working lives less secure. According to Higher Education Statistics Agency (HESA) data, women lecturers and researchers are set to outnumber men in universities, at the professorial level the numbers speak for themselves: of 16,485 professors, 2,885 are women, with only three universities having equal numbers of male and female professors in 2006 – Worcester, Winchester and the Institute of Education. For useful information, see www.hesa.ac.uk.

It is important to recognize that the statistics on gender and educational achievement, and on subject choice, are not easy to interpret and understand. For example, if girls are out-performing boys at the top of the attainment hierarchy, what does this mean for girls who are still performing in the lower reaches of it? Are the girls at the bottom at a disadvantage compared to girls at the top, or is it only boys at the bottom this can be said about? Do boys not achieve at school as much as girls because they do not have to, as they know they will eventually have better-paid jobs than girls, in the main? If that is the case, would equalising opportunity in schools lead to greater inequality in the workplace, as boys increased their already existing advantage? The key issue is how far we can examine the statistics on gender independent of other social factors that may impinge upon achievement. Similarly with subject choice – many feminists have argued that girls tend to choose to study the more expressive subjects, which then translate into less well paid jobs in the labour market, while boys select the more instrumental subjects, which place them at an advantage later. There are two implications of these choices. Do boys therefore miss out on developing the social skills that girls achieve through their choice of subject? Are some boys and girls making socially constructed choices rather than informed choices about their subjects, which have consequences for later work lives? For a discussion of these issues, see Collins *et al.* (2000).

There are other difficulties with the way that sociologists examine and interpret statistics on gender and achievement. Stephen Gorard has criticized the idea that there is a crisis in boys' education on the basis of a different way of looking at statistics on underachievement (see Gorard and Smith 2004, for example). Rather than boys continuing to fall further behind, Gorard argued that the achievement gap had remained fairly stable, and was slightly narrowing in the early twenty-first century, Moreover, when looking at GCSE results, he found that there is little difference in achievement between boys and girls at the lower end of the range of grades, but that the gender gap increased at the top of the grades. Connolly (2008) argues that, while it is interesting to examine the range of grades in this way, the important point to examine is the C grade, as this represents in the public and employers' minds a 'pass', and the statistics show that there is a small but important gap here, with girls outperforming boys at this threshold grade, regardless of social class or ethnicity (Connolly 2006).

## EXPLANATIONS OF GENDER DIFFERENCES IN EDUCATIONAL ACHIEVEMENT AND SUBJECT CHOICE

Let us now consider three types of explanation to account for the above patterns of attainment and choice:

1. Genetic explanations.
2. Outside school explanations.
3. Inside school explanations.

### Genetic explanations

Genetic-based explanations of gender differences in attainment were influential in psychology during the 1970s, though the biological determinist approach has a long history. The crucial belief of biological theories is that gender differences are natural and therefore unalterable. Educationally, then, it would be right and proper to treat boys and girls in schools differently, because their natural inclinations are towards different adult roles. Any socially constructed differences between men and women were built on and constrained by these natural differences (see Hutt 1972). For example, theories were advanced that females excelled at language-based subjects because of their greater verbal and reasoning abilities, yet underperformed in mathematical and science-based courses because of lower levels of innate spatial ability, which restricted their understanding of shape and form.

These biological theories of innate intelligence have been strongly criticized. Kelly (1982) suggests that gender differences in spatial ability may be attributed to the types of toys children play with rather than their genetic make-up. Furthermore, genetic explanations cannot adequately account for the narrowing of gender differences in mathematical and science-based subjects since the mid 1980s – if the differences were biologically determined we would expect them to remain constant over time (complete Exercise 6.3 below to develop your understanding of these criticisms).

A variation on this theme is represented by New Right ideologies, as put forward by Roger Scruton (see Williams 1989), which suggest that the biological and natural instincts of the sexes determine a particular sexual division of labour in the home, and the gender segregation of the male-dominated public sphere and the female world of the private home. These gender arrangements are seen as a 'natural necessity'.

(A)(E)

## Exercise 6.3

Write a list of criticisms of the genetic explanation for differences in achievement between the sexes. Here are two to get you started:

1. Genetic explanations cannot account for the success of girls and women in education in recent times. If intelligence is innate and fixed, how can the change in fortunes of boys and girls be explained?
2. Kelly's research into science shows how it becomes seen as a masculine subject through its social rather than natural construction, such as images in textbooks, use of examples that relate to boys' experiences, domination of male science teachers, domination of boys in science classrooms.

## Outside school explanations

Feminist sociology has been influential in developing a macro approach to gender inequalities in education. Three social (as opposed to genetic) explanations can be identified within the outside school approach:

1. Childhood socialization.
2. Employment opportunities/employment opportunities and women.
3. Patriarchal relations.

### Childhood socialization

Early socialization may well account for the eventual choices and routes taken by girls and boys when they go to school. Mothers talk to and treat girl and boy babies differently, expecting girls to be more placid; different toys are given to newborn babies depending on their gender; and girls and boys are dressed in different colours to identify with their gender. At home, girls my be expected to adopt a more domestic or caring role, even when quite young. The media advertise girls' and boys' toys in line with stereotypical images of adult roles, with girls' toys being associated with the domestic sphere and those for boys associated with masculine pursuits outside the home. Supermarket toy shelves and play/toy shops generally are a testament to the segregation of children's expected roles. Girls may be kept closer to home than boys and given less freedom outside. Hence, according to Norman *et al.* (1988), sex role stereotyping is well under way before children go to school. Role models of parents can be quite traditional even when the mother works outside the home, and these act as part of the early socialization process (do Exercise 6.4 below for a contemporary take on this). Of course, socialization continues in school, where early reading schemes have been seen to reinforce gender stereotyping (Lobban 1974), teachers' expectations of behaviour may tend to be gender specific, boys may dominate classrooms and receive more attention than girls to the extent that teachers, both male and female, cannot remember some girls' names, even though those of quiet boys could be remembered (Stanworth 1983). These studies are now quite old, but their findings resonate into the 2000s.

## Exercise 6.4

ⒹⒶ Draw a grid like the one below and complete it over the course of a few days to analyse who does what in your home. There are spaces for you to add your own examples of additional activities.

| Type of household activity | Mainly carried out by females Put a tick to indicate each time the job is done | Mainly carried out by males Put a tick to indicate each time the job is done |
|---|---|---|
| Washing-up; loading/ unloading dishwasher | | |
| Vacuuming | | |
| Cleaning | | |
| Ironing | | |
| Cooking | | |

(An) When your grid is completed, what conclusions can you draw from the information you have gathered?

(E) Extension activity: draw a similar grid for your school or college class, with appropriate activities for a classroom, to see if the results are as you expected.

Feminists such as Sharpe (1976) maintain that differences in child social-ization serve to generate masculine and feminine cultural identities. Secondary agencies of socialization such as the media and peer groups are said to reinforce gender identities established during primary socialization within the family. For example, many teenage magazines (McRobbie 1991) targeted at female audiences present ideologies of beauty, marriage, domesticity and subordina-tion that serve to strengthen the messages of femininity that families instil into their female members. Gender socialization of this sort is significant because it helps us to understand why females traditionally have 'latched on' to subjects such as home economics and the arts, which have a feminized image, rather than subjects such as technology and science, which are packaged in a mascu-line way. Therefore, sex role theorists, such as Byrne (1978) have argued that the cycle of discrimination against women is created by parents and teachers reinforcing sex stereotypes, which then become the basis for discriminatory practices.

(I)(A)

## Exercise 6.5

Exercise 6.5 requires you to do some independent work. Go on to the internet and search for accounts of outside school explanations of gender differences in educational attainment and subject choice. Use the material you have found to fill in the chart below. When completing the chart you need to explain how each agency of socialization steers females away from scientific and technological subjects and towards the arts. You should also cite empirical studies wherever possible to support the points you make. We have started to fill in the chart for you.

A summary chart illustrating the way childhood socialization affects educational attainment and subject choice, by gender

| Agency of socialization | The process by which educational attainments and subject identities are determined | Empirical studies |
|---|---|---|
| Family role models | | |
| Toys played with | Whereas males are given active construction toys to play with, such as Meccano and chemistry sets, females are encouraged to play with passive caring toys such as dolls and cookery sets. As a consequence, females do not develop the scientific aspirations and aptitudes that males do. | Kelly (1982) |
| Peer group | | |
| Newspapers and magazines | | |
| Advertisements | | |
| Games | | |

During the 1980s a series of research studies challenged the assumption that girls were socialized into one particular form of femininity, or that girls did not challenge the notions of feminine roles with which they were presented. For example, Connell (1986) argued that feminism itself had helped to bring about radical changes in the ways girls perceived themselves, so they no longer constructed their identity in mainly domestic terms. Rather, women now saw themselves as much as workers as homemakers. More recently, Riddell (1992) found that schoolgirls had a dual notion of their futures, linking their subject choices at schools to the local labour market (especially working-class girls) while also accepting that motherhood and domesticity were important parts of their identity as women. But the girls in Riddell's study were not passive in this process of socialization. Rather, they had absorbed both accepting and undermining messages about traditional female roles. In addition, different gender codes were expressed by working-class and middle-class girls, with middle-class girls opting for academic education and thus gaining the approval of the middle-class female teachers whom they most closely resembled.

It is also important to note that Riddell found that parents' conceptions of femininity were also complex, and varied according to class position. While middle-class parents were more supportive of the principle of equal opportunity, middle-class men were most opposed to any positive action to achieve it. Working-class men were the most supportive of traditional gender codes. In both classes, a minority of mothers strongly supported changes in women's social position. So the view that there is a uniform socialization into one specific gender code is mistaken. Rather, there are conservative and radical views concerning gender roles, and different groups of parents choose elements of those agendas in different proportions, which then balance out in their children in different ways.

Sue Sharpe's study underpins the changing nature of socialization and education for girls. In her first study, in 1972, Sharpe (1976) found that girls wanted to leave school early and only aspired to traditional types of 'women's work', with marriage and family being their main motivation. By 1994, in Sharpe's follow-up study, girls wanted to marry later, fewer wanted to have children, and an increasing number thought work and independence were more important than marriage. Francis (2000) also argues that changes in wider society, such as increasing female employment opportunities, have had a significant effect on the ways girls develop their own constructions of femininity (see Exercise 6.6 below to understand the changes in female participation in the workforce).

## Employment opportunities

### Item D

Women constitute nearly half of the workforce according to *UK Family Trends 1994–2004.* More than two-thirds of mothers work outside the home – 68 per cent in 2003. Women return to work sooner after having children than they did in the past, and they also tend to work longer hours than they used to. Women are still the mainstay of the part-time labour force. At the same time, the proportion of men in work is decreasing. For men, the picture is quite different. Their economic activity rates are on a downward slide, falling from 91 per cent in 1979 to 88 per cent in 1991. If the trend continues, women will become a majority in the workforce before too long. However, there has been very little change in the gender segregation of the labour market, especially in the manual trades such as plumbing, building and IT, with women accounting for only 1 per cent in the construction industry (EOC 2004).

The kind of work women do tends to be different from that of men. Women are much more likely to:

- Work in the service industries: 82 per cent of working women have jobs in the service industries, compared with 54 per cent of men. This is particularly evident in the health-associated professions, personal services, and clerical and teaching occupations, where women outnumber men significantly.
- Work part time: 42 per cent of women with jobs are working part-time, according to the *Labour Force Survey* (1991). This involves nearly 4.5 million women workers. Married women are twice as likely as non-married women to be part-time employees; half of married women workers are part-timers compared with just over a quarter of non-married women workers.

*Source*: Adapted and updated from Denscombe (1993).

## Exercise 6.6

)Ⓐ 1. By how many percentage points did the economic activity of men decline between 1979 and 1991, according to Item D?

)Ⓐ 2. In what ways do the jobs women do more than men, as described in Item D, reflect traditional views of gender roles?

)Ⓐ 3. Suggest one reason why the 'kind of work women do' (Item D) helps to explain subject-specific attainment and subject choice.

### Employment opportunities and women

The issue of employment opportunities for girls is linked in sociology to the concept of 'cultural reproduction'. That is, sociologists are interested in the ways in which society acts to produce adults who ultimately have similar life-chances or opportunities to those of their parents. In the case of females, the situation is complicated by the 'domestic option'. Traditional ideology allocates homemaking and child rearing as the prime responsibility of women, and 'earning' as the main activity of adult males. Clearly, in a world where adult male unemployment is high and adult female employment is prevalent, these traditional definitions of gender identity are likely to be strained. Yet while the labour market is now an acceptable goal of female education, cultural reproduction of the genders continues.

In particular, sociological focus has been on the choice of subjects to study by males and females, and on the specific question of why girls continue to choose subjects that are likely to lead to disadvantage in the labour market, in terms of job security and levels of reward. At one level, traditional ideas about femininity and therefore 'proper' jobs for girls would seem to be the answer to this problem. However, the labour market is changing rapidly and new forms of feminine identity are emerging that would seem to militate against this apparently easy relationship between the traditional notions of femininity and less prestigious jobs.

Cultural reproduction theory has shifted from a deterministic model, in which young people of either gender are slotted automatically, with little choice, into appropriate job roles for a capitalist society, to one in which the active participation of individual girls and boys is recognized. Thus, while there are structural constraints in schools that form and channel subject choices, such as the options set against each other (part of the inside school explanations) or the powerful influence of parental pressure, sociologists such as Connell *et al.* (1982) stress the wide scope for individual choices within these constraints.

More recent work on cultural reproduction has challenged its usefulness in a postmodern world characterized by deindustrialization. Weis (1990), for example, argues that postmodern societies, with their emphasis on service industries rather than heavy manufacturing, no longer require boys to follow their fathers into industrial jobs, and girls to follow their mothers into domesticity. Rather, postmodern industries require flexible workers. It was argued earlier (see Chapter 4) that girls have a wider range of options to define their femininity than boys do to identify their masculinity (Francis 2000). In the past, home was the main locus of identification with femininity; now work outside the home is part of girls' conceptions of their role (Sharpe 1994). Gender identities are therefore likely to shift under the impact of this development. The introduction of the national curriculum can therefore be seen not as a commitment to equal opportunities for girls and boys, but as a result of the need to train more young people in the scientific and technological skills needed by a postmodern economy (see Myers 1989). The result may be to establish women as a reserve army of labour across a wider number of occupational sectors.

*Patriarchal relations*

Many feminists have argued that the ideology of patriarchy in society at large is a major cause of inequality in schools. The ideology of patriarchy suggests that the dominant ideas in society tend to favour men, and operate to keep women in subordinate positions. For example, Arnot (1991) argues that the introduction of the Technical and Vocational Educational Initiative, with its emphasis on gender equality through increasing female choices, in fact did little to achieve gender equality. As Arnot put it, 'providing equal freedoms within unequal social relations had little chance of creating equal opportunities'. What she is suggesting is that, given a free choice, girls and boys tend to respond according to society's views of what is proper for each gender, so that girls tend to avoid choosing science and technology subjects. Therefore, there should be greater compulsion in schools to ensure that there are common experiences for girls and boys, which will in turn ensure that equality of opportunity comes about. Evidence from the uptake of modern apprenticeships underlines gendered choices, with girls taking up the majority of places on Early Years and Education, Hairdressing, Health and Social Care, and boys dominating in Motor Vehicle, Plumbing, Construction and IT. Choices of GNVQ/AVCE courses also follow this pattern, with girls opting or being counselled to take courses related to health and social care, and boys more likely to be doing those related to business. See www.learningandskillscouncil.

During the 1980s, the rise of New Right ideologies tended to reinforce patriarchal relationships in society as a whole, and this had an impact on education. However, the effect of New Right ideas was not always as straightforward as might have been expected. Certainly New Right writers were hostile to the notion of equality for women, seeing it as an 'ideological extravagance', and hostile to the central importance the New Right gave to the family (see Campbell (1987) for an account of the New Right's attitude). The assumption made by New Right thinkers was that men would specialize in work in the market place and women in household work. This had implications for the type of education each gender was to receive. New Right ideas reflected traditional roles, with boys being prepared by schools to be the main wage earner, and girls to be homemakers and child rearers (see David 1983). This in turn had implications for the types of subjects girls were to be encouraged to choose in schools.

However, the impact of these ideologies has been blunted by several factors. Arnot (1992) argues that feminism has developed to the extent that women have been able to resist a simple 'back-to-basics' movement, in which women are supposed to be responsible for the home and men for work, so that the experiences of women after the First World War in being returned to domesticity have not been repeated. Campbell (1987) found that changes in occupational structures ensured that in the 1980s there were many middle-class career women in the ranks of the Conservative Party who could resist the simple equation of females with domesticity. As a result, women did not take up a mainly domestic role during the 1980s, despite the impact of recession and job losses. According to a report by the Equal Opportunities Commission (EOC) in 2005, there have been notable successes in women's employment. In 1975 only 4.3 per cent of MPs were women, compared to 19.7 per cent in 2005, and in 1975 only 7 per cent of solicitors were women, compared with 42 per cent in 2005. We also know the educational success story that in GCSEs girls are doing better than boys and now constitute well over 50 per cent of undergraduates. The EOC also found that while equal pay has still to be achieved, single women without children have closed the pay gap when compared to single childless men.

*Outside school explanations – an evaluation*

## Exercise 6.7

Below are a number of evaluation points of the outside school explanations. Identify which are the strengths and which the weaknesses. Record your answers in a two-column table that clearly separates the strengths from the weaknesses. When you record your answers, rank them in order of importance. Justify your ranking to another sociology student.

1. They are an improvement on earlier, genetic-based explanations as they recognize the importance of social processes.
2. The explanations have served to generate further research.
3. They neglect the effects of inside school processes and therefore act as a smokescreen for the failure of the education system.
4. Aspects of the explanations are dated. Many young females have aspirations outside the home, and women are now in more powerful occupational positions.
5. They suffer from ideological bias.
6. As a set of explanations, they attempt to link the different parts of society together and show the interdependence of different aspects of society.
7. The process whereby early experience leads to later effect is never clearly stated. It is often just assumed.
8. They tend to oversimplify the effects of cultural and social forces in society.
9. These explanations stress cultural factors as well as social ones; for example, the importance of the media in influencing views on gender.
10. They suggest that the early experiences of people are important, affecting the later course of their lives.

### Inside school explanations

As with the outside school approaches to gender differences in attainment and subject choice, the impact of feminist theory and research has been influential in shaping the various explanations offered. Feminists claim that a powerful hidden curriculum operates inside schools that reinforces the gender-stereotyped socialisation they experience in the family and wider society. Kessler *et al.* (1985) describe the ways in which the whole of school life is permeated with messages about what is correct masculine or feminine behaviour in the school's 'gender regime'. Arnot (1982) suggests that schools use a 'gender code' to endorse or attack particular forms of masculinity or femininity; in other words, schools are involved in a legitimation process concerning appropriate gender behaviour and outcomes.

However, it is important to note that feminism has become somewhat fragmented and it is difficult to discuss the impact of feminism as a whole, rather than a number of different feminisms. As the politics of identity has replaced social class as the major formative force in individual lives, feminism itself has also split along lines of identity. Thus it has become usual to refer to liberal feminism, radical feminism, socialist feminism and black feminism in analysing schools in particular, and education in general. Each of these strands is likely to emphasize different explanations for the disadvantage experienced by girls in the education system. For example, liberal feminism has traditionally been associated with the social democratic approach to education, in which freedom of subject choice is an important principle. Radical feminists have been more critical of schooling, focusing on the patriarchal nature of the curriculum and the 'androcentric' or male-centred nature of many of its practices. Socialist feminists have emphasized the relationship between girls' experiences in schools and their destinies in the labour market – that is, also their class position, and black feminists have focused on the distinct and double oppressions to which black girls are subject (see Chapter 7).

The solutions to gender inequality put forward by feminists therefore vary according to what type of feminist they are. Liberal feminists, according to Yates (1985), seek to change girls' feelings and attitudes towards schooling by recommending 'girl-friendly' schooling. Yates is critical of policies such as encouraging girls to take up chemistry, because this is putting forward a model of girls as 'deficit boys'. The implication of this policy is that, by making girls' experiences in education as much like that of boys as possible, equality will be achieved. Radical feminists, on the other hand, tend to advocate more fundamental changes to the education system to ensure equality, such as girls-only schools or positive discrimination policies.

What is perhaps most significant about the hidden curriculum is the way it ensures that science and technology have masculine images. This is of consequence because the masculine packaging of science and technology greatly deters female participation and interest.

Let us now consider the different ways the hidden curriculum affects educational attainment and subject identity. The aspects to be covered are as follows:

1. School books.
2. Students.
3. Equal opportunities.
4. Teachers' expectations and attitudes.
5. Patriarchal curriculum.
6. Lack of positive role models.

### School books

A traditional feminist view of school books is that they reinforce a view of females as passive and dependent on men. Particular focus has been placed on fairy tales and the messages about gender roles they encode (or contain in their imagery and language). Some sociologists have emphasized the way that fairy tales reflect the dominant and sexist values of the society in which they were developed (see Bottigheimer 1987). Such views have not gone unchallenged, with sociologists such as Bettelheim (1991) arguing that children identify with the characters regardless of the gender involved. Thus neither the gender of the reader nor that of the character is important in the 'decoding' of the fairy tale. However, feminist fairy tales, which seek to represent females in different ways, have not displaced the traditional stories, which continue to sell in their thousands.

In terms of textbooks, Kelly (1987) argues that there is a masculine bias in science texts, in which women are either passive or invisible (do Exercise 6.8 below to explore this issue). Thus the examples used in these texts tend to utilize male images and ignore famous female scientists. Similarly, Culley (1986) argues that computing textbooks tend to show men in decision-making positions and females carrying out deskilled tasks such as inputting data.

In the 1980s, feminist sociologists reviewed the way that fairy tales and other teaching materials had been studied and rejected a simple 'reading' of them that cast the female reader as a passive recipient of the sexist messages in the text. Rather, research in the 1980s sought to determine readers' reactions to such literature and expose the many different functions that such texts could have for different readers (see, for example, Taylor 1989). The conclusion of this reassessment is that a specific effect for fairy tales cannot be taken for granted, but rather that 'romantic' fiction has many functions for female readers, and not just a gender socialization response.

---

(A)
## Exercise 6.8

For this exercise we would like you to carry out a content analysis of the science and technology textbooks used at your school or college. This will require you to identify, among other things, the number of times females and males are used in pictures and illustrations and the nature of their roles in them, the gender of famous scientists referred to, and the degree to which the examples used in the books are gender specific. You will find it easier to do this exercise with another sociology student so that you can share the workload. You should also consult your teacher/lecturer or a research methods book so that you are clear about how to do a content analysis.

---

### Students

Many feminist writers – for example, Kelly (1987) – have focused on the ways in which boys take control of science and technology lessons – for example, by monopolising equipment for experiments and creating a male-dominated space. This has affected the ability of female students to participate fully in science lessons. Culley (1986) noticed the same process in computing lessons, where male domination of the computers created an uncomfortable social space for those female students who wished to participate. In addition, many studies of the classroom have found that boys tended to dominate when discussion was opened up to pupils, not only in the time taken by boys, but also in determining what gets discussed. As a result, teachers' attention is more focused on boys than girls (Baxter 2002). Attempts to empower females in science and computing lessons have not always been received with good grace by those in the classroom.

Francis (2000) reviewed research from the past and conducted research of her own into achievement at school. She concluded that despite her research being nearly twenty years on from Baxter's, boys still dominate classrooms and their teacher's time, and the curriculum is still patriarchally focused in areas such as science, IT and history. However, the achievements of girls have greatly improved, and in all Key Stage tests (with the exception of Key Stage 2

**Table 6.1** Percentage of males/females achieving five or more GCSEs at grades A*–C

|           | 2000 | 2002 | 2006 | 2007 |
|-----------|------|------|------|------|
| Males     | 44   | 46   | 54   | 45.8 |
| Females   | 54   | 56   | 64   | 58.4 |

*Source*: Adapted from DCSF (see www.dcsf.gov.uk).

Maths and Key Stage 3 Science (DfES 2004)), in GCSEs and A Levels, girls outperform boys (see Table 6.1).

Both boys and girls who receive free school meals (FSM) achieve less than those who are non-FSM. FSM is used as a measure of deprivation or lower social class position, as it is a means-tested benefit received by families with a very low income to enable their children to have a free meal at school. Hence social class is still an important factor in explaining the educational achievement of boys and girls. See 'Bringing It All Together' at the end of Chapter 7 for more detailed consideration of the interplay between class, gender and ethnicity.

If we consider participation rates for girls and boys, we find more girls than boys at the age of 16 are in full-time education and, according to UCAS, more women are in higher education than men (see page 70 and the table in Exercise 6.2, p. 136).

*Equal opportunities*

Hostility to equal opportunity programmes has often come from the students themselves, both boys and girls. While girls may be ambivalent about such initiatives, they often see that some benefits might result from them. Boys, on the other hand, have only things to lose and therefore tend to be much more against any attempt to redress the gender disadvantage. However, the attitude of boys in everyday classroom life has also been a focus of feminist research. In particular, sexual harassment of female pupils and teachers has been investigated. This area is a minefield of gender relations, with opposing sides either claiming its widespread existence (Jones and Mahony 1989) or denying its extent and importance (see Halson 1989). It is also well documented how language use and male–female interaction in the classroom is used to deny classroom equality, and is often expressed in hostile ways, with boys using girls as a negative reference (see Spender 1982). The strategies of denial used by boys include interruption, denigration and trivialization of female talk.

These activities are important aspects of the identity construction of males. Conceptions of masculinity in school are forged in relationship to females (and for white children, in relation to black and Asian children). Weis (1992) shows that white, working-class males in America define themselves in terms of not wanting to be like blacks or females. Their construction of their own sexuality and ideas about what is acceptable behaviour are therefore forged in opposition to other groups, at least in part. Schools are therefore not neutral in the process of identity construction, but they do operate in contradictory ways. While schools tend to encourage a male-dominant ethos, they conversely allow space for females to explore their own identities, in an environment that encourages questioning as well as conformity. Schools can thus allow the possibility of an extension or alteration of gender identity as well as a reinforcement of gender construction within the family. See Connolly's work on masculinity and school in Chapter 4, and the work of Francis (2000).

### Teachers' expectations and attitudes

There has been a great deal of sociological interest in teachers' attitudes towards equal opportunities for women, with teachers often been seen as one of the main stumbling blocks to the achievement of equality for girls in schools. As Weiner (1985) points out, school-based attempts to combat inequality have often been met with hostility from teachers themselves. The conclusions of such studies tend to accept that there are a number of teacher ideologies and operating principles that relegate the issue of gender equality to a relatively low priority in schools. For example, teachers are often in favour of individual choice of subjects as a matter of principle. They do not consider the outcomes of those choices in terms of gender equality, but accept a gender-differentiated curriculum as the natural result of individual choice. According to Riddell (1992), this ignores the social (for example, peer group pressure) and ideological (for example, ideas about 'proper' work for women) constraints within which individual students make their choices. Moreover, there has also been a belief among teachers that sex-stereotyped attitudes are the product of family socialization, and that there is little, if anything, that teachers can do to alter or counteract such socialization. Indeed, many teachers remain opposed to the concept of even trying, seeing equal opportunities policies as ultimately political and therefore unacceptable in schools. This corresponds closely to New Right attacks on the 'political correctness' of such policies, which they see as undermining the natural order of things.

However, resistance to gender equality also operates at the individual level. Hicks (1988) found that many female teachers are in two minds about their dual role as worker and housewife, and as a consequence they often see male teachers as better educators than females, because males are able to concentrate on their careers more than women can. As for male teachers, Spear (1985) has found that many science teachers are hostile to equal opportunity initiatives and express traditional attitudes supporting a subordinate role for women, both at work and at home.

Empirical research into gender relations in the classroom has shown a remarkable degree of consensus about the differential classroom experiences of boys and girls (see Wilkinson and Marrett 1985). The conclusion seems to be that boys behave in a more assertive way, are given more teacher time, and are generally more prominent in classroom interactions than girls. This is so irrespective of whether the researcher is looking at teacher–pupil or pupil–pupil interaction. For example, Sadker *et al.* (1991) have found that boys receive more criticism from teachers than girls do, but also more praise. While other sociologists have reported that boys and girls receive equal amounts of praise (Stake and Katz 1982), some, such as Whyte (1984), regarding the GIST (Girls into Science and Technology) project, have found that in some subjects girls receive more teacher attention than boys.

However Öhrn (1993) argues that these studies underestimate the resistance that many girls exhibit in the classroom to their relative invisibility. This resistance, she argues, often takes the form of over-accommodation to the rules. By making very public displays of conformity to the rules of the classroom, girls achieve a situation where minor infringements are ignored or 'not seen' by the teacher. But when it comes to examining the allocation of jobs in the classroom to boys and girls, sociologists are more in agreement that these are distributed in sex-stereotyped ways. For example, Platt and Whyld (1983) have found that boys are asked by teachers to move furniture, while girls are asked to make tea and wash up afterwards (carrying out Exercise 6.9 below allows you to research this for yourself in science lessons).

According to Livesey and Lawson (2005), labelling and stereotyping is applied more negatively to boys, since the change in levels of achievement have become clear, with teachers more likely to label boys as lazy and underachieving, Girls, on the other hand, may be labelled more positively as high achievers with fewer behavioural problems.

Equal opportunities and high expectations are now part of teacher training programmes across the country. Built into the Initial Teacher Training (ITT) programmes, student teachers must provide evidence of achievement in these areas of their work if they are to gain qualified teacher status. Contained in the first Standards area of the 2009 Postgraduate Certificate in Education (PGCE) course as laid down by the Teacher Development Agency (TDA) is that student teachers must provide evidence of their competence in their 'professional attributes' 'to have high expectations of children and young people ... taking steps to ensure equal and fair treatment of all pupils'. Another example is they must know how to use 'national statistics information to evaluate the effectiveness of their teaching ... and to raise levels of attainment'. Hence there may be some changes to the operation of classroom over the coming years. Teachers may be becoming increasingly aware of their role in creating expectations in the children they teach, and ways in which they can avoid discrimination in their pedagogical practices. Labelling and self-fulfilling prophecies may become a less significant part of children's experiences at school.

Ⓐ

## Exercise 6.9

This exercise requires you to carry out some observational work in a science and/or technology classroom. You will examine the extent to which teaching in this environment favours any particular gender, and the degree to which the science and/or technology classroom is dominated by male students. It is important that you consult your teacher/lecturer or a research methods book so that you are clear about how best to carry out the observation. It is essential that your research is ethically sound. Part of this will require you to obtain the permission of the relevant teachers in your school or college before carrying out the observation.

### Patriarchal curriculum

While the ideas associated with progressive education would seem to favour gender equality, some sociologists have argued that the 'liberal' approach in schools of the 1960s and 1970s ironically had the opposite effect to that intended, and reinforced rather than undermined gender stereotyping. For example, Clarricoates (1980) argues that the result of child-centred progressive styles of teaching, where children are allowed freedom of choice and speech, has been to promote gender differences, as young children re-enact gender power struggles from outside school within the classroom. In this respect, Walkerdine (1981) has found that not only do very young children use sexually abusive language in the classroom, but also that this is unchallenged by the teacher.

There has also been a debate amongst sociologists about the impact of the national curriculum on gender differentiation in schools. Riddell (1992) explores the issue of subject choice in terms of the way that allowing free choices tends to reinforce gender differentiation in schooling. Thus the impact of parental and teachers' expectations about the future roles of children tends to steer girls away from the high-status subjects of science and towards those subjects whose value in the labour market is lower. Therefore, for some feminists, such as Byrne (1985), the introduction of a national curriculum, in which girls are constrained to study science to the same level as boys, at least until the age of 16, is a step towards equality. Kelly (1988) also welcomes the introduction of compulsory science for girls as one of the ways of redressing the advantages boys have gained from an individualized curriculum.

The expansion of coursework has been argued to favour girls in that it demands consistent, independent work over time, which supposedly suits girls. However, with the introduction of changes to examinations in 2008, the coursework option has largely been abandoned.

In looking at girls and science, equal opportunity initiatives such as WISE (Women into Science and Engineering) have focused on the number of women participating in these curriculum areas and ignored the content of the curriculum. Bentley and Watts (1987) suggest that three different approaches to the science curriculum should be recognized. First, there is girl-friendly science, which seeks to make the science curriculum start with issues that grab the attention of girls, and make the content of science lessons address girls' interests. Second, there is feminine science, which seeks to replace 'masculine', aggressive, competitive behaviour in the science laboratory with a more supportive and collaborative approach that is more appealing to girls. Third, there is feminist science, which challenges the way that science is carried out and calls for a greater recognition of intuition in the scientific method, which would increase girls' chances of scientific achievement. On this last point, Kelly (1988) argues that this assumes that, rather than just being 'invisible', women have not been part of scientific endeavour at all.

Feminist criticism of the national curriculum has focused on the simplistic solution to gender inequity it seems to offer. Rather, these critics argue that the case for more girls doing science, which the national curriculum demands from schools, needs to be placed within the context of larger developments in society. For example, Elliott and Powell (1987) suggest that the deskilling of jobs is occurring in all sectors of the economy, including occupations associated with science and technology. As it is women who tend to fill the most lowly and least-skilled jobs in all sectors, encouraging girls to take science and technology may result in yet another area of the labour market in which they could be exploited. Indeed, Elliot and Powell argue that encouraging women to move away from the aesthetic and creative worlds in which they have often excelled, and towards the world of science, reinforces both the 'deficit model' of women's achievements and the masculine view that these worlds are somehow less important than the world of science.

While the most blatant cases of gender segregation in the school curriculum have been tackled, often with some success and often involving across-the-board improvements in girls' achievements, there are still many areas in which under-achievement has not been redressed. Deem (1992) points out that it is mainly white, middle-class girls who have benefited from changes in schooling so far, but this leaves many white, working-class girls and boys, and black and Asian girls, at a disadvantage. Scraton (1987) argues that the most gender-segregated subject of all, physical education (PE), has not been examined seriously by those concerned with equality. The debate has yet to be resolved between those advocating girls-only teams as a way of increasing female self-confidence and physical skills, and those who support mixed teams as a way of challenging male–female relationships founded on physical strength.

### Lack of positive role models

The issue of role models operates at two levels in the case of educational inequality. The traditional approach is to argue that there is a lack of positive role models for girls in the higher positions of school and work, which has the effect of damping down female aspirations and limiting their achievement over their lifetime (see Exercise 6.10 below). So, even when girls succeed at school, they do not compete for the better-paid jobs in the numbers that their achievements would suggest.

---

#### Item E

Sociological evidence suggests that, at all levels of the education system, women are less likely to occupy the higher rungs of the professional ladder. This is supported by the two tables in Item E. Inequalities of this sort are significant, because it means that females have less positive role models to look up to than do males. As a consequence, female attitudes and aspirations may be less ambitious than those of males, and in turn this may depress educational performance. The education system generally, however, has been seen to undergo a process of feminisation, whereby aspects of the curriculum, pedagogy and schooling have become increasingly female-friendly. The majority of education employees are women – from classroom assistants, support staff, office staff and dinner ladies to teachers and managers. Men are more prevalent in the upper echelons – as head teachers, especially in primary schools, and senior managers.

Distribution of all academic staff by grade and gender in 2006/7: all UK universities

|  | Female | Male | Total | % Female |
|---|---|---|---|---|
| Professors | 2,885 | 13,600 | **16,485** | 17.5 |
| Senior lecturers and researchers | 12,375 | 21,275 | **33,650** | 36.8 |
| Lecturers | 24,590 | 27,340 | **51,930** | 47.4 |
| Researchers | 16,815 | 19,925 | **36,740** | 45.8 |
| Other grades | 15,255 | 15,935 | **31,190** | 48.9 |
| **Total academic staff** | **71,920** | **98,075** | 169,995 | 42.3 |
| Non-academic staff | 121,585 | 72,585 | **194,170** | 62.6 |
| **All staff** | **193,500** | **170,660** | **364,165** | **53.1** |

*Source*: HESA(Higher Education Statistics Agency) (2008). See http://www.hesa.ac.uk.

## Exercise 6.10

Read Items E and F

1. What percentage of head teachers are female in secondary schools?
2. Which teaching scale does Item E indicate is the one that females are more likely to be represented in?
3. Use the chart on academic staff in universities in Item F to support the claim that females are less likely to reach the highest occupational positions in the higher education sector.
4. Explain why women might meet a 'glass ceiling' in the education sector. What might be the characteristics of jobs such as senior managers and head teachers that put women off?

Item F

Teachers in service: full-time regular qualified teachers in the maintained schools sector, 1997–2004, by phase, grade and sex (percentages)

| England | 1997 | 1998 | 1999 | 2000 | 2001 | 2002 | 2003 | 2004 | 2005 | 2006 |
|---|---|---|---|---|---|---|---|---|---|---|
| **Nursery and primary** | | | | | | | | | | |
| **Heads** | | | | | | | | | | |
| Men | 44.3 | 42.2 | 41.0 | 40.3 | 39.2 | 38.1 | 37.0 | 35.4 | 34 | 33 |
| Women | 55.7 | 57.8 | 59.0 | 59.7 | 60.8 | 61.9 | 63.0 | 64.6 | 66 | 67 |
| All teachers | 100.0 | 100.0 | 100.0 | 100.0 | 100.0 | 100.0 | 100.0 | 100.0 | 100.0 | 100.0 |
| **Deputy heads** | | | | | | | | | | |
| Men | 28.5 | 27.2 | 27.0 | 26.1 | 25.2 | 24.9 | 24.7 | 24.0 | 23 | 22 |
| Women | 71.5 | 72.8 | 73.0 | 73.9 | 74.8 | 75.1 | 75.3 | 76.0 | 77 | 78 |
| All teachers | 100.0 | 100.0 | 100.0 | 100.0 | 100.0 | 100.0 | 100.0 | 100.0 | 100.0 | 100.0 |
| **Classroom and others** | | | | | | | | | | |
| Men | 11.7 | 11.8 | 11.8 | 11.8 | 11.9 | 11.9 | 11.9 | 12.2 | 12 | 12 |
| Women | 88.3 | 88.2 | 88.2 | 88.2 | 88.1 | 88.1 | 88.1 | 87.8 | 88 | 88 |
| All teachers | 100.0 | 100.0 | 100.0 | 100.0 | 100.0 | 100.0 | 100.0 | 100.0 | 100.0 | 100.0 |
| **All teachers** | **100.0** | **100.0** | **100.0** | **100.0** | **100.0** | **100.0** | **100.0** | **100.0** | | |
| Men | 16.9 | 16.6 | 16.4 | 16.2 | 15.9 | 15.8 | 15.7 | 15.7 | 16 | 16 |
| Women | 83.1 | 83.4 | 83.6 | 83.8 | 84.1 | 84.2 | 84.3 | 84.3 | 84 | 84 |
| All teachers | 100.0 | 100.0 | 100.0 | 100.0 | 100.0 | 100.0 | 100.0 | 100.0 | 100.0 | 100.0 |

Item F (Continued)

| England | 1997 | 1998 | 1999 | 2000 | 2001 | 2002 | 2003 | 2004 | 2005 | 2006 |
|---|---|---|---|---|---|---|---|---|---|---|
| **Secondary** | | | | | | | | | | |
| **Heads** | | | | | | | | | | |
| Men | 74.3 | 72.3 | 71.2 | 70.5 | 68.7 | 68.4 | 67.8 | 65.9 | 64 | 64 |
| Women | 25.7 | 27.7 | 28.8 | 29.5 | 31.3 | 31.6 | 32.2 | 34.1 | 36 | 36 |
| All teachers | 100.0 | 100.0 | 100.0 | 100.0 | 100.0 | 100.0 | 100.0 | 100.0 | 100.0 | 100.0 |
| **Deputy heads** | | | | | | | | | | |
| Men | 64.9 | 64.6 | 63.9 | 63.2 | 61.7 | 60.9 | 59.5 | 58.2 | 58 | 56 |
| Women | 35.1 | 35.4 | 36.1 | 36.8 | 38.3 | 39.1 | 40.5 | 41.8 | 42 | 44 |
| All teachers | 100.0 | 100.0 | 100.0 | 100.0 | 100.0 | 100.0 | 100.0 | 100.0 | 100.0 | 100.0 |
| **Classroom and others** | | | | | | | | | | |
| Men | 46.4 | 45.8 | 45.4 | 45.0 | 44.1 | 43.6 | 43.1 | 42.7 | 42 | 42 |
| Women | 53.6 | 54.2 | 54.6 | 55.0 | 55.9 | 56.4 | 56.9 | 57.3 | 58 | 58 |
| All teachers | 100.0 | 100.0 | 100.0 | 100.0 | 100.0 | 100.0 | 100.0 | 100.0 | 100.0 | 100.0 |
| **All teachers** | | | | | | | | | | |
| Men | 47.8 | 47.1 | 46.7 | 46.2 | 45.8 | 45.4 | 44.8 | 44.3 | 44 | 43 |
| Women | 52.2 | 52.9 | 53.3 | 53.8 | 54.2 | 54.6 | 55.2 | 55.7 | 56 | 57 |
| All teachers | 100.0 | 100.0 | 100.0 | 100.0 | 100.0 | 100.0 | 100.0 | 100.0 | 100.0 | 100.0 |

*Source*: DCSF (2007) 'Statistics of Education: School Workforce in England' (available at: http://www.dcsf.gov.uk/rsgateway/DB/VOL/v00063/index.shtml).

As shown in Item F, it has been the case that women are under-represented in the senior management of schools and the upper echelons of higher education. In primary schools, the overwhelming majority of teachers are female, but men are more likely to reach senior management positions. It is also the case that black women teachers are few and far between (see East *et al.* 1989). This lack of women in positions of power within schools is argued to be detrimental to female schoolchildren, who come to see male domination of organisations as the natural order of things (do Exercise 6.11 below to explore this in the area of science).

One aspect of the feminist reaction to the lack of positive role models for girls in schools was to look to anti-sexist educational initiatives, not just with respect to the curriculum and female experience in the classroom, but also to the hierarchies of schools themselves. A crucial part of the anti-sexist package was the development of local education authority policies that attempted to promote equal opportunities for both women and men, and for different ethnic groups. These included proper procedures for interviewing, and quotas for the management structures of schools. While anti-sexist initiatives have been criticized by New Right writers in the same way that anti-racist policies were (see Chapter 7), the effect of such initiatives, according to Parmar (1989), has been to introduce the 'politics of identity', in which different groups of women have been divided from each other according to the 'hierarchies of oppression' they face. Thus the experience of black women is seen as being different from that of white women, and homosexual women are subject to heterosexist oppression, which their 'straight' sisters are not. Similarly, Walker (1989) argues that feminism may have prised open opportunities for middle-class girls, but it has done little for girls from the working class. This is partly because assertive behaviour on the part of middle-class girls is approved of as a preparation for male-dominated working life, while similar behaviour by working-class girls is seen as 'trouble-making'. The implication of Walker's work is that class is still an important influence on the educational outcomes of girls, and not just their gender.

Ⓐ

## Exercise 6.11

In a number of science and technology faculties across Britain, more males than females can be found in positions of responsibility. This may account for females being less likely to identify with and excel in such subjects. Your task for this exercise is to investigate the hierarchies of responsibility that exist in your schools' or colleges' science and technology faculties, and the numbers of males and females that occupy each position. Draw a diagram, like a family tree, to show who holds each position. Start with the 'top' jobs, such as Head Teacher, Principal, Chief Executive.

---

The second issue concerning role models in schools is their relationship to the under-achievement of boys, especially at the Primary level. It is argued that, because male teachers are in a significant numerical minority in primary schools (see Francis and Skelton 2005) then the primary classroom is 'feminized' and does not encourage boys to do their best and therefore they underachieve (Martino and Frank 2006). The mechanism for the translation of a female numerical majority into a feminized classroom culture is through behaviour management techniques. The process that is supposed to happen is that women teachers establish more lenient discipline regimes than male teachers, and boys do not respond as well to more caring approaches to discipline but are more likely to respect a tougher approach that is associated with maleness and masculinity (Mills 2008). However, researchers such as Francis *et al.* (2008) found that boys did not necessarily perceive their male teachers as having a more robust discipline regime than their women teachers. In exploring this issue, Read (2008) looked at the ways in which teachers talk to pupils in order to manage their behaviour. She developed a distinction between a 'disciplinary discourse' (tough and robust talk, usually associated with hegemonic masculinity) and a 'liberal discourse' (more open to negotiation and associated with femininity and middle-class masculinity). She found that the utilisation of such discourses was not influenced by the gender of the teacher, as both male and female used both types of discourse in different circumstances, but with the disciplinary discourse predominant. This counters the notion that the primary classroom has in some way been feminized.

*Inside school explanation – an evaluation*

Ⓘ Ⓐ Ⓔ

## Exercise 6.12

Here are a number of partly completed statements relating to the strengths and weaknesses of the inside school explanations. Your task is to complete the statements by selecting appropriate sentences from those offered below.

Strengths:

1. These offer a counter-balance to earlier structural explanations.
2. They reveal the ways in which educational.......
3. The explanations have had a major impact on social policy,......

4. They have opened......
5. They also emphasize some......

Weaknesses:

1. They offer an over-socialized view of people.
2. They emphasize some social forces......
3. They are often based on small-scale qualitative research,......
4. Despite the claim that they are interactionist in approach,......
5. There is a tendency in some of these approaches to end up......

Matching strengths sentences:

(a) success may be socially constructed.
(b) wider social world and the way these influence what goes on in the classroom.
(c) It is reasonable to consider factors within schools as well as outside.
(d) up the 'black box' of schools.
(e) for example, on the way teachers are trained, equal opportunity initiatives in schools and so on.

Matching weaknesses sentences:

(a) 'blaming the teacher' for all that is ill in education.
(b) many of these studies offer simplistic and deterministic views of the classroom.
(c) but do not consider other important structural causes that may influence the school.
(d) which is low in reliability.
(e) Not all females are put off science in the way suggested.

---

## FEMALES – THE EDUCATIONAL ACHIEVERS

In the early 1990s came the first indications that the imbalance between male and female achievement was changing. The evidence for this emerged first from the results of the Key Stage tests taken at ages 7, 11 and 14, from GCSE examinations, and then from A Level results. These showed that the gap between female and male attainment was widening in the favour of females in arts and humanities subjects, and with the exceptions of Key Stage 2 Maths and Key Stage 3 Science the traditional advantage of males over females was narrowing. Three interpretations have been put forward for these changes:

1. Boys falling behind.
2. Social policy aiding females.
3. Changing attitudes.

## Boys falling behind

This approach suggests that it is not just that females are achieving better than before, but that there is a problem with boys and education that has not yet been fully explored by sociologists. The reasons given for this falling behind are varied, but according to Barber (1994) they are connected to males developing much less positive attitudes to education than do females. This negative attitude is manifested in a number of ways, including lower work rates among male students and signs of disaffection, such as increased truancy and behaviour problems. It is also suggested that male peer groups tend to develop less favourable attitudes towards education and this creates peer group pressure. In 1994 *Panorama* (BBC1, 24 October) drew on American research to show that parents spend less time reading and discussing books with their sons than with their daughters. It was suggested that this could be linked to a reluctance among males to read, and their poorer standards of literacy. This view has been influential in persuading some educationalists that any agenda for equal opportunities initiatives needs to address male under-achievement as much as that of females. However, feminists would argue that this explanation tends to play down the real progress being made by female students and to divert attention back to boys. Weiner *et al.* (1997) have argued that the media have created a moral panic about boys' under-achievement which has produced a powerful discourse about male academic performance, with class and ethnic dimensions, and which detracts from the celebration of the performance of girls. While girls have made progress, Weiner *et al.* argue there are still subject choice patterns, especially in post-16 education, which suggest that educational performance has not brought about more general equality between the sexes. It is also suggested that the 'discovery' of male under-achievement is exaggerated, and that some males have always struggled to be successful in education.

Mitsos and Browne (1998) have also concluded that male under-achievement may be connected to teachers having lower expectations of boys, boys being more likely to be excluded from school, a culture of masculinity that is anti-school, and a changing labour market in which there are fewer traditional male jobs. Their conclusion is that there is a 'crisis of male identity', but this does not inhibit males from still holding the top jobs in society.

Generally, the statistics based on examination performance are pointing to the fact that both girls and boys are improving, and this point is discussed in more detail later (see 'Bringing It All Together' at the end of Chapter 7).

## Social policy aiding females

*GIST (Girls into Science and Technology)*

This view suggests that a number of policy changes have been effective in encouraging female students to achieve in those areas where they have traditionally done less well. The first initiative was GIST (Girls into Science and Technology), followed by WISE (Women into Science and Engineering), which was designed to encourage female students to opt for science, technology and engineering. This included policies such as arranging visits from female scientists to act as positive role models, developing curriculum materials that reflect female interests, non-sexist careers advice, and the raising of teachers' consciousness regarding gender role stereotyping. The media were also used to promote and advertise these areas to women. However, critics of this explanation suggest that it is difficult to pin down a general increase in female standards to this particular initiative, as GIST was fairly narrow in scope and applied in only a few selected schools. Nor were these policies necessarily always followed through, because they were expensive to implement.

*Single-sex classes*

Another initiative that has been claimed to be successful is the introduction of single-sex classes. This builds on the arguments in favour of single-sex schools. Female-only classes provide positive role models – as, for example, the science teacher too is female. In science lessons, having no boys in the class removes the domination of laboratory equipment by boys, and also allows female students to answer questions and follow their interests. The positive outcomes of female-only classes are said to be an increase in female confidence and a more positive attitude towards science. Critics of this approach argue that female-only classes do not guarantee that teachers' attitudes are changed or that sexist materials are not used. As with GIST, this approach has only been adopted by a few schools as it is relatively expensive to implement.

*GCSE*

The introduction of GCSE, as opposed to O Level and CSE, is argued to have favoured females. The principles behind GCSE are that students should be able to show what they 'know, understand and can do'. In order to achieve this, coursework has been introduced as a prominent feature of GCSE courses. This component is said to favour the consistent and conscientious work that is characteristic of female students. Similarly, the increased emphasis on oral assessment is believed to favour female skills. Also, the widespread introduction of joint science GCSEs has led to increased performance among females, as their strong biology orientation has pulled up their general grade in science. However, the effect of these innovations is likely to be limited. For example, coursework marks are limited in GCSE, so there are clear constraints on the amount of benefit female students can be said to gain. Nor is it clear that female students possess the attributes given to them, such as working consistently harder than males. There is, for example, a clear link between class and females' attitudes towards school work (see Chapter 4).

ⓘⓐⓔ

## Link Exercise 6.1

Using material from this chapter and Chapter 3, assess the extent to which the introduction of the national curriculum in 1988 may have helped to improve females' academic performances in mathematics, science and technology.

### Changing attitudes

This view suggests that female attitudes towards education and work have changed significantly. This is partly because more young women have rallied to the feminist call for gender equality (Arnot 2002), and partly because of an increase in the employment opportunities available to them. Thus it is claimed that women are now more independent-minded and ambitious, and with their higher expectations they are less likely to want to marry and start a family at a young age – education, work and career have become a new focus of gender identity (Sharpe 1994). Wilkinson (1994) also shows that employment has taken over from starting a family as the main aim of young women, and that this shift in social attitudes is having a strong bearing on educational aspirations and performance.

However, it is important not to overestimate the degree of change in attitudes. Sharpe (1994) indicates that, in her 1990s study, many of the females – like those in the 1970s research – anticipated life as a 'dual worker', combining paid employment with family and domestic responsibilities. Sharpe also acknowledges that the desire to gain educational qualifications may partly reflect females' recognition of the fragility of the labour market in a period of recession.

We should also point out that the increased employment opportunities are less impressive than at first sight. It may be that the 'glass ceiling' has been raised slightly, so that women are found in significant numbers in middle-management positions, but females are still under-represented in the top echelons of management and over-represented in the dead-end, part-time work they have traditionally dominated. This lack of gender equality is recognized by Sharpe (1994), and she sees it as potentially denting the expectations and aspirations of females in the 1990s.

)(A)

## Exercise 6.13

The explanations we have put forward for the recent advances in female academic attainment are some of the first to have been offered. The improvement in female levels of achievement could also be explained by the decline in actively discriminatory practices in education, and the teaching profession becoming more aware of the importance of implementing equal opportunities policies in classrooms and schools. Schools and colleges have now developed and are implementing their own equal opportunities policies. Furthermore, there have been a number of wider social policies introduced by the government, which have produced arguably more equality in education – such as the national curriculum, for example. The effects of earlier legislation such as the Sex Discrimination Act (1975) and the Equal Pay Act (1975) may also have had a wider impact in society as well as in schools to bring about more equalitarian attitudes. There is no doubt that the explanations presented here will be supported and/or rejected to varying degrees, and new ones will come along. It is important that you keep yourself up to date with the issues as they appear in the press and books. Make sure you keep your eyes open and make notes on any relevant material that comes your way.

---

## Exam Focus

This activity is aimed at helping you to order your arguments logically, so that the evaluation aspect of your response shows through. To do this activity properly, you will need to refer to Items reproduced elsewhere in this book. Review the main pieces of research and evidence in this chapter and in Chapter 5 to help you organize your arguments in a logical order.

### Question

Using information from the Items in this chapter and in Chapter 5, evaluate sociological contributions to an understanding of the hidden curriculum, as it affects female pupils. (20 marks)

What follows is a real examination answer by an 18-year-old student. However, the paragraphs have been jumbled up and your task is to arrange them in a logical order. Once you have done that, highlight the sentences or passages you think are analytical and evaluative.

Do not try to get a 'right' answer, but seek to find a logical progression. It could be useful to begin by deciding which is the introduction and which the conclusion. By the way, this answer would have attracted full marks.

## Student's answer

## CANDIDATE A

*Paragraph 1*: Clarricoates, however, adds this important dimension, as she found that teachers maintained that males were intellectually more elite, despite girls getting consistently higher marks.

*Paragraph 2*: Stansworth takes a more holistic view of schools and sees that they are male dominated, and so until they change, female achievement will not improve. Her study is particularly useful as it shows how the whole structure and ethos of a school affects the hidden curriculum, which in turn affects females.

*Paragraph 3*: Shaw proposes single-sex education, and Arnot single-sex classes in mixed schools. Their suggestions could be seen as a response to a worsening situation, though it must be remembered that their contributions (as far as they are explored here) are not empirically based and on their own provide insufficient evidence.

*Paragraph 4*: Since the early biological arguments of Tiger and Fox, and Murdoch, sociologists have looked for social reasons why females tend to under-achieve. The hidden curriculum is something that interactionists have been particularly interested in, as they see it as a central part of schooling that directly affects female pupils.

*Paragraph 5*: Gender inequalities and experiences shaped by a pupil's sex are issues that are not isolated to schools. Douglas and Sharp show that parental expectations affect how females regard their education. Marxists argue that teachers are unwitting agents of capitalists, and that the ruling class shapes schools so that females will either be wholly domesticated or become part of the reserve pool of labour for the feminized industries. It is safe to say, though, that the hidden curriculum practised in schools includes values that are not necessarily exclusive to schools, so Marxist and functionalist theory is relevant here.

*Paragraph 6*: As we see in Item C, Spender identifies boys receiving two-thirds of teacher time. This implies that teachers see it as 'natural' for boys to do well and therefore pay special attention to ensuring they achieve. Spender's research is important as it identifies one important way that attitudes of teachers affect females. However, it could be argued from this observation alone that in fact girls are more self-sufficient and require less attention, whereas boys are 'needy' and require more.

*Paragraph 7*: We can see then that studies that focus on the school contribute quite well to our understanding of the hidden curriculum, though they could be accused of teacher bashing and are not placed within the context of the whole society. Nevertheless, they seek to uncover the experience of pupils themselves from their point of view.

*Paragraph 8*: However, studies that deal directly with the hidden curriculum could be successfully applied to schools and hence are valuable contributions.

*Paragraph 9*: Kelly shows how the formal curriculum, hand in hand with the hidden curriculum, can affect female pupils. She is concerned about the low percentage of girls in science and sees this as a result of attitudes that treat it as a boys' subject. Kelly is most in favour of GIST.

*Paragraph 10*: In studying the hidden curriculum (which is defined as the informal value systems, attitudes and norms within schools), interactionists and interpretivists have used qualitative methods, actually going into schools and doing empirical research to explain female underachievement. Thus their research is particularly valid as they give us an insight into the day-to-day running of schools and, through the practice of *Verstehen* and ethnographic techniques, tell us what the experiences of females actually are in relation to the hidden curriculum.

*Paragraph 11*: In Item E, we see that gender can be an important criterion for teachers' labelling of students, which may lead to a self-fulfilling prophecy. Howard Becker also shows that the 'ideal pupil' notion that teachers have is that of a white, middle-class male, not a female. If it is true (as in Item D) that teachers' qualities are influential, then as females become aware that teachers have these sorts of attitudes they may feel discouraged.

## Question

What explanations might sociologists offer for the different levels of achievement between the sexes in science subjects. Which explanation do you find the most convincing, and why? (20 marks)

   The question gives you a specific focus for any material you may have on gender and educational achievement. You must take care to apply any material you use to the issue of science subjects. Also, the question requires more than one explanation, so you should provide a range of explanations – as many as you can. The evaluation part of the question asks you to set out your reasons for thinking that one is more convincing than another. However, you do not have to come out in favour of one explanation, as you may find a combination more convincing. Nevertheless, you do have to say why you have come to this conclusion if you are to gain the evaluation marks.

## Important concepts

equality of opportunity • socialization • patriarchy • subject • choice • cultural • reproduction • deindustrialization • reserve • army of labour • teachers' expectations • feminist perspectives

## Critical thinking

- Consider the reasons for the changes in achievement and attainment rates for females in education since the 1970s. Is discrimination less apparent now, in the twenty-first century?
- What is the importance of the interplay between socio-economic background and gender in education? Is there a relative importance to the factors inside (teachers' roles) and outside school (parents' influence) which influence gender and performance?
- Are changes in the labour market that enable women to compete with men the main impetus for the overall changes in women's position in society?

*Chapter 7*

# Explaining Ethnic Differences in Educational Achievement

By the end of this chapter you should:

- be able to describe ethnic differences in educational achievement
- understand some of the problems associated with official statistics on educational achievement
- be able to assess different explanations of ethnic differences in educational achievement
- appreciate that the educational achievements of ethnic minority students are mediated by social class and gender, and understand the interplay between these three social factors
- have reflected critically on government policies concerned with ethnic minority education
- have practised a structured exam question yourself

## INTRODUCTION

Like interest in gender, interest in ethnic differences in educational performance began to take off in the 1980s, under the impact of renewed sociological interest in issues of identity. Prior to the 1960s, while, there was some sociological interest in ethnic issues, it was largely confined to those who had a special interest in the area. However, during the 1960s and 1970s, increasing numbers of sociologists began to be critical of the ethnocentric views of the white-dominated sociological establishment (see West 1993), in which the educational experiences of all children were analysed from a mainly white viewpoint. African-American sociologist, Joyce Ladner (1973), argued that this neglect of ethnic issues was not accidental but the product of the wider ideology of American society, which had consistently marginalized black experiences except when they were seen to 'deviate' from mainstream society.

By the early 1990s, sociologists were increasingly interested in postmodernist issues, which emphasized the ethnic dimension as an important component of the 'new' politics of identity and difference, in which the old certainties of social class had disintegrated in the face of competing loyalties of gender, ethnicity, disability and sexual identity. For example, Carol Nicholson (1989) follows up Foucault's emphasis on the 'Other' in education. Foucault was concerned with power and the way that there is always an 'Other' who is pushed aside and marginalized by dominant forces in society. Nicholson argues that we should be listening to the stories of marginalized groups in schools, such as 'people of colour', and their experiences of a curriculum and education that has disempowered such groups.

Since various governments have been collecting statistical data on school performance, a clear hierarchy of achievement has emerged and can easily be accessed using government websites. The descending order of attainment from Key Stages 2, 3 and 4 using the government's classification system for ethnicity is shown in Table 7.1 (see Bringing It All Together on page 202 for some criticisms of these measures of attainment/performance).

**Table 7.1** Descending order of attainment, by ethnicity, at Key Stages 2, 3 and 4, 2006

| Key Stages 2 and 3 | Key Stage 4 |
| --- | --- |
| Indian | Indian |
| White | White |
| Bangladeshi | Bangladeshi |
| Black Caribbean | Pakistani |
| Black African | Black |
| Pakistan | |

Source: Adapted from data on the DCSF website (see http://www.dcsf.gov.uk/).

### Exercise 7.1

Write down as many criticisms as you can think of about these statistics. (Hint: Can a pupil who is good at sport be included in these measures?)

In covering this area we shall follow a similar format to that of the previous two chapters. We shall begin by establishing the extent of ethnic differences in educational achievement, and then consider three different approaches that have attempted to explain the observed inequalities: (i) a genetic approach, which looks at differences in intellectual capacity between ethnic groups; (ii) outside school explanations (non-genetic), which reflect socio-cultural, socio-economic and societal factors outside the school environment; and (iii) inside school explanations, which address individual and institutional racism operating within schools and colleges. We shall also give consideration to various social policy initiatives that have emerged in the pursuit of improving the educational experience and attainment of ethnic minority pupils. At the end there is a section that brings together the relationships between social class, gender and ethnicity in explaining educational achievement. The section shows how treating groups homogeneously is likely to draw misleading conclusions and miss some of the underlying factors that have persisted in determining education performance since the Second World War.

## EVIDENCE OF ETHNIC DIFFERENCES IN EDUCATIONAL ACHIEVEMENT

A range of statistical evidence exists to support the idea that educational attainment varies by ethnic group. For example, in the USA, Ladson-Billings (2006) showed that in 2005 African-American and Latino students scored persistently lower than white pupils in standardized tests of reading and mathematics. The statistics in Items A and B below provide information on inequalities in performance from secondary schools through to higher education in the United Kingdom, and Exercise 7.2 will help you to examine these.

## Exercise 7.2

### Item A

Key Stage 4 (age 16) GCSE results by ethnic group 2006 (percentages)

| | 5+ A*–C including English and Maths | 5+ A*–C or equivalent | 5+ A*–G or equivalent |
|---|---|---|---|
| White British | 47.6 | 59.9 | 90.7 |
| Indian | 60.3 | 72.4 | 96.7 |
| Pakistani | 39.5 | 53.9 | 94.0 |
| Bangladeshi | 40.6 | 57.7 | 89.8 |
| Black Caribbean | 30.5 | 47.1 | 90.5 |
| Black African | 41.6 | 54.8 | 92.0 |

Source: Adapted from Strand (2008), p. 7.

### Item B

In 2008, according to the Institute for Employment Studies, some 15 per cent of new undergraduate students are from minority ethnic backgrounds. This percentage is higher than the proportion of ethnic minority people in the wider population. In subject areas such as Medicine and Mathematics, the percentage can be as high as 30 per cent. Ethnic minority students seem to be attracted to the more vocational subjects, which can lead to good employment prospects, rather than the humanities, with the exception of the key subject of education – that is, training to teach

1. Study Item A. Which ethnic group seems to perform least well in the education system?
2. Using Item A, calculate the percentage difference between the number of Black Caribbean and the number of Asians achieving five grade A*–C GCSEs.
3. Give some reasons for the differences in performance at GCSE indicated in Item A.
4. What is the problem with using the term 'ethnic minority'?
5. Give some reasons why the proportion of ethnic minority students at university is higher than in the wider population.

The emergence of a significant number of mixed heritage children, and in particular, white/black Caribbean has complicated an already complex picture (see Haynes *et al.* 2006) as regards the achievement of ethnic minorities. Sociologists are careful to avoid over-generalisation about ethnic achievement because it is difficult to encompass very different groups within general statements. For example, Tikly *et al.* (2004) show that, while white/black Caribbean children are under-achieving, the same is not true for white/Asian pupils, who achieve more than most other groups. It could be that the latter group are from higher social classes than the former, and what we are seeing is a class effect rather than an ethnic one (see Chapter 5).

When sociologists are interpreting statistics such as the ones you worked with in Exercise 7.2, it is important that they look at them critically and do not just take them for granted. An important distinction to keep in mind is the difference between 'equality of opportunity' and 'equality of outcome'. Most measures of educational under-achievement are concerned with 'outcomes', such as university entrance, examination performance and so on, and it is possible that ethnic minorities may have equality of opportunity, but still (for a variety of reasons that we shall explore) have inequality of outcome. One of the main criticisms of statistics about ethnic minority 'under-achievement' is that they are undifferentiated. That is, ethnic minorities are all lumped together in a few categories, where important differences could be hidden. A good example of this 'collapsing' of categories is in Item A of Exercise 7.2.

Even when there is a more comprehensive categorisation, some difficulties still remain. For example, the amount of evidence about the educational achievement of Jewish and Cypriot children is relatively limited, and it is therefore difficult to make comparisons (see Taylor, 1988). There is also the problem of how to break down large ethnic categories into 'real' divisions. For example, is it valid to look at the achievement of African-Caribbean children whose families originated from different islands in the West Indies? When does any effect associated with migration cease to be important – five years, ten years, one generation, two generations, never?

An important distinction between groups of ethnic minorities has been introduced by Gibson and Ogbu (1991). They argue that there is a real difference in the educational experiences between what they call 'voluntary' minorities and 'involuntary' minorities. For the voluntary minorities who have recently migrated into a country, education offers a way forward into a situation that is usually better than the one from which they have come. They are therefore likely to adapt to the cultural habits required for successful schooling, despite the discrimination they will also experience. Involuntary minorities are those with a caste-like position in society who already have a history of exploitation and discrimination in the 'host' country. This marginalisation of the involuntary group provokes a more hostile rejection of the education process, which, combined with their structural position (such as lack of employment opportunities, even if they do gain qualifications), leads to educational under-achievement.

However, a large number of studies during the 1980s argued that the statistics showed that, while certain categories of South Asian children were performing at the same level as their peers, African-Caribbean children were underperforming significantly (see, for example, Verma and Pumfrey 1988). Figueroa (1991) warns against taking these findings as the whole picture and is critical, for example, of the Swann Report (DES 1985), arguing that its data under-represented black, middle-class children, who were likely to achieve higher qualifications than their black, working-class counterparts. Other sociologists have suggested that social class, rather than ethnicity on its own, is an important factor in the levels of educational achievement attained by ethnic minority children (see Maughan and Dunn 1988). Figueroa (1991) goes on to argue that much of the research on ethnic minority children is small-scale and has been carried out in inner-city areas, where average performance is lower than the national average regardless of ethnicity. He therefore challenges the representativeness of such studies. Hence, it is prudent to be careful about these statistical findings. For example Jones (1993) argues that the educational gap between whites and ethnic minorities, in particular those of African-Caribbean origin, is narrowing among the younger age groups.

Differential outcomes between ethnic groups occur not just in education, but also in government training schemes. The Commission for Racial Equality (CRE 1994) has shown that, while there is little difference between the success rates of white and ethnic minority trainees in terms of gaining a qualification on a government training scheme, there are large differences in the success of the two groups in getting a job at the end of the scheme. In a government survey of the Youth Training Scheme, only one in four young blacks had found jobs after leaving the scheme, compared with one in three of disabled trainees and one in two of whites (see Bevins and Nelson 1995). Moreover, there has been a trend for ethnic minority trainees to be placed on schemes that are less likely to lead to full-time employment. The government therefore introduced 'Modern Apprenticeships' in September 1995, where equal opportunity guidelines are built into the selection procedures. See Chapter 2 for more material related to social policy and change.

①

### Exercise 7.3

Try to update the statistics we have presented on ethnic inequalities in educational performance. You could start this search by referring to the most recent editions of *Sociology Update* and *Social Trends.* Refer to page 16 in Chapter 2 for a list of useful websites. If your search is successful, repeat questions 1 and 4 in Exercise 7.2.

## EXPLANATIONS OF ETHNIC DIFFERENCES IN EDUCATIONAL ACHIEVEMENT

Having familiarized ourselves with the extent of ethnic differences in educational attainment, we now draw on three types of explanation to account for them:

1. Genetic explanations.
2. Outside school explanations.
3. Inside school explanations.

### Genetic explanations

As in the case of social class and gender, certain psychologists have explained ethnic differences in educational performance in terms of biological differences in intelligence. In the USA, Jensen (1969) claims to have shown that black people consistently attain lower scores in IQ tests than do white people. He concludes from this that black people have lower intelligence levels than their white compatriots, and this is the reason why they under-achieve in the education system. Despite being greeted with widespread criticism, genetic explanations of differential educational achievement have controversially resurfaced in the USA. In their book *The Bell Curve – Intelligence and Class Structure in American Life,* Herrnstein and Murray (1994) conclude that black people are genetically less intelligent than white people, who in turn are less intelligent than people who originated in Asia. Herrnstein and Murray not only contend that this accounts for black people's lower levels of achievement, but also their higher levels of criminality. As with the earlier work of Jensen, Herrnstein and Murray have been subjected to fierce criticism. Remind yourself of some of the most important criticisms of genetic-based explanations of differential educational attainment by referring back to Chapter 5.

The controversy aroused by Herrnstein and Murray's book echoes a continuing debate in the social sciences between those who have argued for a large measure of inherited intelligence and those who claim that environmental factors are more important in determining levels of intelligence. What is different about Herrnstein and Murray's arguments is that they do not fix the proportion of intelligence that is inherited as high as did previous biological determinists, but they do argue that attempts to improve the situation of black people in the USA through social policy are likely to fail, for the simple reason that they will never overcome the genetic differences that separate rich from poor and black from white. It is this that critics of Herrnstein and Murray have attacked, arguing that they are making a political rather than a scientific point in reassuring the rich (and white) that their wealth is deserved because they are more intelligent than the poor (and black). So, while Herrnstein and Murray are very careful not to draw any direct racist conclusions from their data, as earlier writers have done, and indeed take great pains to argue that it is individuals and not groups that matter, their opponents have accused them of performing an ideological function – that is, justifying great inequality as in some way being the natural order of things.

## Outside school explanations

Five social (as opposed to genetic) accounts of ethnic differences in educational performance have developed from the outside school approach:

1. Family life.
2. Language.
3. Social class.
4. Racism in society and minority youth responses: theories of resistance.
5. Religion.

### Family life

This home background explanation looks inwards at the material conditions, family structures and attitudes of different ethnic groups. Early explanations for ethnic minority under-achievement focused on such issues as the low incomes and inadequate housing of ethnic minority families, which, like social class explanations, were seen as detrimental to educational achievement. The 2001 Census confirms that employment rates are lower for ethnic minorities, with Pakistani and Bangladeshi groups being four times more likely to be poor than a white family. Indian families had incomes similar to the comparable white family. A further variation of this theme, and one that has a more contemporary impact, is the idea that the one-parent family structure that characterizes a significant minority of African-Caribbean households creates difficulties for them when it comes to supporting their children's educational needs. According to *Social Trends* in 2004, 22 per cent of white families are headed by single parents and 11 per cent of all Asian British families are single-parent households, compared with 48 per cent for Black Caribbean families. New Right commentators have focused on the one-parent family structure as a major cause of social problems, and have put forward policies that seek to discourage the formation of such families. They are seen as being in some way pathological. However, high-income-earning single-parent families have few educational problems, which suggests that under-achievement is more to do with material deprivation and poverty than single parenthood. Furthermore, it has been suggested by some sociologists that African-Caribbean family networks place a lower value on educational success and are less encouraging of their children's education than other ethnic groups – for example, those of Indian origin. On the other hand, the larger family size of some South Asian families is also seen in a pathological way – that large families have a negative effect on the educational progress of the children in such situations (see Dawson 1988). However there is some evidence from the USA that the aspirations of African-Americans are very similar to those of white Americans (see Banks 1988), so that while there may be differences in attitudes towards education between ethnic groups, it is not the case that black families universally instil negative attitudes towards education in their children. Further evidence that black families do indeed value education is the existence of 'Saturday' or 'Supplementary' schools, where children attend classes out of normal school time, either to learn about their own heritage and religion or extend the traditional learning taking place during the week in school. Indeed, Mac an Ghaill (1991) has argued that the existence of such schools indicates a dissatisfaction among minority parents with the official education of their children.

The effect of the focus on family structure and attitudes to education has been to develop a 'deficit' approach to ethnic minority children, in which their culture and life-style is seen as in some way deficient. Theorists of the New Right, such as Flew (1986), have argued that it is a mistake to assume that inequality of outcome is a consequence of inequality of opportunity. Rather, Flew draws on the work of the American economist Sowell (1981) to argue that group differences are not the result of discrimination, but that differences in educational outcome between ethnic groups is a result of differences in culture. However, this approach has been criticized for providing a 'victim-blaming' explanation (see Massey 1991), in which there is seen to be little wrong with the education system itself, but that the fault of under-achievement lies in the background of the 'victims' of under-achievement. Flew's ideas are therefore based on the notion that cultures can be judged as superior or inferior according to their outcomes, in terms of social behaviour, literature, art and so on. This has led other New Right theorists such as Scruton (1986) to argue that the solution for under-achievement is for ethnic minorities to embrace British culture in the education system, while using voluntary associations to preserve their own.

ⓘ

## Exercise 7.4

This exercise is designed to encourage you to appreciate the way in which the cultural background of certain Asian families is conducive to educational success. As you complete the exercise, bear in mind that some sociologists contend that the positive cultural factors you will identify are lacking in African-Caribbean families. Your task is to study Item C, which offers a short 'newspaper-type' feature about African-Asian families (families of Asian origin who have migrated from Kenya, Tanzania and other African countries) and school performance. When you have read the item, identify four factors that could explain the educational success of African-Asian students.

### Item C

**Why Chinese students do well at school**

While most of his English and Black school friends are out enjoying themselves, Chen Fu is at home doing homework. He does not mind the discipline that this involves as it is part of the way he has been brought up by his parents.

In the years since they came to the United Kingdom from Tanzania, the Chen family have built up a chain of Chinese food supply shops and now live over their main shop in Leicester. Fu's father also works as an adviser to other Chinese retail outlets, while his mother runs one of the shops herself.

Chinese parents are very ambitious for their children and are committed to educational success. 'You have to do well at school if you are a Chinese boy,' says Fu, 'otherwise you are thought of as a failure by the wider Chinese community.'

This attitude is reflected in research that shows that Chinese children outperform children from other backgrounds in education. The achievement of Chinese students can be compared to the two groups that most often fail to develop their potential: local white children and children from African-Caribbean backgrounds.

This suggests how important it is to have parents who value education and put pressure on their children to succeed.

## Language

This is again a home background explanation, but focuses on the educational problems that arise through language. It has been argued that certain Asian students, such as Bangladeshis, experience communication problems because, for many, English is their second language. Thus they may find it hard to understand and be understood by their teachers. Moreover, they may experience difficulties reading textbooks and examination papers. In the case of African-Caribbean students, it is suggested that they encounter educational problems because the 'creole' dialect or 'patois' they speak does not fit the standard English taught in schools. Typical difficulties they experience include misunderstanding the meaning of everyday expressions, and being understood by teachers. However Taylor (1981) points out that there is a crucial difference between those who are perceived as having English as a second language (for example, Gujerati speakers) and those who are perceived as speaking black British English. Whereas speakers of English as a second language may attract funding to help them with their 'problem', those who employ patois are likely to be seen as 'linguistically deficient' and are assumed to have no other language than low-status black British English. There is therefore some evidence to suggest that teachers label African-Caribbean students as being less able because of the 'broken' English they speak. This has been shown to demoralize African-Caribbean students, with the result that they begin to resist schooling. For example, Mac an Ghaill (1988) found that a group of anti-school male African-Caribbeans deliberately used patois as an expression of rebellion against teachers and school. See the summary of Labov's work in Chapter 5 (page 103), which outlines how the interpretation of language by the 'powerful' group can lead to particular cultural understandings or misunderstandings by not seeing the language in context and the purposes it serves. Reay (2007) also looked at how children perceive their accents and use of language to be less worthy than other forms of speech. She goes on to say that forms of assessment, though purported to be about raising standards, are more about dominance and control, which creates 'academic stars' of middle-class pupils and failures in other groups, such as working-class and minority groups. There is also a correlation between the poorest children and the worst-performing schools. Millar (2005) looked at how factors such as ethnicity and class play an important part in deciding to which school a pupil goes. Parental choice is limited largely to parents from particular middle-class backgrounds.

The Swann Report (DES 1985) argued that the crucial factor in language teaching was that all students should have a good command of English. The report did not like the idea of separate provision of English as a second language, arguing that this would be divisive. The committee also suggested that the maintenance of community languages should be the responsibility of the minority communities themselves. They argued against community languages as the medium of instruction, but in favour of the teaching of community languages as part of the languages curriculum of a school. Figueroa (1991) argues that this is to marginalize the community languages and undermine the idea that all cultures are of equal value, as well as placing some bilingual students at a disadvantage. Research evidence from a variety of countries suggests that mother-tongue teaching in the early years of schooling assists children in learning the dominant language of the country (see Beltz 1985).

The concept of 'cultural capital' has been used by sociologists to explain the function of language in structuring the under-achievement of ethnic minority pupils. The 'language on display' in a classroom is an important part of the judgements that teachers make about the educational performance of their students. As Thompson (1984) argues, teachers assume that they speak the same language as their pupils, but teachers in fact operate with a dominant form of language, to which not all students, and in particular working-class and ethnic minority children, have equal access. This dominant form of language constitutes part of a cultural capital that operates to disadvantage certain groups within schools. However Bourdieu (see Chapter 4), who developed the notion of cultural capital, has been criticized by other sociologists, such as Mehan (1992), for being over-deterministic about the outcomes of schooling. Bourdieu is accused of denying the importance of resistance to their disadvantage by those who are disadvantaged. The operation of cultural capital is seen by these critics not to be an automatic process, in which ethnic minority children are doomed to under-achievement by their lack of schooling-friendly language.

### Social class

One line of argument concerning outside school explanations is that the differential educational performance of ethnic groups reflects the social class backgrounds of those groups as well as their ethnicity. It is claimed that minorities such as Indians and African Asians do well educationally because they have the economic advantages of being middle-class, while groups such as Bangladeshis, Pakistanis and African-Caribbean boys under-perform in the education system because they experience the material disadvantages of being working-class. However, the debate concerning the effects of social class versus ethnicity is not a simple one. Some studies have tried to compare the effects of these two variables directly (see Vasquez 1992). However Jeffcoate (1984) argues that it is reasonable to suppose that, as the majority of African-Caribbean children come from manual backgrounds, they are subject to the same disadvantages as white working-class children. Others have compared class with gender (Reay 2007; Connolly 2006). However, Figueroa (1991) warns against any simplistic equation of class and ethnicity. He points out that the factors of class and ethnicity (as well as gender and culture) are interwoven in complex ways, and that it is too simple to assume that African-Caribbean and other ethnic minorities form an underclass whose experiences are all similar. Clearly, there are middle-class African-Caribbeans who may experience racism without sharing the material disadvantages associated with the working class. Furthermore, the interplay between factors of class, culture, ethnicity and gender will vary according to circumstances; one factor may be dominant when related to a particular issue – parental choice, say – and another may hold sway on a different issue, such as subject choice. In the case of mixed heritage students, Haynes *et al.* (2006) argue that it is important to relate socio-economic disadvantage (as measured by the Free School Meals criterion) to the gendered perceptions of teachers about their identity (see also Gillborn and Mirza 2000)

(A)
## Link Exercise 7.1

If we accept that social class cuts across ethnicity to account for ethnic differences in attainment, we must acknowledge the influence of material factors in determining educational performance. It is certainly true that Bangladeshis and African-Caribbeans are among the poorest ethnic groups in Britain. Drawing on the work you did on social class in Chapter 4, identify and explain three ways in which the depressed educational achievements of Bangladeshi and African-Caribbean students can be explained by material deprivation.

### *Racism in society and minority youth responses: theories of resistance*

This is a societal explanation that is advanced by O'Donnell (1992), among others. O'Donnell points out that all ethnic minorities face prejudice and discrimination in Britain. However, he argues that it is the response to this discrimination by different ethnic groups that helps us to understand differential educational performance. He observes that African-Caribbean males often react with anger and oppose white institutions, including education. In contrast, Indians, despite being resentful of racism and show anger, do not always reject the powerful white institutions. It follows, then, that African-Caribbeans (particularly males) are more likely to under-perform because they show strong resistance to schooling, while Indians perform well because they use the education system to their advantage – they keep their heads down. Warren (2005) argues against a simple rejectionist view of black Caribbean boys' responses to the racism they experience at school. Rather than a rejection of schools, their bad behaviour can be seen as a reaction to a lack of respect by certain teachers, while they retain an overall attachment to school as a way of 'getting on'.

More radical theorists have drawn on the work of Willis (1977) (see also Chapter 4) to develop resistance theory. Willis argues that subordinate groups in schools do not just passively accept their disadvantage, but develop strategies for resisting the practices that lead to their under-achievement. Giroux (1983) argues that these strategies may be adaptive as well as resisting, but that strategies of resistance, such as those adopted by ethnic minorities, have the potential to liberate the oppressed from their exploitation. It is by treating individuals as being able to 'mediate' (negotiate or alter) their 'lived existence' that ethnic educational disadvantage may be overcome. However, critics of Giroux, such as Senese (1991), argue that resistance, far from liberating ethnic minorities, may have the effect of making their situation worse. Rather than adapting to the linguistic and other demands of schooling, which may lead to success, Senese argues that resistance can lead to a further marginalisation of resisting groups, that they develop an anti-intellectual attitude and have little interest in the real world around them. Mac an Ghaill (1991) and Mirza and Reay (2000) point to the general dissatisfaction of black Caribbean communities with white institutions which fail their children, and the development of Saturday or supplementary schools to cater for the educational needs of children from these communities, as noted above.

## Religion

In 2004, 33 per cent of Muslims of working age had no qualifications – the highest proportion for any religious group (see Exercise 7.5 below). They were also least likely to have degrees or equivalent qualifications. Across all religions, women are generally more likely than men to have no qualifications.

## Exercise 7.5

People of working age with no qualifications, by religion, 2004, Great Britain

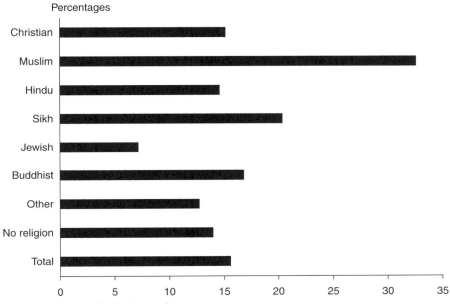

*Source*: www.nationalstatistics.gov.uk.

Refer to the figure above and answer these questions.

1. After the Muslims, which religious group had the lowest level of educational qualifications?
2. Which religious group had the highest level of qualifications?
3. How could the interplay between class and ethnicity explain the differences in educational attainment of religious groups? (Hint: Consider the unemployment patterns of some minority groups.)

*Outside school explanations – an evaluation*

### Strengths:

1. They have exposed the weaknesses of earlier genetic-based explanations because they highlight the need to look at the social rather than the biological causes of ethnic differences in educational attainment.

2. The outside school explanations have served to bring about social policy initiatives to improve the educational experiences of ethnic minority children – for example, provisions for teaching English as a second language.
3. A range of empirical evidence exists to support, to a greater or lesser extent, each of the outside school explanations. For example, the Swann Report (DES 1985) gives great weight to socio-economic factors, as stressed by the social class explanation.

---

Ⓔ Ⓘ | **Exercise 7.6**

**Weaknesses:**

For this exercise you are asked to provide one weakness of each of the explanations within the outside school approach. Start by offering your own criticisms, then confirm or supplement these by referring to a suitable text.

---

### Inside school explanations

As we have seen in previous chapters, inside school explanations focus on the concept of the hidden curriculum. Many sociologists believe that the hidden curriculum operating in schools is a racist one and therefore discriminates against ethnic minority students. Some debate exists about whether this racism is intentional or unintentional. Either way, the evidence suggests that the racist hidden curriculum serves to create a resistance to schooling on the part of certain ethnic groups, and leads to their eventual under-achievement.

---

Ⓘ Ⓐ | **Exercise 7.7**

Exercise 7.7 again requires you to do some independent work. It should prove to be relatively easy as you will come across ideas that have been well covered in earlier chapters. Start the task by reading school-based explanations of ethnic differences in educational attainment. You should then use the information you have gleaned to fill in the chart below, which has been partially completed for you. When completing the chart, you need to explain how each aspect of the hidden curriculum depresses educational performance and cite empirical studies to support the points you make. You may also find some useful information in this chapter.

The inside school approach to ethnic differences in educational attainment

| Aspect of the hidden curriculum | The process by which educational 'failure' occurs | Empirical studies |
|---|---|---|
| Racist books Racist students | Ethnic minority students experience racial harassment in schools; for example, verbal and physical abuse. This may lower self-esteem and confidence. Some students play truant for fear of abuse and attack. | |
| Teachers' expectations and attitudes | | Mac an Ghaill (1988) Gillborn (1990) Mirza (1992) Crozier (2005) |
| Streaming | | |
| An ethnocentric curriculum | School curricula are ethnocentric. They fail to tap into the cultural routes and experiences of ethnic minorities. For example, literature courses evolve around English authors such as Shakespeare, and history courses focus on European history. The ethnocentric nature of the curriculum ensures that black students feel *alienated* from schools. For some ethnic groups, a 'British' education may at best be irrelevant and at worst offensive. Motivation and commitment to schooling become difficult for some ethnic minority students. | |
| Lack of positive role models | | |

## The national curriculum and ethnicity

It has been argued that the national curriculum disadvantages pupils from minority backgrounds in that it reflects 'white, Anglo-Saxon culture' with a specific European focus, and distorts the history of imperialism and colonialism. Furthermore, the 1988 Education Reform Act stated that religious education should reflect Christian traditions. History has traditionally been taught from a perspective of the colonizers, and the experiences of the colonized largely neglected. However, more recent revisions to history specifications could be seen to redress this somewhat by teaching about slavery and the struggle for independence in India and Africa. Modern foreign languages have been mainly European languages, with the more numerous Asian languages in Britain being largely side-lined. Japanese, Chinese, Punjabi, Hindi and Gujerati are available as GCSE and A Level specifications, but they are often provided in schools as 'supplementary' subjects and taught after normal school hours or on Saturdays. Literature has also been dominated by English writers such as Shakespeare, Dickens, Jane Austen, the Brontës, Thomas Hardy and so on, but once again specifications have changed more recently and included writers from wider cultural backgrounds, such as Toni Morrison's novel *Beloved*, which is written from the perspective of an American slave.

### A selection of studies on inside school explanations

In the tradition identified by Cole (1992), it was history and geography textbooks that were mainly responsible for putting forward imperialist and racist views of non-white peoples. Wright (1986) suggests that two popular geography textbooks of the 1980s continued to put forward unacceptable views of black people. Descriptions of black people in these textbooks are often negative, involving words such as 'coarse' and 'drooping', while descriptions of white people are couched in positive language, using words such as 'fine' and 'fair'.

While there is evidence that some overt racial prejudice still exists among teachers (see Gillborn 1990), Klein (1993) argues that many teachers hide behind a 'colour-blind' approach, in which they claim not to see the colour of the child, but which has the effect of denying an important part of the child's ethnic identity.

Jeffcoate (1984) argues that the evidence for teacher stereotyping of ethnic minorities is 'flimsy, to put it mildly'. He argues that there are so many problems with the research into teacher expectations, both ethical and practical, as to negate any findings in these studies. He also argues, that, while there is evidence of racist sentiments in staffroom discussion, there is also evidence (Hammersly 1981) that these attitudes do not spill over into teacher behaviour in the classroom. This is exemplified by the existence of successful black students, who overcome any adverse effects of teacher stereotyping and inside school factors. Byfield (2008) found that successful black students not only had supportive parents who wanted them to succeed, but that they were also able to mobilize supportive teachers (both black and white) to achieve their educational goals. The support of religious communities was also seen as being important in counteracting any negative impact of schools.

Attempts to reduce the ethnocentric nature of the formal curriculum in schools have been characterized by Hulmes (1989) as focusing on the lifestyles of ethnic minorities rather than their life chances. The result of this is a curriculum that only recognizes ethnic minority experiences at the level of music, dancing, religious ceremony and cuisine. Furthermore, Blair (2003) has pointed to teaching strategies and methods based on cultural norms and values that are unfamiliar or hard to understand for minority ethnic pupils.

In the USA, Kozol (1991) has shown that a large number of financial and political constraints are in operation, whose effect is to deny poor minority children an appropriate share of basic educational resources. He examines the legal and financial systems that operate in American cities to produce what he calls 'savage inequalities', and shows how attempts to redress these founder on a system that perpetuates racial and social exploitation. McNeil (2005) argued that the high-stakes testing established in the USA had the effect of disadvan-taging children from ethnic minorities. By defining what is tested as 'legitimate' knowledge testing devalues other forms of knowledge, such as local or commu-nity knowledge. In particular, multicultural knowledge or knowledge drawn from the experiences of ethnic minorities is not seen by the testing regime as being legitimate.

Assessment of ethnic minority children, specifically African-Caribbean chil-dren, was found by Wright (1986) to be influenced more by the teacher's evaluation of their behaviour in the classroom than their actual cognitive abil-ity. Therefore, rather than viewing the educational problem of black children in terms of under-achievement, Wright argues that it should be seen in terms of disadvantage. This could explain why a higher proportion of black Caribbean students are classified as having special educational needs (SEN) – 28 per cent compared with 18 per cent of white pupils (Livesey and Lawson 2005) Foster, *et al.* (1996) argue that black Caribbean boys are over-represented in lower sets at school because of their unacceptable behaviour. Diane Abbott (a black Labour MP) has argued that white female teachers in particular are frightened by the behaviour of black boys in schools, and this leads to the higher like-lihood of their exclusion. Hence labelling by teachers can have a significant effect on performance and achievement.

When it comes to mixed heritage students, there is another dimension to teacher labelling, which is a distinctive aspect of an inside school explana-tion. The stereotyping of mixed heritage students as having 'identity problems' led teachers to dismiss their behavioural problems as stemming from their confusion over what ethnicity they were. This expectation that mixed heritage students suffer from low self-esteem because of their confused identity led to the labelling of such students as low achievers (Tizard and Phoenix 2002). However, the students themselves did not in the main feel confused about their identities, but were frustrated by how they were perceived by their teachers. Teacher perceptions of the family backgrounds of mixed heritage students was also stereotypical, in that they were perceived as living with their lone white mothers, when the majority in Haynes' research (Haynes *et al.* 2006) were in stable, dual-parent households.The lack of positive role models for children in schools has been highlighted as a significant factor in explaining the lower aspirations and under-achievement of children from minority groups (Blair 2003). In a National Union of Teachers survey carried out in 2003 entitled 'Pushed to Prove Themselves', ethnic minority teachers claimed they needed constantly to prove themselves and work harder than their white counterparts. Also, they regularly came across both overt and covert racism in their schools, which they felt had an effect on their promotion prospects.

Gillborn (2002) argues that schools are institutionally racist, in that many of the processes and procedures in relation to the running of the school, classroom practices and teaching, as well as the formulation of the curriculum, 'generally under-rate the abilities of black children'. Black children can be disproportionately assigned to lower streams or low-ability groups (in 2002, research showed that black children were more likely to be classified as having SEN in the Pupil Level Annual School Census), disadvantaged in schemes such as 'gifted and talented', and the development of vocational courses.

### Institutional racism

While not being a new concept, the notion of institutional racism came to the fore after the death of teenager Stephen Lawrence and the resulting MacPherson Report into the killing. MacPherson argued that police were an institutionally racist organisation in that the prejudices and discrimination against black people in society were part of the very fabric and culture of the police service. Despite the upper echelons of the police evidently being anti-racist, the day-to-day activity of policing and the canteen-culture of the beat officers patently *was* racist. Mitsos (2003) has used a similar argument about the nature of schools. This means that structural inequalities are mediated through the day-to-day activities of the school. Racism is embedded in institutions such as schools, though racism can also be individual and overt. Crozier (2005) argues that teachers hold pathological views of Afro-Caribbean children that define them as 'troublesome', and have the effect of limiting the children's aspirations and achievements. Moreover, teachers who may be aware of this institutional racism are unsure about how to handle it or develop counter-strategies to combat the effects of institutional racism in schools.

### Link Exercise 7.2

Using material from Chapter 3 and other sources, explain how the introduction of the national curriculum in 1988 may have served to hinder the opportunity of ethnic minorities to achieve well at school. (Hint: Think about the ways in which the curriculum has been made more Eurocentric.)

*Inside school explanations – an evaluation*

### Exercise 7.8

1. Read the evaluation statements that follow. Identify which are the strengths and which are the weaknesses. Record your answers in a two-column table that clearly separates the strengths from the weaknesses. Leave room in each column to complete task two.
2. On the basis of previous evaluations of inside school approaches (see Chapters 4 and 5), identify two other strengths and weaknesses that could be applied to inside school explanations that purport to explain ethnic differences in educational performance. Record your answers in the table you began for task one.

### Evaluation statements

(a) The approach attempts to see things from the social actors' point of view and therefore allows insight.
(b) Some research evidence (Foster, 1990) demonstrates that not all teachers are racist.
(c) The explanations have helped us to understand the nature of social inequality and injustice.
(d) Some sociologists argue that racism in schools cannot be a complete explanation because Indian and African Asian students experience such racism yet perform well educationally.
(e) It could be argued that the explanations overstate the case. A number of schools have adopted multicultural and/or anti-racist approaches to education that reduce the level of racism that inside school approaches judge to exist in schools.
(f) Most of the findings are based on qualitative research and therefore are high in validity.

## THE INTERACTION OF GENDER AND ETHNICITY

In this chapter we have already seen how social class cuts across ethnicity to determine educational performance. However, we also need to consider the way in which gender interacts with ethnicity.

---

### Exercise 7.9

Study Item D carefully and then describe the ways in which educational performance varies between ethnic groups according to gender.

---

### Item D

Highest qualification held,[1] by sex and ethnic group, 2004,[2] Great Britain (percentages)

| | Degree or equivalent | Higher education qualification[3] | GCE A Level or equivalent | GCSE grades A*–C or equivalent | Other qualification | No qualification | All |
|---|---|---|---|---|---|---|---|
| **Males** | | | | | | | |
| White British | 18 | 8 | 30 | 19 | 10 | 14 | 100 |
| White Irish | 23 | 6 | 24 | 12 | 17 | 18 | 100 |
| Mixed | 22 | 6 | 24 | 20 | 13 | 15 | 100 |
| Indian | 30 | 6 | 17 | 11 | 22 | 15 | 100 |
| Pakistani | 15 | 4 | 15 | 16 | 22 | 29 | 100 |
| Bangladeshi | 11 | 2 | 10 | 12 | 25 | 40 | 100 |
| Black Caribbean | 11 | 6 | 26 | 24 | 15 | 18 | 100 |
| Black African | 24 | 9 | 18 | 14 | 25 | 12 | 100 |
| Chinese | 33 | 4 | 13 | 10 | 21 | 19 | 100 |
| **Females** | | | | | | | |
| White British | 16 | 10 | 19 | 29 | 10 | 16 | 100 |
| White Irish | 25 | 13 | 15 | 15 | 16 | 16 | 100 |
| Mixed | 20 | 7 | 22 | 27 | 13 | 11 | 100 |
| Indian | 21 | 6 | 16 | 16 | 24 | 18 | 100 |
| Pakistani | 10 | 4 | 14 | 20 | 18 | 35 | 100 |
| Bangladeshi | 5 | 2 | 12 | 17 | 15 | 49 | 100 |
| Black Caribbean | 15 | 13 | 16 | 33 | 14 | 10 | 100 |
| Black African | 17 | 9 | 15 | 15 | 26 | 18 | 100 |
| Chinese | 29 | 6 | 10 | 8 | 26 | 21 | 100 |

*Notes*:

1. Males aged 16 to 64, females aged 16 to 59.
2. January to December. See Appendix: Part 4, *Annual Population Survey*.
3. Below degree level.

*Source*: *Annual Population Survey*, Office for National Statistics.

One of the gender differences you should have observed from the statistics in Item D is that Black Caribbean women are more successful educationally than their male counterparts. Such differences have been well explained by Fuller (1980), Mac an Ghaill (1988) and Mirza (1992). All these sociologists reach similar conclusions, which interestingly challenge the determinism inherent in the inside school approaches. They point out that African-Caribbean females feel and resent negative labelling and racism in schools, and like African-Caribbean males, they develop a resistance to schooling as a consequence. However, unlike African-Caribbean males, they do not form strong anti-school subcultures, which they realize lead to educational 'failure'. Instead, they adopt an approach of instrumental compliance that allows them to obtain the qualifications they desire so that they can 'prove their teachers wrong' and obtain the middle-class occupations they aspire too. To sum up, the differential educational performance between African-Caribbean males and females can be understood in terms of the degree of school resistance exerted. African-Caribbean males resist more strongly than females and are therefore less able to exploit the educational system for their own purposes.

However Mirza (1992) argues that this leaves the problem of why black girls' educational achievements do not lead to better jobs. She rejects the stereotypical views held about girls being mainly concerned about families and children. Instead, to explain their under-achievement she looked at the socioeconomic location of the school, the stratified nature of local labour markets and the poor quality of careers advice. In each case, issues of gender, class and race were important in channelling black girls into career routes that failed to take their educational achievements into account.

Sociologists have therefore pointed out that ethnicity is not a separate experience from gender or class, but is nested together with those characteristics. Fuller (1980) argues that the experiences of ethnic minority girls in schools cannot be assumed to be similar to those of black boys or white girls, but that they will develop their own identity in response to experiences specific to them. She concludes that black girls often suffer from double or even triple disadvantage if they also come from working-class backgrounds. The way that black males construct their identities in schools differs from the way that black girls do precisely because they are male, and because they have different experiences from black girls. For example, Cooper et al. (1991) detailed evidence to show that black boys are over-represented in SEN provision compared with white boys, black girls and Asian boys.

## ETHNICITY AND EDUCATIONAL POLICY

The emergence of significant ethnic minority communities in Britain after the Second World War has had a profound impact on many schools, especially those in cities, and has prompted a series of government policies on ethnic minority education. The main thrust of early educational policies *vis-à-vis* ethnic minorities was 'assimilation', which stressed the swiftest possible integration of ethnic minorities into the dominant culture. Lynch (1986) argues that policies such as providing special centres for those migrants whose first language was not English were based on the idea of the superiority of the dominant culture. It would be inaccurate to regard all education in the 1950s and 1960s as an expression of this point of view, as many local authorities were concerned with equality rather than assimilation.

Ethnic minority responses to assimilationist policies were negative, and Carter (1986) documents the emergence of Saturday schools for African-Caribbean children as a way of motivating the children to succeed. The provision of separate schools for different ethnic minorities continues to be a controversial issue, with many Islamic groups seeking to establish state support for Islamic schools in the same way that Christian schools are supported. However, opposition to such schools comes from a wide spectrum of political positions, from New Right theorists to Women Against Fundamentalism (see Klein 1993).

The two main social policy initiatives that have emerged in Britain since the mid-1970s to meet the educational needs and problems of ethnic minority students are multiculturalism and anti-racist education. As with the case of separate schooling, these are highly controversial political issues, causing a great deal of disagreement among sociologists and politicians.

### Multicultural education

Multicultural education is a policy supported by liberal sociologists and educationalists. The policy aims to encourage schools to recognize the cultural diversity of Britain's ethnic population. There is an attempt, above all, to move away from ethnocentric curricula. Schools that have adopted this initiative have, for example, integrated black authors into literature lessons, taught global history, and celebrated events such as Diwali. This is seen to be a positive form of social policy that creates tolerance and understanding in society and raises the educational performance of ethnic minorities by allowing them to draw on their own cultural backgrounds. Proponents such as Banks (1988) argue that in the USA the adoption of a multicultural approach reduces ethnic conflict in schools and aids the educational achievement of ethnic minority children.

However, multicultural education has come under attack from both radical and New Right positions. New Right critics have lumped together multiculturalism, political correctness, feminism and gay rights issues as an attempt by neo-Marxists to dominate the education system, and produce what they see as brainwashed students who are unable to challenge suspect ideas for fear of being damned as racist (see Siegal 1991 for an example of the American New Right argument). In Britain, Flew (1986) also argues that multiculturalism has a revolutionary intent – maintaining ethnic minorities as members of a discontented force who are ready to act as the shock troops of some future socialist revolution. He is critical of explanations of ethnic under-achievement that rely on the concept of racism, arguing that it is a vague and unhelpful concept. Beneath Flew's and other New Right theorists' attacks on multiculturalism is a concern for the preservation of a national identity, as formed by an imperialist past with no recognition of the cultural diversity existing in contemporary Britain. For example, Pearce (1986) sees multicultural education as undermining the native British way of life.

Radical critics argue that multiculturalism does not go far enough and does not address directly the central concept of racism. Parekh (1986), for example, sees multiculturalism as an attempt to keep ethnic minorities quiet, while ignoring the social and political conditions that led to their disadvantage. Radical opponents of multiculturalism argue that it has achieved little in terms of equality of opportunity for ethnic minorities. They call for a much more proactive approach to the issue of ethnic minorities in schools, an approach that has been called anti-racist education.

## Anti-racist education

Anti-racist education is a policy that is more broadly supported by radical sociologists and educationalists. It is a more challenging form of social policy than multicultural education, and aims to examine and oppose racism in both schools and society in general. Schools following anti-racist policies have attempted to remove racism from their teaching, school organization, curricula, reading schemes and assessment methods. This has involved them offering in-service training time to raise awareness about racism, and appointing a larger number of ethnic minorities to senior teaching posts. It is believed that this type of educational policy combats racism and therefore provides a more favourable society in which ethnic minorities can achieve.

As might be expected, this too has come under attack from theorists of the New Right, along similar lines to their critique of multiculturalism. In the USA, Ravitch (1990) has attacked anti-racist education as a threat to the common conception of nationhood – a concern that is important in such an ethnically diverse nation as the USA. In Britain, the concerns of the New Right have led O'Keefe (1986b) to argue that those involved in race relations promote disharmony, and that anti-racist teachers are effectively 'race spies' in the classroom.

The government and schools themselves have become concerned about the low achievement of some minority groups, and have introduced practices to bring about an improvement in performance. These range from providing support for students in classrooms by using a teaching assistant to work with identified pupils, sometimes from the same ethnic background as the support staff, to appointing staff to deal specifically with 'behaviour management' issues within the school. Other examples are out-of-school learning support designed to raise the achievement of specific groups with specific needs. Out-of-doors education has gained considerable momentum in recent years, with primary school children in particular being taken outside the confines of the classroom in the belief that it will stimulate their own learning when put into an environment which is exciting and challenging and begin to formulate their own questions.

Other policies have been designed and implemented to tackle issues that have an effect on deprived groups in society and a greater impact on minority groups. Education Action Zones (EAZs), and Social Exclusion Units (SEUs) were set up in the later 1990s. EAZs attracted funding from the government to attract more and better qualified teachers into the most deprived areas with the lowest educational achievement, to boost attainment levels. SEUs aimed to tackle truancy issues and stem the increase in school exclusions. Research into the effectiveness of such policies will emerge over the longer term, but if these policies are viewed as being similar to compensatory education initiatives we might conclude that they fail to tackle underlying causes of educational disadvantage and disaffection and will therefore have a limited long-term impact.

Ⓘ Ⓔ

## Exercise 7.10

Using the material in this chapter and other sources, evaluate the effectiveness of multicultural and anti-racist education policies. To complete the task you will need to look into some of the criticisms that have been made of the two initiatives. We recommend that you consult O'Donnell (1991, 1992) to help you to do this. As part of your evaluation, explain which of the two policies you feel are most likely to improve the educational chances of ethnic minorities – and make sure you justify your decision. Consider the impact of some of the more recent initiatives you may have had experience of yourself, such as the use of teaching assistants, out-of-doors education and so on.

More recent developments in the field of policy on ethnicity have drawn heavily on postmodern ideas, and in particular on the idea of 'critical pedagogy'. Critical pedagogy is critical of the Marxist assumption that there is a correspondence between the economy and schooling, and the New Right's insistence on cultural uniformity as an objective of education. Instead, they argue that education for children should be about their possibilities, and teaching them to recognize that we live in a fragmented and uncertain world. For example, McLaren (1991) argues that globalization and increasing ethnic plurality in British society necessitates a 'decentring' (moving away from) of what is described as racist and Eurocentric discourses (or ways of thinking) in education. Instead, teachers should be developing a 'postcolonial pedagogy'. This means that those who are subject to racist practices and ideology should be developing, as active agents, both challenges to racist ideas and patterns of behaviour in the classroom. Postcolonial pedagogy is therefore about the need for education to empower disadvantaged groups so that they begin to speak with their own voices. However, Ellsworth (1989) describes this process as having a very high level of abstraction, with the result that postcolonial pedagogy has little to offer in the way of practical classroom management and specific techniques of empowerment.

## Evaluation of Labour policies and education

Writers such as Whitty (2002) have argued that, while Labour reversed some of the Conservatives' free market policies on education, such as the creation of Grant Maintained Schools and brought them back under Local Authority control as well as focusing on areas of deprivation, their general approach still has much in common with that of the Conservatives. They continued in the 'privatization' of some aspects of education such as the School Meals Service, bolstering parental choice and the development of a traditional curriculum. However Trowler (2003) presents a more positive overview, pointing to the significantly increased funding, the creation of EAZs and Excellence in Cities, which targeted deprived areas; the focus on literacy and numeracy in primary schools; and the emphasis on ICT in all schools, as areas where the government has made a difference.

## THE INTERRELATIONSHIP BETWEEN SOCIAL CLASS, GENDER AND ETHNICITY

We have seen in this chapter the importance of looking at class, gender and ethnicity as aspects of an individual's being. Postmodern sociologists argue that, increasingly, it is the issue of identity that is at the centre of an analysis of the individual in society, and that characteristics such as class, gender and ethnicity are important components of individuals' construction of their identity. While individuals and groups mark themselves off from each other through the use of 'signifiers' (symbols, consumer goods, styles), it is important to note that there are structural effects on identity, such as the experiences individuals have in schools, because of their significant social characteristics. The implication of the increasing fragmentation of culture in postmodern societies is that it is increasingly difficult to write about the experiences of social groups as being common to all members. The interplay of ethnic, gender and class factors in the performances of different individuals is likely to lead to more complex patterns of achievement and under-achievement in the education system.

There is a further difficulty in understanding this interplay. The classical way that relative achievement has been measured is through statistical analysis of examination results by social factors. The mathematical techniques employed for these analyses have become increasingly sophisticated, so that the effects of individual factors can be measured. However, Gorard (2000) points out that the analysis of achievement gaps can produce two different responses, depending on how the analysis is carried out. One type of analysis will lead to the conclusion that achievement gaps are increasing, and another type that they are decreasing. Therefore it is difficult to be certain what is happening in the complex interplay of class, gender, ethnicity and achievement.

---

### Exam Focus

Read the Items and look at the guidance related to the exam question below. Then try to answer the question by yourself.

## Item E

The under-achievement of African-Caribbean, Pakistani and Bangladeshi pupils in British schools involves some of the same processes that lead to the under-achievement of working-class children. These groups become progressively eliminated as they move through the education system and as various processes take effect. Several studies have shown that teachers' expectations of children from ethnic minority backgrounds can have a marked impact on performance. While teachers are unlikely to be overtly racist, their misunderstanding or misinterpretation of cultural signs and behaviour leads to stereotypical labelling and treatment of children from minority groups. Teachers can have a Eurocentric focus in their approach to the delivery of the curriculum which does not take into account other cultures and ethnic groups.

*Source*: Adapted from Mitsos (2003).

## Item F

According to an Ofsted report (2000; see http://www.ofsted.gov.uk) all the main ethnic groups were achieving higher grades than ever before. However, there are variations in performance of different ethnic groups. Black pupils are more likely than other groups to be permanently excluded from school, and the proportion of African-Caribbean pupils gaining five grade A*–C GCSEs has dropped from 39 per cent in 2000 to 36 per cent in 2002, according to the Youth Cohort Survey which looked at the educational experiences of 18,000 young people in England and Wales. By contrast, Indian pupils are most likely to gain five grade A*–C GCSEs, with over half of Indian boys achieving these standards and two-thirds of Indian girls reaching this level. Pakistani and Bangladeshi girls and boys were only half as likely to reach the same levels.

*Source*: Adapted from Denscombe (2004).

## Question

Evaluate sociological explanations of the 'poor school progress' made by some children from African-Caribbean and Asian homes (Item F). (8 marks)

The question here directs your attention directly to Item F, where specific information about the educational achievement of black and Asian students is given. Item F therefore provides you with some of the explanations put forward, which you should expand on and evaluate with regard to their importance. You should also note that Item E provides hints about explanations for ethnic minority performance. The important thing is to apply the information given on teachers' expectations to ethnic minority pupils, and it would be even better if you could provide some supporting evidence, in the form of studies that look specifically at teachers' expectations and ethnic minority achievement. The lesson to be learnt here is that the Items often contain useful bits of information for a question, even when you are not specifically directed to go to them. It is therefore worthwhile taking a little time to make sure you have read through the Items carefully before you begin to answer questions.

Let us look at how an answer to this question might be structured, drawing on an answer given by a student in a real examination.

## Section 1: The introduction

Consider the following introduction:

> Overall, it is widely regarded that black and Asian children do less well in the school system compared with their white counterparts. The position of ethnic minority children is more complicated than this, as the Swann report shows that the majority of Asian children do as well as their white counterparts, but that groups such as Pakistanis and Bangladeshis do less well. West Indians are the group that tend to do the least well in the education system. Only 5 per cent have one or more A level, and only 1 per cent go on to university. The explanations of these differences have concentrated on either factors from outside school or factors inside the school.

This is a good opening paragraph, because the candidate has set out some very important points that should inform the rest of the answer. The candidate has shown that she or he is aware that ethnic minorities cannot be lumped together as a whole, but that nevertheless there are important differences in educational attainment between some ethnic minorities and their white counterparts that need to be explained. They also show the marker how the answer is to proceed, by laying out the alternative types of explanation put forward.

## Section 2: Genetic explanations

For the second section it would be appropriate to show why sociological approaches have rejected the biological determinist approaches of the geneticists and psychologists, and looked to the experiences of ethnic minority children both within and outside the school system. The section need not be very long, but it is important to set the context. This section should have an evaluative aspect, by looking briefly at the evidence for and against genetic explanations.

## Section 3: Inside school explanations

The answer should then turn to explanations from experiences inside the school. It is important that you provide a range of such explanations and do not just concentrate on only one. You can find a couple of explanations in the items themselves, but must apply them specifically to the issue of ethnicity and achievement. Where possible, you should support the points you are making by referring to appropriate studies, and if there are any specific criticisms of these, include them to give this section an evaluative edge.

## Section 4: Evaluation of inside school explanations

In this section you should consider the strengths and weaknesses of the explanations put forward, showing how they may be important in explaining certain aspects of ethnic under-achievement, as well as how they may be limited in fully explaining it. You may wish to consider the theoretical underpinnings of these explanations, and how important these are in assessing the approach.

## Section 5: Outside school explanations

Here, you should consider a range of explanations that look beyond the school gates. Follow the principles contained in Section 3 above. However, you should begin this section with a sentence that links inside and outside explanations in an evaluative way. For example, 'Because of these weaknesses in the inside school explanations, some sociologists have offered an alternative view that emphasizes the experiences of ethnic minorities outside school.'

## Section 6: Evaluation of outside school explanations

Continue to demonstrate your evaluation skills by considering the advantages and disadvantages of these approaches, using the guidelines in Section 4.

## Section 7: Class, gender and ethnicity

In this section you should demonstrate your understanding of the complexity of the issue under discussion by looking at the complex interaction between class, gender and ethnicity. Refer back to your introductory paragraph to see from where the theme should be developed.

## Section 8: Conclusion

There are many ways in which you can come to an evaluative conclusion. You do not always have to sit on the fence, but can support one or a couple of explanations, as long as you have argued for them during the course of your answer and have considered some alternatives, which you are rejecting. A straightforward 'sitting on the fence' conclusion is illustrated by the following paragraph:

> If you join together all these explanations of 'poor school progress' it will give you a more accurate account of why some ethnic minorities do not do so well, because, as we have seen, there are many factors that help to explain 'poor school progress'.

Now write your own response to the question, using the above structure, but come to your own conclusion, as this will strengthen the evaluation of the different explanations you include. You should also try to include an introduction that sets out the route your answer will take.

## BRINGING IT ALL TOGETHER – HOW CLASS, GENDER AND ETHNICITY INTERRELATE

So far we have examined how the social characteristics of class, gender and ethnicity have an impact on the educational performance of children in schools. However, for the purposes of clarity, each of these factors has, in the main, been considered separately. In this section we want to look at how they interrelate, and in so doing, how we might shed new light on our understanding of educational attainment.

### Complexities

To begin with, though, we want to emphasize that the study of educational performance is by no means straightforward. There are important complexities of which we should at least be aware.

#### What is meant by performance?

'Performance' itself is a contested concept. What counts as performance traditionally has had a rather narrow focus, in that it is almost invariably taken to mean performance in national tests and examinations, such as the national curriculum tests, GCSEs/GNVQs/AVCEs, Applied A Level, and A/AS Levels. Some sociologists might regard this as little more than the uncritical acceptance of 'official definitions' that fail to address or even consider alternative measures such as those associated with artistic merit, sporting ability, cultural awareness and tolerance, and so on. In addition, performance relates, in part, to subject/course choice, particularly for post-14 education, in so far as this will tend to determine to some extent career outcomes.

### How is performance defined?

Even if we accept test/examination-related definitions of educational performance, then it is clear that different definitions will lead to very different views as to what counts as under-performance. Thus, in relation to traditional qualifications such as GCSEs, there are at least three possible measures of performance: achieving grades above or below a grade D; achieving below grade D in English and Maths; or achieving at least five grade A/A*– C (Cassen and Kingdon 2007).

Each of these measures will produce its own statistical outcome, and result in a different pattern or trend over time that measures 'performance' and 'under-performance'. For example, as The Bow Group has reported, between 1997 and 2007 the numbers leaving school without at least five basic G grades at GCSE including English and Maths has increased to nearly 90,000 (Skidmore 2008; see also http://www.bowgroup.org/ harriercollection-items/The%20Failed%20Generation.pdf). However, during the same period the percentage of pupils achieving five grade C passes or better has risen significantly.

Table 7.2 indicates how different measures of underperformance determine different outcomes.

**Table 7.2** Measures of performance by gender and eligibility for free school meals (FSMs) at GCSE (percentages)

|  | FSM – Girls | No FSM – Girls | FSM – Boys | No FSM – Boys |
|---|---|---|---|---|
| No passes at grade G or above | 10 | 4 | 13 | 5 |
| No passes at grade G or above in English and Maths | 17 | 5 | 20 | 6 |
| No passes higher than grade D | 40 | 16 | 55 | 37 |

*Source*: Adapted from *Tackling Low Achievement*, Joseph Rowntree Foundation, July 2007, p. 13.

To the extent that policy is based on evidence, it follows that each measure is likely to result in a different policy emphasis, designed to address the nature and extent of the problem. For example, if the focus is on 'no passes higher than D', then resources might be concentrated on improving the performance of marginal D/C students, which might have the additional benefit of apparently enhancing overall attainment as expressed in league tables. On the other hand, if the measure is 'no passes at G or above in English or Maths' then policies such as the national literacy and numeracy strategies might result. In this way, different measures influence both the funding of schools and the practices of teachers. In addition, we should note that the choice of measure can be a matter of political judgement and convenience on the part of government rather than being based on purely educational considerations.

### The time-line

It is also important to remember that educational performance is not set in stone. There are trends over time that should be recognized if we are to fully understand the issues. For example, in relation to gender and performance at KS2, the data shown in Table 7.3 apply.

**Table 7.3** Percentage of pupils achieving Level 4 or above in Key Stage 2 tests

|  | 1997 | 1998 | 1999 | 2000 | 2001 | 2002 | 2003 | 2004 | 2005 | 2006 |
|---|---|---|---|---|---|---|---|---|---|---|
| **Reading** | | | | | | | | | | |
| Boys | 63 | 64 | 75 | 80 | 78 | 77 | 78 | 79 | 82 | 79 |
| Girls | 71 | 79 | 82 | 86 | 85 | 83 | 84 | 87 | 87 | 87 |
| All pupils | 67 | 71 | 78 | 83 | 82 | 80 | 81 | 83 | 84 | 83 |
| **Writing** | | | | | | | | | | |
| Boys | 45 | 45 | 47 | 48 | 50 | 52 | 52 | 56 | 55 | 59 |
| Girls | 62 | 61 | 62 | 63 | 65 | 68 | 69 | 71 | 72 | 75 |
| All pupils | 53 | 53 | 54 | 55 | 57 | 60 | 60 | 63 | 63 | 67 |

*Note*: Key stage 2 refers to school years 3–6. Pupils are tested in reading and writing when they are in Year 6, aged 10 or 11.
*Sources*: Data compiled from DfES 2006 – see http://www.dcsf.gov.uk/ – and *Tackling Low Achievement*, Joseph Rowntree Foundation, July 2007, p. 76.

These figures indicate that the notion of 'failing boys' might be regarded as simplistic, but the fact that the gender-gap has remained largely unchanged means that the performance of both girls *and* boys has *steadily improved* over the period in question and at approximately the same rate. Hence, the notion that 'boys', as a single autonomous category of learner, are failing can be challenged.

## It's not only about class, gender and ethnicity

Another complexity lies in the recognition that the educational performance of children depends in part on factors other than class, gender or ethnicity. The quality of the learning process itself, as practitioners would accept, relates to the quality and professionalism of teachers, and this will vary. For example, according to The Institute of Public Policy Research, poor secondary-school teachers can mean the difference between passing and failing at GCSE (IPPR 2008; see http://www.ippr.org.uk/). Similarly, how schools are organized, class sizes, the quality of leadership within schools, their ethos and values, resources more generally and so on, are all likely to have an influence on how well children do, and result in significant regional and local variations in achievement. In contrast, earlier research focused on factors connected to the home background of children and the attitudes of parents concerning the education of their children as key influences on education performance, achievement and progress. These factors are related to the differential attainment patterns of working-class and middle-class children.

## Class, gender and ethnicity

Having highlighted some of the issues associated with understanding educational attainment, the importance of combining class, gender and ethnicity can be further explored. It must be remembered that research in this area should be designed (but sometimes isn't) as much as is possible, to reflect the realities of children and their performance, and what is clear is that children do not enter school as simple bearers of class *or* gender *or* ethnic identities. There will be considerable overlap and interplay between these social factors; gender identity may be a dominant characteristic in relation to subject choice, for example, but social class background is a defining factor in relation to 'performance'. Similarly, social class could reinforce or undermine ethnic identity. This point illustrates again the complexities of social life and the need to design research accordingly. In addition, single-factor statistics are often misleading and can result in false conclusions regarding the causes of underperformance. In short, several social, cultural and educational factors may interplay at different times to bring about particular experiences and achievement in education for a particular child.

Tables 7.4, 7.5 and 7.6 illustrate this point by summarizing unpublished data relating to performance by ethnicity in KS2 national tests in English for an unnamed school in Bedfordshire (University of Bedfordshire, Department of Sociology and Criminology, 2008).

If we examine performance by ethnicity alone (see Table 7.4), it appears on most measures as if children of Caribbean heritage do significantly less well in schools than those from many other ethnic groups. (This is also the case with children of Pakistani, Bangladeshi and black African heritage, as seen earlier in this chapter). This under-performance also continues into higher education, with these groups being under-represented in UK universities (HESA 2006).

These figures indicate that, in the school in question, white pupils outperform pupils of Caribbean origin by 20.7 per cent, and seem to suggest that African-Caribbean children as an ethnic group are less academically able.

**Table 7.4**   Performance by ethnicity – KS2 English (percentages)

|  | Results | | Total |
|---|---|---|---|
|  | Target+ | Below target |  |
| White | 68.3 | 31.7 | 100.0 |
| Caribbean | 47.6 | 52.4 | 100.0 |
| Total | 61.3 | 38.7 | 100.0 |

*Note*: Target+ denotes the percentage of pupils achieving level 4 or better.
*Source*: Unpublished data, P. Brown, Department of Sociology and Criminology, University of Bedfordshire, 2008.

**Table 7.5**   Performance by ethnicity and gender – KS2 English (percentages)

| Gender | Ethnicity | Results | | Total |
|---|---|---|---|---|
|  |  | Target+ | Below target |  |
| Male | White | 61.1 | 38.9 | 100.0 |
|  | Caribbean | 27.3 | 72.7 | 100.0 |
| Total |  | 48.3 | 51.7 | 100.0 |
| Female | White | 73.9 | 26.1 | 100.0 |
|  | Caribbean | 70.0 | 30.0 | 100.0 |
| Total |  | 72.7 | 27.3 | 100.0 |

*Note*: As Table 7.4.
*Source*: As Table 7.4.

**Table 7.6** Performance by ethnicity and relative poverty – KS2 English (percentages)

| Relative poverty | Ethnicity | Results | | Total |
|---|---|---|---|---|
| | | Target+ | Below target | |
| Non-FSM | White | 84.4 | 15.6 | 100.0 |
| | Caribbean | 75.0 | 25.0 | 100.0 |
| Total | | 82.5 | 17.5 | 100.0 |
| FSM | White | 11.1 | 88.9 | 100.0 |
| | Caribbean | 30.8 | 69.2 | 100.0 |
| Total | | 22.7 | 77.3 | 100.0 |

*Note*: Relative poverty is an indicator of socio-economic background; it is defined in terms of Non-FSM (not eligible for free school meals) and FSM (eligible for free school meals); see also Table 7.4.
*Source*: As Table 7.4.

The sorts of data presented in Table 7.4 have sometimes been cited as evidence that the distribution of performance by ethnicity is an expression of the distribution of genetic ability, and that some 'races' are naturally less able than others (see page 177). However, this is a fallacious argument, for if we *combine* ethnicity with gender, it is clear that while *male* Caribbean pupils do tend to under-perform, *female* Caribbean pupils do almost as well on average as other female groups, and better than most white males (see Table 7.5).

If performance was simply a matter of genetic inheritance, it would be impossible to explain these gender differences within ethnicity. This is because both male and female African-Caribbean children typically have, in ethnic terms, the same parentage and therefore the same genetic make-up. That is not to say, of course, that an *individual's* performance is wholly unconnected to innate intelligence or ability. However, we are dealing here with social aggregates and not individuals, and social factors rather than 'natural causes' should be our main focus of enquiry.

We can further illustrate the importance of combining social factors in relation to educational performance by looking at the relationship between socio-economic background and ethnicity for the same school (see Table 7.6).

These data show that while there is an ethnic impact on performance, the effect of socio-economic background is much more significant for white pupils than it is for those of Caribbean origin, with white pupils from a relatively affluent background being among the best performers, while those from a relatively deprived background being among the worst.

We can examine this issue in more detail by drawing on national figures – see Table 7.7.

Those on FSMs perform less well than those who are not eligible, and this is the case for all ethnic groups. However, there are important differences – for example, the impact of relative deprivation seems to be particularly pronounced for White British pupils, whereas Black Caribbean pupils seem to under-perform significantly in both categories (non-FSM and FSM). Overall, the figures suggest that performance for some ethnicities cannot be explained with reference to socio-economic status alone. Table 7.8 illustrates this point.

These figures show that Indian and Bangladeshi pupils perform much better than would be expected if performance was based solely on the result of the impact of relative deprivation. Black Caribbean pupils, on the other hand,

**Table 7.7** Proportion of pupils, by selected ethnic groups and relative poverty (FSM), achieving five or more A*–C grade GCSEs/NVQs, 2003 (percentages)

|  | Non-FSM | FSM |
|---|---|---|
| Black Caribbean | 37 | 24 |
| Pakistani | 47 | 34 |
| Bangladeshi | 50 | 43 |
| White British | 56 | 20 |
| Indian | 68 | 47 |

*Source*: Adapted from Department for Education and Skills, *Ethnicity and Education – The Evidence on Ethnic Minority Pupils*, 2005, p. 13.

**Table 7.8** The effect of selected ethnicities and deprivation on GCSE results, 2003

|  | Expected differences | Actual differences |
|---|---|---|
| Black Caribbean | −6 | −18 |
| Pakistani | −8 | −10 |
| Bangladeshi | −16 | −5 |
| White British | +1 | +1 |
| Indian/Other Asian | −3 | +8 |

*Notes*: Expected difference – expected difference from the national average for all pupils (standardized at 0) as a result of the impact of relative deprivation (FSMs); Actual difference – actual difference national average for all pupils (standardized at 0).*Source*: Adapted from Department for Education and Skills, *Ethnicity and Education – The Evidence on Ethnic Minority Pupils*, Department for Education and Skills, 2005, p. 16.

perform at a much lower level than would be expected, whereas for White British pupils in particular, deprivation seems to explain most of the variation:

> The educational attainment of White British pupils was particularly vulnerable to low parental social class, mothers with no educational qualifications, relative poverty (entitled to Free School Meals (FSM)), living in single parent households, living in rented housing and living in deprived neighbourhoods. These factors impact negatively on attainment within most ethnic groups, but seem to be associated with disproportionately low attainment among White British pupils. In effect, White British are the most polarized ethnic group in terms of attainment: White British pupils from high (socioeconomic) homes are one of the highest attaining ethnic groups, while White British pupils living in disadvantaged circumstances are the lowest attaining group. (DCSF, 2008; see http://www.dcsf.gov.uk/, p. 2)

and

> Eligibility for free school meals is strongly associated with low achievement but significantly more so for White British pupils than for other ethnic groups. (Joseph Rowntree Foundation, 2007, p. xi)

Tables 7.6 and 7.7 also indicate that Caribbean pupils from relatively affluent backgrounds tend to under-perform in relation to white pupils, an observation that is also reflected in the Department for Children, Schools and Families (2008) and Joseph Rowntree Foundation (2007) national reports. In addition, Black Caribbean boys significantly underperform in comparison with other male-ethnic groups, as Table 7.9 illustrates.

**Table 7.9** Proportion of male pupils, by selected ethnic groups, achieving five or more grade A*–C GCSEs/NVQs, 2003 (percentages)

| | |
|---|---|
| Black Caribbean | 25 |
| Pakistani | 36 |
| Bangladeshi | 39 |
| White British | 46 |
| Indian | 60 |

*Source*: Adapted from Department for Education and Skills, *Ethnicity and Education – The Evidence on Ethnic Minority Pupils*, 2005, p. 13.

## CONCLUSION

We have suggested that educational policy designed to address issues associated with performance in schools should be evidence-based. In addition, by their nature, single-factor statistics are likely to be unreliable in developing an understanding of what the real issues are. By combining class, gender and ethnicity, however, as in the discussion above, we are better able to draw appropriate and relevant conclusions.

Overall, in terms of policy-focus, therefore, the groups for whom low attainment is the greatest concern are:

- White British boys and girls, and Black Caribbean boys, from low (socio-economic) homes. These are the three lowest attaining groups;
- Black Caribbean pupils, particularly but not exclusively boys, from middle and high (socio-economic) homes who underachieve relative to their White British peers.

(DCSF, March 2008, p. 3)

---

### Important concepts

- resistance • globalization • Eurocentrism • racism
- multiculturalism • anti-racism • institutional racism

---

### Critical thinking

- Consider why there has been such a consistent pattern in the underachievement of ethnic minority groups in the British education system.
- Is the impact of social class just as important when sociologists try to provide explanations for ethnic minority educational disadvantage and poor performance?
- Would anti-racist training of teachers and the appointment of a more representative teaching workforce reduce the disaffection of black children and create more positive roles models for these children?
- How far do you agree that school-based policies to address underachievement will be limited in their impact, as it is the wider structural inequalities in society that are the root cause of under-achievement.

*Chapter 8*

# Functionalist Explanations of the Role of Education and Training

By the end of this chapter you should:

- appreciate the ways in which the socialization role of schools and training programmes can be seen in a positive light
- be familiar with functionalist views on the allocation role of education and training
- understand the views of those who maintain that education performs a positive vocational function for society
- be able to assess functionalist approaches to the role of education and training

## INTRODUCTION

When considering the role of education and training we are concerned with examining the functions that schools and training courses perform for society. In sociology, this has traditionally been the main concern of the functionalist perspective. Functionalists see society as a system of interrelated parts, in which each part has functions to perform for the whole of society. They have therefore always been concerned with the relationship between education and the economy.

However, the relationship between the economy and the education system is not a straightforward one, in that schooling has historically not only been seen as a preparation for the world of work, but also as schooling into the wider culture of society. Industries have until recently offered their own specific training programmes, through apprenticeships, on-the-job training and so on. Though industrial training programmes have often been linked to education courses in colleges of further education, during the 1980s and 1990s the education system took on a more explicit vocational role, as the government sought to improve the preparation of young people for the world of work.

When the British economy was dominated by Fordist characteristics such as mass production and a low-skill, low-wage workforce, the amount of job training needed was limited. However, Finegold and Soskice (1988) claim that the characteristics of a post-Fordist economy demand, in part, a highly skilled workforce, and that therefore the training system in Britain should change to meet the new circumstances. While other sociologists accept that there will be a demand for highly skilled labour in the post-Fordist economy, they also warn that development will not be the same in every sector of the economy, and that there are likely to be sectors in which under-employment and low skills are dominant (Brown and Lauder 1992). Functionalists, however, offer an optimistic analysis of the role of education and training. They maintain that education and training perform a positive function for all in industrial and post-industrial societies. Schools and training schemes are said to achieve this through three related economic roles:

1. Socialization – their role in instilling norms and values.
2. Allocation – their role in slotting people into 'appropriate' occupational positions.
3. Vocational training – their role in equipping young people with practical and technical skills.

Each of these roles will now be examined in turn.

## THE SOCIALIZATION ROLE

Functionalist sociologists claim that schools and, more recently, training programmes, act as a form of secondary socialization that follows primary socialisation within the family. This socialisation is said to be an essential means by which modern societies perpetuate themselves. The most emphatic statements of the functionalist view on educational socialization come from Durkheim (1956) and Parsons (1959). Both these theorists claim that educational systems perform an integrative and regulative function by transmitting socially 'agreed' norms and values. The transmission of such norms and values (see Exercises 8.1 and 8.2) is said to occur through both the formal curriculum (for example, timetabled subjects such as English and history) and the hidden curriculum (for example, the punishment and reward systems operating within schools). It is through the internalization of society's norms and values, it is believed, that individuals learn to become good 'social citizens', and societies achieve social cohesion and stability. Acceptance of particular ways of behaving is important for the operation of the economy, because many types of work can be boring. The instillation of a 'work ethic' and the development of good work habits, such as punctuality and honesty, are important for the successful operation of an industrial economy. Moreover, an industrial economy needs workers who, at the bare minimum, have the basic skills of numeracy and literacy.

However, the socialization role of schooling can be seen as more than just the instilling of basic values, skills and attitudes. Drawing on the work of Foucault, Hoskin (1990) argues that modern (as opposed to traditional) forms of government are only made possible through education. In traditional societies, compliance with government is obtained by coercion or force, while in modern societies, social discipline is obtained through the education process, which seeks to regulate the population by offering individuals 'emancipation' through education. That is, education holds out the promise of a better, freer life to those who pursue it.

## Exercise 8.1

Identify three norms and three values that functionalists believe characterize Western societies.

## Exercise 8.2

In 1994, John Major's Conservative government launched a 'back to basics' campaign. This policy was partly an attempt to stem the alleged breakdown in social mores. Your task for this exercise is to conduct a newspaper search, possibly using the internet, to find out some of the key norms and values that John Major wanted institutions such as the family and schools to instil into young people. The following example should help you to get started:

- Individuals should grow up knowing 'right from wrong'.

Ⓐ

## Link Exercise 8.1

It can be argued that one of the reasons why Conservative governments in the 1980s and 1990s supported the new vocationalism is because initiatives such as TVEI, CPVE, YT, ET ((G)NVQs/AVCEs), Applied A Levels (see Chapter 3) aim to make students and trainees 'attitudinally better employees'. This is said to be achieved by instilling key work values such as punctuality. Identify four other work values that may be socialized into students and trainees when following a new vocational course.

## THE ALLOCATION ROLE

Functionalists such as Davis and Moore (1945) and Parsons (1959) maintain that education performs an important allocation or selection role by matching students on the basis of their talents or abilities to the jobs to which they are best suited. It is argued that the function of allocating people into appropriate occupational roles is essentially achieved through the certification process operating within education and training systems. Thus schools, universities and training schemes examine students at different levels and offer graded qualifications that sift and sort people into different but fitting job positions. In this way, it is believed, the most able and talented in society ultimately occupy the most functionally important jobs, having achieved high-status qualifications with good grades; while those with low-status qualifications with poor grades find themselves in the least important jobs.

The role allocation function of schools is judged to be all the more important in advanced industrial societies as the occupational structure has grown and become more complex and diverse. For example James Avis (1993) argues that educational methods such as group work, records of achievement, profiling and so on are developed by what he calls 'curriculum modernizers' to meet the needs of a post-Fordist economy. Under Fordist economic conditions, manual workers were needed who would follow instructions and carry out fairly simple and repetitive tasks. Therefore the qualifications the education system needed to provide such workers with were also fairly basic and concerned limited and formal skills such as literacy.

In a post-Fordist economy there is a need for more highly skilled workers who are flexible, responsible and, most of all, committed to the aims of the organisation. Therefore, the employer needs to know much more about a prospective employee than in the past, and is interested in the whole person, not just her or his basic skills. For example, the employer needs to know about the ability of an employee to work co-operatively, or how creative he or she is. Qualifications therefore need to reflect these attitudes and motivations, through monitoring an individual's performance in group work or problem-solving tasks. The vocational qualifications such as GNVQ, AVCEs and now Applied A levels are geared towards this type of assessment, as well as sorting individuals according to key skills such as numeracy, communication and information technology skills.

Ⓐ
## Exercise 8.3

This exercise is designed to enhance your appreciation of the hierarchy of qualifications that are needed to fit into a modern, stratified society.

Copy out the table below and fill in the necessary qualifications needed to undertake the various occupations that fall under the Registrar General's social class schema. If you get stuck, try to find out the answers using an appropriate sociology website – useful websites are www.atss.org.uk or the careers website www.connexions-direct.com.

| Social class | Example of occupation | Necessary qualifications |
|---|---|---|
| Class I (Professional) | University lecturer | |
| Class II (Intermediate) | Teacher | |
| Class III n (Skilled non-manual) | Police officer | |
| Class III m (Skilled manual) | Electrician | |
| Class IV (Partly skilled manual) | Telephone operator | |
| Class V (Unskilled manual) | Office cleaner | |

Ⓐ
## Link Exercise 8.2

Functionalists make three main points with regard to the allocation function of schools and training programmes: (i) the selection that takes place is conducted in an educational environment that offers equality of educational opportunity; (ii) schools and society at large reward individuals on meritocratic criteria; and (iii) education and training offers an important avenue for social mobility. This link exercise is designed to get you to follow through these key functionalist assumptions.

Your task is to copy out and then complete the chart provided below by carrying out the following instructions:

1. Using information from Chapter 2, define (i) equality of educational opportunity; and (ii) meritocracy. Referring to what you already know, define social mobility (note that there are different types).

2. Drawing on material from Chapters 2 and 3, explain how various educational policies have helped to create a more open society.
3. Using the internet, locate different pieces of empirical evidence to support the functionalist assumptions that equality of opportunity is offered in educational institutions; that meritocracies exist; and that schooling acts as a vehicle for social mobility.

| Functionalism | Equality of educational opportunity | Meritocracy | Social mobility |
|---|---|---|---|
| Definition | | | |
| Underlying theoretical assumption | Schooling is neutral in that it treats all social groupings equally. It therefore allows everyone to demonstrate their talents to the full. | Structured social inequality is accepted because there is a fair contest for unequal rewards. Educational and occupational success is achieved and is based on merit. | Given equality of educational opportunity and the existence of a meritocratic society, education acts as a route for social mobility. Modern and postmodern capitalist societies are characterized by fluid social class structures. |
| The positive effect of educational policies: creating an 'open' society | | | |
| Empirical evidence in support of the functionalist views | | | |

## THE VOCATIONAL TRAINING ROLE

The key theorist to address this function of schooling and training is Schultz (1977). The role of education and training in transmitting vocational skills was explored in Chapter 3, when we examined new vocationalism. However, this key economic role of education was debated by human capital theory (a distinct branch of functionalism) long before new vocational thinkers began to discuss the need for technical and vocational education in schools and colleges.

Human capital theory rests on the assumption that education (particularly technical education) is a productive investment – a means by which societies can bring about and sustain economic growth. It is believed that schools, colleges and universities can act as catalysts for economic growth because they provide highly educated and trained workers who have the necessary knowledge and skills to make effective use of the advanced productive technologies found in modern industries. Schultz's arguments for investment in people were influential in the creation of policies to deal with Third-World poverty during the 1960s. However, the failure of human capital programmes to bring about development in the Third World led to the rise of alternative views of vocational training, in which the market was the mechanism behind the provision of training programmes, rather than government planning. In the 1990s, notions about 'investment in people' and the need of the postmodern economy for highly skilled workers have revitalized human capital ideas. Indeed, all the major political parties agree that there is a need for investment in training, though they differ over the means of delivering the skills the economy requires.

>)(A)

## Link Exercise 8.3

The introduction of the national curriculum in 1988 and new vocational schemes such as Applied A levels and Modern Apprenticeships have been seen as an attempt to ensure that school leavers were 'skilled up' for employment in the 1990s, 2000s and beyond. Drawing on earlier work you have completed, explain how the national curriculum and vocational education ensure that young workers have the necessary practical and technological competences to work in modern industries.

## New Right perspectives on education

The development of socio-political perspectives on education in the late 1970s and 1980s were closely linked with the Conservative Party, and in particular the policies of the Thatcher government. Sometimes difficult to classify sociologically because of their origins in the political sphere, many observers would attach the main tenets of the perspective(s) to functionalism. New Right concepts such as role allocation, individualism, values and meritocracy can be closely aligned with functionalist writers. The Conservative governments of the 1979–97 period introduced many policies which underpinned traditional functionalist thinking. The role of the government was seen to be one in which the creation of the right conditions to foster individual achievement and enterprise was paramount Applied to education, this meant an increasing 'marketised' system, where schools would compete for pupils and parents would have the right to choose which school their children attended. Hence poor schools would have to improve or go out of 'business', and good schools would be the market leaders providing leadership for those that were below standard. The use of competition, through the publication of leagues tables, would be the key to creating the best form of education, with minimum intervention by the government. Standardized assessment and teaching, training rather than education, and socialisation to produce consumers and workers were all key parts of the New Right agenda in relation to education. The election of the Labour government in 1997 led to the continuation of many of the New Right policies and objectives. League tables, parental choice, specialist schools and city academies had all become part of the educational discourse.

### An evaluation of the functionalist approach to the role of education and training

### Exercise 8.4

Listed below are the strengths and weaknesses of the functionalist approach to education and training. Your task is to identify whether the strength or weakness is specific to the functionalist views on socialization, allocation or vocational training, or whether it is a general strength or weaknesses of the functionalist approach to education and training. We have completed one of the answers to help you get started.

### Strengths:

1. Functionalist theorists recognize that education and training systems are related to other institutions, such as the family. *(A general strength.)*
2. It is true that schools and training courses transmit norms and values through their formal and/or hidden curricula.
3. The approach is sensitive to the fact that education systems are in part shaped by the economic needs of society.
4. Some empirical evidence exists to support the claim that the sorting and sifting role of schools operates under egalitarian principles, and that this helps to create a meritocratic and fluid social structure.

**Weaknesses:**

1. The norms and values transmitted by schools and training schemes are not necessarily those of society as a whole, but those of dominant social groups. It is thus a 'class-centric' approach.
2. The benefit of a vocational education has to be questioned. A number of sociologists point to the problem of deskilling, which is the process whereby work activities have the skill taken out of them, either through organizational arrangements or technological change. Others point out that most practical and technical skills can be learnt on the job.
3. The functionalist approach offers a rather impersonal account of the role of education and training. It does not really address the role of schools and training courses in offering a spiritual and humanizing education.
4. It is questionable whether schools offer equality of educational opportunity as they slot students into a range of occupational positions. For example, 'bottom set' pupils are denied certain types of knowledge and experiences, which 'top set' pupils receive.
5. Occupational selection is not always based on meritocratic principles. Social background is often a major determinant, particularly in times of recession when there is an excess of highly qualified personnel.
6. It is doubtful whether all students ultimately internalize the same norms and values. This is because the educational diet of students varies according to their class, gender and ethnic background.
7. The ability of the education and training system to equip young people with practical and technical skills in the 1990s had to be queried. This is because education and training in Britain was still essentially academic, and many vocational initiatives have been judged to be of a poor quality.

(E)

## Link Exercise 8.4

This exercise takes you back to the new vocational initiatives. We would like you to use the information in Item A to elaborate on weakness number 7 above.

### Item A

**Problems with vocationalism**

Vocational qualifications have come under attack from a variety of viewpoints, arguing, often for very different reasons, that they are failing the very students they are designed to assist. From the outset, the 'parity of esteem' with academic courses that they were supposed to attract has not been achieved, for a number of reasons. One line of thought suggests that whenever vocational courses are introduced, they are 'done in a hurry', with little thought given to training needed for teachers in the new qualifications. This particular criticism has been levelled at the GNVQs, vocational A levels, Applied A levels and vocational Diplomas. The counter-criticism is that, no matter how long was given to the lead in time, opponents of vocationalism would say that it is never enough!

A more fundamental criticism concerns the targeted audience for vocational qualifications and the way that they are perceived as being 'different' from those who take traditional A levels. The argument goes that academic qualifications are not suitable for every 16–19-year-old, because not every student wants to study an academic subject as they move into adult life. However, the implication here is that traditional academic skills, such as extended writing, theoretical knowledge and higher-level skills, which are difficult, disadvantage these non-traditional students. The answer then must be to offer a different type of experience that does not involve these academic skills. Initial attempts to produce vocational qualifications therefore downgraded the amount of knowledge that was needed and relied more on non-traditional assessments such as projects and teacher-marked worked. The result was that the vocational qualifications were therefore seen as 'easier' options and did not achieve the parity of esteem that was intended. As vocational exams were made more like A levels to combat this, they disadvantaged the very students they were supposed to be attracting into education and training beyond the age of 16.

## Contemporary functionalist themes in education: the case of Faith Schools

Although Faith Schools have long been a feature of the modern education system and had their legacy in being the only providers of education to the poor in the nineteenth century, a debate has taken place in the early twenty-first century about the increasing number of different types of such schools. Functionalism's emphasis on the role of values in integrating individuals into society through the educational process has a resonance with the issue of Faith Schools, where there is a defined emphasis on the moral dimension of schooling. However, because there are many different forms of Faith School, they provide an interesting issue for exploring whether schools do provide that integrating force, or whether they can divide as well as unite. The debate about the integrative potential of different Faith Schools takes place in the context of Citizenship education, and whether Faith Schools are a help or a hindrance in promoting social harmony and the integration of citizens into a postmodern society with all its diversity (see Conroy 2009 and Exercise 8.5 on page 223).

In 2001, the government published a White Paper which said that it intended to create more state-funded Faith Schools including schools for religions 'such as Islam and Judaism'. In 2007, there were over 6,000 state-supported Faith Schools in Britain, mainly primary schools and mainly Christian, but including 37 Jewish, 2 Sikh, 7 Muslim, 1Seventh Day Adventist and 1Greek Orthodox (Walford 2008). These constitute a small but significant proportion of maintained schools in the UK. Included in this tally are two Christian Academies in the north-east of England established by Reg Vardy and allegedly basing their religious education lessons on creationism; an Islamic academy in Leicester established alongside a new Church of England academy, and partly funded by the Samworth family. The Academy programme has been used by religious bodies as a way of establishing their own schools very cheaply, as the required input from the sponsor can be delivered in kind rather than just in cash (Beckett 2007).

Sociologists in America and Australia (Glanville *et al.* 2008) have been interested in why there seems to be a correlations between religious participation and a number of 'positive developmental outcomes' in young people. These range from low rates of delinquency, high levels of psychological well-being, health enhancing behaviour and good academic performance to higher verbal ability in girls. Glanville's research points to the effect of intergenerational integration and interaction, whereby multiple generations are in constant contact and there is communication with parents having involvement in the social networks of their children and vice versa. Some of these factors could go some way to help us to understand the effect of Faith Schools in British society.

The evidence is clear that students at Faith Schools do better in terms of educational qualifications than those at mainstream comprehensive schools, Critics of Faith Schools argue that their apparent higher performance rates are related more to the selection of the intake, than the quality of teaching and values of the school community. Gillard (2007) showed that there was a social class bias in the recruitment of children to Faith Schools, with a lower proportion of students there being eligible for free school meals. When the value-added measures are considered, their success is much less clear, with only the Jewish schools performing well in this measure of educational achievement (see Schagen and Schagen 2005).

A second line of attack on Faith Schools concerns their perceived failure to integrate their members into the wider society, because they are focusing on the narrow perspective of their own faith. In some areas of the country, and in particular in London, it has been argued that Faith Schools are a way in which the white population can avoid attending schools that are populated mainly by ethnic minorities (see Dench *et al.* 2006 on Bangladeshi-dominated schools). As the social mix of Faith Schools in terms of class and ethnicity (and occasionally gender) is narrower than in mainstream schools, the argument is that they are therefore a force for division rather than integration, as proposed from a functionalist perspective. Others argue that the promotion of particular values within Faith Schools can avoid the fragmentation that the existence of different types of Faith Schools implies (Short 2003). Supporters argue that such schools develop a sense of community and belonging, which helps to integrate individuals into society.

However, the teaching of values in Faith Schools is not a straightforward issue, with commentators disagreeing on whether the values stem from a spirituality associated with the particular faith or from an agreed morality that originates in the specific schools, and often from the Principal (see Colson 2004). Colson found that the four schools he investigated had different processes for developing common values, and also differed to the extent to which they permeated aspects of school life, from admissions policies to sex education lessons. Each of the four Principals did not see external forces as being significant in the development of the school's values, which suggests that any integrative role of such schools is not derived from a societal view, but from an individualistic one.

Another concern is that one-faith schools might promote religious and other forms of intolerance. There is little evidence that Faith Schools promote views that other religions are by their difference wrong or evil. On the contrary, the fact that religious education is taken seriously, even with a strong denominational emphasis, has been cited as a factor in attracting students of different or no faiths into them (see Colson 2004). On the other hand, Gillard (2007) argues that, by imposing a particular form of collective worship on the students and putting forward a particular agenda, Faith Schools essentially deny students their human rights. The crux issue here is the attitude of faith-based schools towards homosexuality. The bitter debate in the Anglican Church about the role of gay clergy illustrates the potential for isolating and stigmatising gay people, even in caring institutions (see Garrod and Jones 2009). As one of the core beliefs of the book-based religions is the wrongness of homosexuality, then faith schools might find it difficult to integrate their gay students into the school, never mind the wider society. Rather than performing an integrative function for gay young people, they may act and teach in ways that present homosexuals as outsiders.

A related criticism is aimed at the ways in which religious teaching may distort or even undermine the curriculum, and here the issue of creationism is at the forefront The debate about the teaching of creationism or its offshoot, intelligent design, is more heated in the USA than in the UK. Notably, the city academies established by Reg Vardy have a creationist agenda. While they have to follow the national curriculum and teach evolution, it is the way that it is taught by creationist scientists that has provoked controversy. In terms of functionalist argument, it is the conflict between two world-views that suggests the integrative role of Faith Schools is minimal.

There have been other conflicts about the role of religion in education in relation to religious observance, the expression of religious values and attitudes and religious dress in mainstream non-faith schools. An important case arose in 2002 when a student from a Luton school, Shabina Begum, who wanted to wear traditional full-length jilbab Muslim dress at school and was sent home as she had disobeyed the school's uniform policy. She took her case to the High Court and initially won the case that her human rights has been infringed but on appeal the school's case was upheld, with the court declaring that the school had 'a legitimate aim which was the proper running of a multi-cultural, multi-faith, secular school' (*Guardian*, 15 June 2004).

(E)

## Exercise 8.5

What are the advantages and disadvantages of Faith Schools for the individual and society? Complete the table below. A suggestion for each has been completed to help you get started.

|  | Advantages | Disadvantages |
|---|---|---|
| **Individual** | Helps to define and foster a sense of personal identity | Groups cut off or isolated from mainstream education and society. |
| **Society** | **Advantages** Integrates individuals into society by valuing different types of religious belief and expression | **Disadvantages** Could bring out isolation from the wider society and/or hostility or intolerance to those who hold values or attitudes perceived to be a variance with dominant group(s). |

| Important concepts |
| --- |
| meritocracy • allocation role • socialization • human capital theory |

## Critical thinking

1. How might the allocation role of education apply to modern society and the qualifications currently available in schools and colleges?
2. Do functionalists offer an overly positive view of the nature of education given the levels of 'failure' in the system?
3. Compare and contrast the perspectives of the New Right and postmodernism, and consider their relationship to traditional functionalism.

*Chapter 9*

# Conflict and Postmodern Explanations of the Role of Education and Training

By the end of this chapter you should:

- appreciate that the socialization role of schools and training programmes can be seen in a negative light
- be familiar with Marxist views on the allocation role of education and training
- understand conflict interpretations of the vocational role of education
- be able to assess Marxist approaches to the role of education and training
- understand postmodern approaches to education
- have reflected on student answers to an exam question
- have practised a structured exam question yourself

## INTRODUCTION

Conflict theory covers a range of modern approaches to sociological issues, all of which accept that the basic characteristic of societies is the conflict between different groups within them. Conflict explanations of the role of education and training cover similar ground to the functionalist explanations we considered in Chapter 8. Thus they are concerned with examining the way in which the socialization, allocation and vocational roles of schools and training courses perform economic functions for societies. However, unlike functionalist explanations, which offer a positive analysis of education and training, conflict theorists offer a pessimistic analysis. It is maintained that schools and training programmes do not serve the interests of everyone in society, but only those of a ruling minority. Feminist sociologists reflect on the way in which education and training shapes gender identities and aspirations, through socialisation and rewards, and allocates students and trainees on the basis of gender rather than merit or ability. Weberian sociologists share similar concerns. They give consideration to the way in which education and training socializes students into distinct status cultures, and the way in which role allocation is based on class and status rather than meritocratic criteria. Postmodern theories criticize the 'modernist' stance of both functionalist and conflict theories.

The first part of this chapter addresses the ideas of Marxist sociologists. Marxist theorists tend to focus on the ways in which education and training can be seen to maintain capitalism by reproducing the class system and legitimising unequal class relations. Exactly how schools and training courses function to serve the needs of capitalist societies in this way will be explored through a consideration of three roles:

1. The socialization role.
2. The allocation role.
3. The vocational training role.

Each of these roles will now be examined in turn.

## THE SOCIALIZATION ROLE

Marxist sociologists share with functionalist sociologists the belief that schools and training schemes transmit norms and values that create social stability in society. However, whereas functionalists believe that this stability is based on the internalisation of socially 'agreed' norms and values that benefit everyone, Marxists believe it is based on the internalization of dominant ideologies that benefit only a ruling minority. This Marxist position is taken by structural Marxists such as Althusser (1972) and Bowles and Gintis (1976). The important concept employed by structural Marxists is 'ideology'. Ideologies in this sense are ideas that serve the interests of a particular social group and have a 'real' existence; that is, they are not just ideas, but have a material form in the practices and processes of institutions. So a dominant ideology would be one that shaped (or, more strongly, in Marxist terms, determined) the experiences and activities of people in the major institutions of society.

Therefore Althusser sees the education system as part of the ideological apparatus of the state. He claims that education, along with other ideological state apparatuses such as the family, reproduce class-based systems of inequality by creating the belief that capitalist social arrangements are in some way 'just', 'normal', 'natural', and so on. It is the fact that new generations of workers perceive the capitalist system to be 'fair' and 'inevitable' that prevents the system from being challenged, and hence it reproduces itself. Therefore dominant ideologies are absorbed by individuals through their experiences in the important structures of society, such as the education system. The effect of the activities of the ideological state apparatus is to reproduce social relations, so that, for example, the sons and daughters of the working class tend to remain in the working class themselves, while ensuring that the members of the working class acquire a 'false consciousness' by accepting the inequality that disadvantages them.

We shall now examine three ways in which Marxists believe that education systems ensure social acquiescence and cultural reproduction.

## The ideas that are taught

Structural Marxists argue that the formal content of schooling ensures that young people come to accept the status quo. For example, in subjects such as economics, students come to internalize dominant capitalist ideology through learning about such concepts as competition and the profit motive. These concepts are taken for granted and are presented as 'natural phenomena'. Students in schools therefore rarely come into contact with ways of thinking that challenge the existing social order. For example, only a minority of students leave school having learnt about Marxism, feminism, communism, and so on. However, before the introduction of the national curriculum it was difficult to identify the mechanisms by which the formal content of schooling could be controlled by the capitalist class. The dominant ideology amongst educationalists following the Second World War seemed to be some kind of social democracy, in which the curriculum in a school would be settled locally, allowing minority subjects such as peace studies or world studies to gain at least a foothold in the classroom. Moreover, curriculum policies with an egalitarian (making equal) emphasis, such as anti-sexist or anti-racist initiatives, were also allowed to flourish in a school system where curriculum decisions were decentralized.

Theorists of the New Right, represented by think tanks such as the Hillgate group or the Adam Smith Institute (see Whitty 1989), argue that control of the curriculum by teachers and educationalists prior to the Education Reform Act of 1988 led to a lack of accountability in curriculum design, and this allowed left-wing curriculum initiatives such as peace studies to appear in schools.

They therefore argued that there should be state intervention and standardisation of the curriculum throughout the country. This was a reversal of the traditional position of the New Right, which had previously argued for less rather than more state intervention. The implication of central control of the curriculum, by the Department for Children, Schools and Families, and the Qualifications and Curriculum Authority, is that the formal curriculum of all schools is determined by agents of the government and is therefore less open to subversion by 'progressive' teachers.

For example Goodson (1990) argues that the national curriculum is an attempt to reconstruct a national identity for Britain, which has been undermined by the globalization of economic activity. It is argued that computerization and the growth of global communications through fibre-optic and satellite communications has significantly weakened the importance of national boundaries as a source of identity. The re-establishment of traditional subjects, with traditional content, in the national curriculum is therefore an attempt by the government to isolate what is seen as 'progressive' educational subject matter and reaffirm a curriculum that asserts a British or even an English identity. This can be see in the predominance of British history in the provisions of the history elements of the national curriculum and in insistence on the centrality of Shakespeare in the core subject of English.

However, New Right sociologists have pointed out that control of the curriculum by the government is not total and does allow teachers some independence in determining what goes on in their classrooms. Indeed, the government argues that the national curriculum is only a framework that encompasses the two cross-curricular dimensions of equal opportunities between the genders and ethnic minorities. However, as Arnot (1991) points out, equal opportunities can only be built into schemes of work that achieve the targets, assessment objectives and content of the government-determined national curriculum. Nor is there any funding for curriculum innovations that do not meet the criteria laid down by the government. Therefore, it could be concluded that the formal curriculum is now more firmly under the direction of those who support the capitalist status quo (complete Link exercise 9.1 below to assist you in understanding this point).

Ⓘ Ⓐ
## Link Exercise 9.1

Explain how the introduction of the national curriculum in 1988 ensured that 'left-wing' ideas and thinking did not creep into the formal curriculum. (Hint: Think about some of the subjects that were omitted.)

## The values, attitudes and personality traits instilled

Structural Marxists such as Althusser, and Bowles and Gintis, maintain that schools create social compliance through a hidden or unofficial curriculum. They argue that schools socialize students into certain values, attitudes and personality traits that 'fit' the interests of dominant social classes and capitalist ways of working. This instilling of values and attitudes may be overt in certain subjects such as religious instruction, but it is more effective in the subtle and hidden ways in which values are transmitted (carry out Exercise 9.1 below to explore this idea). The values may be obvious, such as a stress on punctuality, which has a clear message for future workers. Or the values may be less directly linked to the world of work, but powerful for all that. An important area of debate concerning the transmission of values has been the teaching styles, or pedagogy, adopted by schools. Marxists would argue that schools create docile workers by giving working-class children few opportunities for independent work, while private schools offer more responsibility for their own learning to the children of the upper class.

The debate concerning teaching styles is based on two stereotypes of the way teachers work. The first is 'traditional' education, which has the image of a disciplined, didactic (teacher talking, student listening) approach, in which the expert teacher transmits his or her knowledge to the attentive student. This 'revelatory model' (a style in which knowledge is revealed to the next generation) is often presented as the way effective education was achieved in the past. The second stereotype is the 'progressive' model, in which teachers and students set out together to discover knowledge for themselves, with the student having much more control over the topics she or he wishes to pursue. Ironically, the private sector is associated with the 'traditional' model and the comprehensive sector with the 'progressive' model. The problem for the Marxist is that, if the models are taught where they are said to be taught, then it is middle-class and working-class children who receive the independent mode of learning, and upper-class children who are more passive in their education. However, Marxists argue that these are stereotypes that do not correspond to what happens in the real world, in which private-school students are required to develop an independent frame of mind through academic research, while children of the working class are much more controlled in their schooling than the progressive stereotype would imply.

### Postmodernist responses

Many postmodern sociologists, among others, have been critical of the idea that there is only one right way to teach. They point out that a single pedagogical route to educational success, whether traditional or progressive, is unlikely to be successful. This is in tune with the postmodernist distrust of 'metanarrative'; that is, any 'story' that tries to explain everything in a world that is fractured, contradictory and inconsistent. For example, a traditional style of pedagogy adopted in Canada and the USA – 'direct instruction' – has been criticized because it is effective only in certain situations; for example, when it is used to teach basic skills (see Hallinger and Murphy 1987). A negative effect of 'direct instruction' is that it leads to dependency and a lack of initiative among students, precisely the qualities that Marxists say the education system promotes in working-class children (see Smyth and Garman 1989).

Similarly, postmodernists argue that more student-centred techniques are not just about empowering individual students in schools. On the contrary, students taking responsibility for their own learning can be viewed as an increase in the surveillance and regulatory activities of schools (see Usher and Edwards 1994). Discipline in the student-centred model is not imposed externally by teachers. Rather, it is composed of self-discipline, so that any educational failure comes to be seen as the result of the individual failing, rather than resources not being provided or disadvantage not being addressed.

Postmodernists therefore argue for multiple models of teaching, which draw upon the experience of teachers and pupils in the classroom, and are not just based on the expertise of 'scientific' researchers (see Hargreaves 1994).

Marxists such as Aronowitz and Giroux (1991) have been influenced by postmodernism in approaching this issue of teaching styles. They begin by moving away from the economic determinism associated with Marxists such as Althusser, and examine the role of teachers as active agents in the education process. They are following the traditional concerns of Marxists by looking primarily at the working class, but rather than merely identifying how the working class is dominated by capitalist ideology in the education system, they are concerned with developing alternative ways of teaching that could transform working-class lives and lead to the empowerment of the working class. They arrive at the concept of 'border pedagogy', whereby teachers are recruited to transform the prospects of working-class children in schools through a different type of teaching, in which social progress and resistance to dominant ideologies are central. In later work, Giroux (1994) argues for a 'post-Marxist' approach to sociological issues and identifies the pedagogies that would effect the transformation of the working class that he seeks.

Giroux therefore argues that border pedagogy should seek to cross the borders of traditional education 'narratives' such as the standard English Literature texts and seek to demonstrate to students that, for example, history is never certain but rather that it is socially constructed, or that the works of literature are situated in specific historical and ideological settings. He uses the concept of the postmodernists in suggesting that texts should be 'decentred'; that is, understood in their historical and social context rather than just read as 'literature'. In terms of pedagogy, Giroux argues that students and teachers should be much more involved in designing their courses, and that teachers should use a variety of teaching styles, including giving more responsibility to the students for their own learning. In developing 'democratic' practices in schools, Giroux is suggesting that working-class students would be empowered and more able to control their own lives within a capitalist system. He believes that the adoption of border pedagogy would change the extent of social class inequality in Britain (see Chapter 4).

However, Giroux and Aronowitz have both been criticized for assuming that teachers would be willing to adopt border pedagogy, and that students would be open to and influenced by the new classroom strategies (see Lynch and O'Neill 1994). Lynch (1990) argues that teachers are part of the state apparatus, and are therefore unlikely to adopt Giroux's border pedagogy. Nor is it likely that teachers would have the freedom to introduce such a radical pedagogy, especially with the increasing central control of education that began in Britain during the 1980s. Moreover, students have shown themselves to be highly resistant to classroom strategies that do not seem to be immediately relevant (see Hannan and Shorthall 1991). They respond to pragmatic and instrumental strategies directly related to the local labour market, rather than strategies linked to concepts such as liberation or empowerment.

(A)
## Exercise 9.1

Explain how the hidden curriculum operating inside schools or training schemes may instill the values of (i) obedience; (ii) punctuality; and (iii) acceptance of authority. (Hint: Think about the positive and negative sanctions that schools employ on a day-to-day basis.)

## The ways in which educational institutions are organized

Bowles and Gintis (1976) contend that the structural organization of educational institutions, as an aspect of the hidden curriculum, has the effect of making young people accept the existing social order. Studying schooling in capitalist America, these Marxist sociologists claim that the internal organisation of schools corresponds to the internal organization of the capitalist workplace. There is thus a 'correspondence principle' operating, in which the experiences of young people in schools is a direct preparation for their experiences in work. Hence, working-class children experience schools as systems of control, in which they are taught the aptitudes and attitudes necessary for low-skill, routinised work. Working-class children are therefore subject to a strict hierarchical control that corresponds to the type of control they will experience in their working lives. On the other hand, middle-class children, it is argued, experience a less formally controlled educational environment, in which they are encouraged to take responsibility for their own learning and to acquire independence of mind rather than the habit of obedience. This hidden curriculum of school organization has the effect of legitimating inequality. So Bowles and Gintis argue that, in the USA at least, schools do not perform the democratic function of promoting the personal development of all children. Nor do they promote equality of opportunity. On the contrary, the organization of schools mirrors the organization of a hierarchical and autocratic industrial system, in which workers are expected to obey without question. If working-class students are alienated by their experiences in schools, then this is also preparation for their experiences in work.

However, this aspect of the work of Bowles and Gintis has suffered a great deal of criticism. Brown and Lauder (1991) argue that there has never been a simple correspondence between the education system and the needs of the economy, as suggested by Bowles and Gintis. Rather, the education system performs several different functions for society, not all of which are economic. For example, Brown (1990) suggests that what he calls the 'first wave' of education in the nineteenth century was more to do with a way of differentiating between the elite and the masses, than with the needs of the early capitalist economy. Moreover, the correspondence principle assumes that those who experience the 'hidden messages' of the organization of the school interpret them (or, in post-modern terminology, decode the messages) in a particular way. It seems highly unlikely that participants in the education system will all 'read' the messages of hierarchy in exactly the same way.

Michael Apple (1982, 1986) developed the work of Bowles and Gintis by examining the hidden curriculum in terms of the role of teachers. He suggests that teachers are being proletarianized, as they are deskilled through the introduction of standardized curriculum packages, and that the profession is becoming feminized. This has the effect of increasing state control over teachers and defining more tightly how they carry out their functions. He is not arguing that teachers are like automatons, with no power of resistance; he believes that schools are sites of struggle, and that both teachers and pupils resist the reproductive processes to which they are subjected. Indeed, Apple argues that the education system has 'relative autonomy', which allows this resistance to express itself. However, the end result is, according to Apple, the reproduction of inequalities.

He also argues that the formal curriculum is class-biased, the reproduction of high-status academic knowledge being a priority in the schooling of those who are not poor or part of a minority. Moreover, when analysing school text-books, Apple argues that the the formal curriculum of schools neglects social conflict and distorts the causes and consequences of conflict, which contributes to the ideological reproduction of capitalism. This approach is supported in the work of Anyon (1981) who, having looked at five schools, argues that what counted as knowledge in these schools varied according to their social class basis, with working-class schools being dominated by a low-status curriculum content. However, Ramsay (1983), in a larger survey of schools, found a great deal of variation among working-class schools, and as Hannan and Boyle (1987) demonstrated, the management and attitudes of teachers can make a difference in determining the ethos of a working-class school, so that not all working-class schools prepare their students for failure.

Ⓐ

## Exercise 9.2

This is the first of two exercises aimed at helping you to appreciate the way in which educational experiences correspond with work experiences. Your task for Exercise 9.2 is to identify the hierarchical systems of authority and control that exist in schools and the workplace. Make sure that you pair off equivalent occupational positions. The top and bottom rungs of the school and workplace hierarchies have been given below to get you started. You should finish with about six different levels in total.

### Hierarchical systems of control

| School | Work |
| --- | --- |
| Headteacher | Managing director |
| Cleaners | Cleaners |

Ⓐ

## Exercise 9.3

This exercise is designed to get you to consider a number of other similarities that exist between school and work. Your job here is to identify the missing correspondences between school and work, and to fill in the gaps.

| School | Work |
|---|---|
| **Ordinary workers have little or no control** | |
| | Workers follow orders. They do not have a say in what goods are made or how they are made. |
| **Acceptance of alienation** | |
| School work; rarely done for its own sake, but for ulterior motives; for example, to gain praise or good qualifications. | |
| **Fragmentation** | |
| The curriculum is broken down and divided into separate 'subjects'. The school day is also fragmented. | |
| **The principle that those with different talents and aptitudes require different rewards** | |
| | The different layers of jobs (managerial, supervisory, skilled, semi-skilled, manual, unskilled) are rewarded differently by varying pay, conditions, etc. |

## THE ALLOCATION ROLE

Marxists share with functionalists the belief that education and training serve to allocate people to or select people for distinct occupational positions. However, the optimistic assumptions that underlie the functionalist theory of role allocation (see Chapter 7) are hotly disputed by Marxists such as Althusser (1972) and Bowles and Gintis (1976). There are three points that Marxists make regarding role allocation by the education system:

1. The education system does not offer equality of educational opportunity.
2. Role allocation is not conducted within a meritocratic framework.
3. Education offers limited opportunities for social mobility.

### The education system does not offer equality of educational opportunity

Marxists make this claim on two levels. First, equality of access does not exist. It is argued that all students do not have the same opportunity to study at schools that offer an equivalent education. For example, the high fees of private schools debar the vast majority of working-class students from attending them (see Chapter 2 for further details). Since the late 1980s, the governments of Britain and the USA, have pursued policies of open enrolment and parental choice in an attempt to empower all 'parent-consumers' of education, and make the education system more responsive to parental needs. Evidence has suggested that these policies do lead to changes in the recruitment patterns of schools, but to the detriment of working-class children. For example, Moore (1990) shows that in the USA the more popular schools have become 'colonized' by better-off parents, and that children from less well-off families have become concentrated in other schools. This is because better-off families are more knowledgeable about how to operate the system to their own advantage, as well as having the means and mobility to move to areas with popular schools. Also, as Edwards and Whitty (1992) show, popular schools begin to select their pupils on the basis of academic ability, upon which their popularity depends, thus creating a 'two-tier system' in which working-class children are concentrated in the less popular schools.

Second, within the state sector of schooling, pupils are not treated equally. Here, Marxists draw on a wide body of evidence to suggest that working-class students are 'cooled' out of the educational system. For example, they make reference to the fact that many teachers hold low expectations of the working class, and that this has a damaging, self-fulfilling prophecy effect on working-class pupils (see Chapter 4 for further details). Aronowitz and Giroux (1991) argue that any working-class pupils that do 'get on' in the education system have to abandon their working-class attitudes, thoughts and actions and become socially mobile. Success in higher education necessitates a change in class identity.

## Role allocation is not conducted within a meritocratic framework

Marxists argue that educational and occupational success is based on social class rather than merit. The process of cultural reproduction works against the meritocratic ideology that surrounds schooling in capitalist societies and ensures that working-class children get working-class jobs, if they get a job at all. The statistics of educational 'success' and 'failure' show that working-class children under-achieve in the education system compared with their middle-class counterparts, and this is a result, in part at least, of the non-meritocratic nature of the education system. According to the Marxists, therefore, the problem facing the education system is how to offer greater equality of opportunity to meet the demand from capitalist corporations for workers with certain skills, while limiting the aspirations of the majority of working-class children. Brown and Lauder (1991) argue that the concept of IQ has been used by the education system to detect 'talent' early in a child's life and to select socially on the basis of class by an apparently 'objective' criterion. The result of IQ testing, according to Evans and Waites (1981) is to further the interests of middle-class children while minimizing working-class resistance to an unfair system.

### Education offers limited opportunities for social mobility

This argument is advanced because of the belief that equality of educational opportunity is not offered in schools and because capitalist societies are not meritocratic. Thus the ideology of meritocracy is a powerful force for preserving the status quo and preventing a truly meritocratic society. Capitalist societies are not meritocratic, because the capitalist system confers huge advantages on those who own and control the means of production, and thus can ensure that the system operates to their own and their children's benefit.

Moreover, the situation has not improved over time. Research by the Sutton Trust (2005) suggested that social mobility in the UK has 'stalled'. Thus those born in 1958 had a greater chance of exceeding the income of their parents than those born after 1970. Since 1970, there has been no improvement at all. The proportion of children gaining 5 or more grade A\*–C GCSEs is closely related to the social class of the parents, and therefore also to social mobility or the lack of it. The Youth Cohort Study (DCSF 2002) data are shown in Table 9.1.

Therefore Marxists maintain that schools and training programmes not only reproduce class inequalities but legitimate them as well. That is to say, they make them seem natural or in some way inevitable. It is argued

**Table 9.1** Children gaining five or more grade A\*–C GCSEs, by social class of parents, 2002 (percentages)

| Parents' social class | Percentage |
| --- | --- |
| Higher professionals | 77 |
| Lower professionals | 64 |
| Intermediate | 52 |
| Lower supervisory | 35 |
| Routine | 32 |

that this ideological role of education and training is achieved by spreading various myths about the 'openness' of the system of role allocation. For example, schools and training schemes create the belief that educational and occupational attainment is based on merit. Thus individuals and social groupings come to accept that those in powerful positions have got there by ability and effort, while those in subordinate positions only have themselves to blame because of lack of talent or effort (to check your understanding of this aspect of Marxist theory, do Exercise 9.4 below).

## Exercise 9.4

Below is a partly completed paragraph that summarizes the Marxist view of role allocation. Copy out the paragraph and fill in the missing words by selecting appropriate words from the list provided.

From a Marxist point of view, schools and training courses serve to......people for jobs. However, the education and training system does not offer......of......opportunity, nor does it operate under......principles, and it does not act as a route for......Schooling actually depresses the......and lowers the aspiration levels of......students. In this way, working-class pupils are......out of the education system. It is almost as if they are supposed to......so that they can take up......'blue-collar' positions. The net result of the role allocation function of schools and training programmes is to......the social class.......

### Missing words

- mobility • class • fail • appropriate • meritocratic
- social • structure • equality • sifted • educational
- talents • reproduce • working • allocate

## Link Exercise 9.2

This exercise is almost identical to one you carried out in Chapter 8. You are required to draw up a chart along the same lines as that in Link exercise 8.2, but this time as it applies to the Marxist role allocation theory. You should begin by copying out the chart provided and then complete it according to the following instructions. There is no need to define the key terms as this has been done previously.

1. Use the material you have read in this chapter to establish the underlying theoretical assumptions of the Marxist theory of role allocation.
2. Use information from Chapters 2 and 3 to explain how various educational policies have served to create a closed society.
3. Making use of the internet, identify several pieces of empirical evidence to support the Marxist assumptions that the education system does not offer equality of educational opportunity; that role allocation is not conducted within a meritocratic framework; and that education offers limited opportunities for social mobility.

| Marxism | Equality of educational opportunity | Meritocracy | Social mobility |
|---|---|---|---|
| Underlying theoretical assumption | | | |
| The negative effect of educational policies: creating a 'closed' society | | | |
| Empirical evidence in support of the Marxist views | | | |

## THE VOCATIONAL TRAINING ROLE

We have seen (in Chapter 8) that the functionalists view the vocational training role of schools in a positive light, arguing that schools provide the skills and work habits that industry requires to function efficiently. Marxists have a different view of this vocational function. Structural Marxists, such as Althusser (1972), do not see schools transmitting a range of practical skills to the workers of the future. Rather, they see education providing working-class children with only basic numeracy and literacy, to enable them to perform the routine and boring jobs they will eventually obtain. This is because Marxists such as Bowles and Gintis (1976) see schools as institutions of social control, rather than as meritocratic or empowering. Conflict theorists such as Paul Willis (1977) have developed this idea by looking at the experiences of working-class boys as they move into the world of work. Willis charts how the 'lads' are involved in preparing for their own future exploitation by employers, and how schools equip these boys with appropriate attitudes towards boring, routine work. Therefore Marxists tend to see vocational preparation in wider 'thought control' terms than do the functionalists.

However, two issues need to be addressed with regard to this vocational role and the relationship between education and society. The first concerns the concept of 'skill' and how schools prepare their pupils for the world of work. Marxists tend to see the development of the capitalist economy in terms of deskilling (see Braverman 1974). By this they mean that, as technology develops under the impetus of cost-saving policies of capitalist enterprises, it tends to result in an increasing loss of skill by both manual and non-manual workers. This results in the ever-intensifying exploitation of workers who, with the loss of their skills, lose much of their power in negotiations with employers. Thus the education system, according to the Marxists, only has to provide workers with the basic skills needed for low-level work.

However, there has been a great deal of debate about deskilling, and whether technological development inevitably means that skills are taken away from the workforce. For example, Thompson (1983) argues that Braverman has exaggerated the extent and significance of deskilling by promoting an idealized view of a skilled workforce in the past. Moreover, postmodernists have argued that the development of new technologies has had a fragmentary effect on the skills of the labour force rather than the uniform effect suggested by Marxists. For example, Harvey (1989) argues that postmodern industry demands different types of workers in flexible labour markets. First, there are the 'core' workers, who have full-time, permanent status and the prospect of being reskilled as technology advances. 'Peripheral' workers are of two types: full-time workers with skills that are readily available in the labour market – for example, clerical skills; and low-skill, part-time, casual workers. Therefore it is not just deskilling that occurs under modern capitalism, but reskilling also, and education systems in the postmodern world will have to deliver workers that are differentiated by their levels of skill.

The second issue concerns the relationship between education and the economy. Marxists see the education system as a means of reproduction; that is, as one of the ways capitalist relations of production are maintained from one generation to the next. Vocationalism in schools is seen as an important aspect of this reproduction, because, for example, new vocationalism (see Chapter 3) seeks to identify the needs of capitalist industry for certain types of labour power, and to develop the educational courses that will meet those needs (see Hodgkinson 1991). However, Marxists such as Bowles and Gintis (1976) argue for a positive and direct relationship (or correspondence) between education and the economy, in which educational change is determined by the needs of the economy.

Other Marxists follow Althusser (1972) in arguing that the education system is 'relatively autonomous'. This means that the state gives it some freedom from the economic requirements of capitalism, but ultimately education does have to fulfil the needs of capitalist industry. Other sociologists, such as Moore (1988), argue that there is no correspondence at all between education and industry, but rather they are autonomous (free-standing) social formations.

Brown and Lauder (1991) argue that there has never been a simple relationship between education and the economy as the Marxists suggest, and call for a new relationship to be forged between them in the light of technological and industrial change. They believe that Britain should be aiming for a high-skill rather than a low-skill economy, and therefore education should be based on the idea that all rather than just a few are capable of significant practical and academic achievements. This involves the creation of a high-trust education system, which will empower students by providing a high-ability education system for all, and what they call the 'power tools' of confidence and analytical skill. This will enable all students to interpret the wealth of information available in the globalized information market of the postmodern world.

## Link Exercise 9.3

Many of the Marxist ideas you have read about above on the vocational training role of schools also apply to training initiatives outside the school environment. For example, many left-wing writers are critical of Youth Training (YT). It is argued that not only does YT often fail to equip trainees with 'transferable skills', but it also reproduces the capitalist status quo. Your task for this exercise is to use the material you read in Chapter 3 on YT to elaborate on the Marxist position on this scheme. You should try to build on the table we have started for you below.

| Reasons why YT often fails to equip trainees with 'transferable skills' | Reasons why YT reproduces the capitalist status quo |
| --- | --- |
| 1. High trainee/staff ratios | 1. A source of cheap labour |
| 2. Too much working and not enough training | 2. |
| 3. | 3. |
| 4. | 4. |
| 5. | 5. |

## An evaluation of the Marxist approach to the role of education and training

(A)
(E)

This exercise is similar to the one you carried out for the evaluation of the functionalist approach to education and training in Chapter 7. You have to identify whether the strength or weakness is specific to the Marxist views on socialisation, allocation or vocational training, or whether it is a general strength or weakness of the Marxist approach to education and training.

We have again completed one of the answers to help you get started.

Strengths:

1. The approach recognizes that the education system is shaped by structural factors – the economic infrastructure of society. Recent evidence would support this view; for example, the national curriculum and the new vocational initiatives have been 'shaped' by the government and industry. Furthermore, as more schools opt out of Local Education Authorities, so the control of education by the state and industry increases.
2. Much empirical evidence exists to support the claim that schools 'cool' or depress the talents of working-class students. Empirical evidence also suggests that occupational position and reward is often based on social background and not on ability.
3. The effect of powerful ideologies is recognized.
4. The approach offers a useful challenge to New Right thinking on vocational education. This is because the negative aspects of vocational education are addressed.

Weaknesses:

1. It offers an over-socialized view of humankind. It is highly questionable whether students internalize the hidden curriculum, as described by Bowles and Gintis, and Althusser. Even Marxists such as Willis are doubtful. Willis's 'lads', you will remember, resisted school and were far from obedient, docile and disciplined.
2. The explanations are too class-based – they lack a gender and ethnicity focus.
3. The approach can often be 'blind' to any evidence that suggests that society is becoming more open and meritocratic. *(A weakness, as it applies to allocation.)*
4. The positive achievements of new vocational courses in raising skill levels and individuals' control over the work process are often ignored.

ⒾⒶ **Link Exercise 9.4**

This exercise is designed to develop your interpretation and identification skills. Use material from Chapters 8 and 9 to identify the similarities and differences between the functionalist and Marxist views on education and training (make sure you cover each of the three roles they talk about.) Record your answers in a chart similar to the one we have started off for you below.

**Similarities between functionalist and Marxist views on education and training**

| Socialization | Allocation | Vocational training |
|---|---|---|
| 1. Schools and training programmes instil norms and values via the formal and hidden curriculum. | | |
| 2. | | |

**Differences between functionalist and Marxist views on education and training**

| Socialization | Allocation | Vocational training |
|---|---|---|
| 1. | | |
| 2. | | |

## POSTMODERN PERSPECTIVES ON THE SOCIOLOGY OF EDUCATION

The perspectives we have discussed so far, both functionalist and conflict, can be classified as modernist in nature. Modernism here refers to particular ways of thinking about knowledge and society that have their origins in the Enlightenment of the sixteenth and seventeenth centuries and beyond. The Enlightenment, often associated with modernism, is characterized by a belief that humankind can obtain demonstrably valid knowledge of the world, and that this knowledge can be used to improve the human condition. For example, if the causes of educational underachievement can be discovered objectively using social scientific methods then this knowledge can be used to reduce or eliminate educational under-achievement. Schools, from this point of view, represent important mechanisms whereby knowledge is transmitted from one generation to the next. In recent years, education and its role in society has been both critically analysed and reformulated from a postmodern perspective. In order to examine the specific contribution of postmodernism to educational debates we shall begin with a detailed description of the education system from a modernist position.

## Modernism and education

Modernist forms of education are typical of Western societies. Education according to modernity would free people from superstition by spreading rational and scientific thinking and a belief in progress. To modernists, as we have seen, it is possible to obtain valid knowledge of the world. Obviously, human beings are not born with this knowledge; it takes time to acquire it, and schools play an important part in that process. Teachers are seen as the repositories of the knowledge that children need, as experts in maths, science, languages, history, geography, social morals and values and so on, and it is their job to ensure that children learn these things through the course of their school careers. In other words, for modernism, education is something that is 'done' by adults (teachers/schools) to children in a relatively hierarchical and authoritarian manner. Adults in school determine codes of conduct for pupils – what they should know, and by what age they should know it.

It follows that modernism implies a particular approach to children and childhood. Childhood is a developmental process, a process of becoming an adult, and comprises a number of elements. First, it is a biological process, a process of physically growing and maturing; second, it is a socialization process whereby children learn about and internalize the cultural norms and values of society; third, it is an educational process through which both core and specialist knowledge is taught, as expressed in the national curriculum, for example; and fourth, it is a nurturing process through which children's physical and emotional needs are met (explore this further in Exercise 9.6 below). This view of childhood is constantly affirmed and reaffirmed through daily interaction within schools and indeed the wider community, and it provides justification for how the education system is organized.

---

(A)
(E)

### Exercise 9.6

What ways can you think of to illustrate how the modernist approach to the four aspects of childhood is reflected in education and educational practices within schools? Try to use your experiences of being at school which could be examples of this – for example, rules regarding how pupils should behave towards one another, or those regarding punctuality might illustrate the socialization process.

- The biological process.
- The socialisation process.
- The educational process.
- The nurturing process.

If we briefly revisit the functionalist and Marxist perspectives already discussed, we can see that, despite their fundamental differences, both can be seen to share the modernist view of education and childhood outlined above (carry out Exercise 9.7 below to confirm this).

For functionalists, the essence of society is a moral order, and schools are an essential part of its establishment and continuity. Any society is (or should be) an efficient and stable system – all parts, including education, working together to promote harmony. Similarly, childhood is seen as a process through which the next generation becomes social in the full meaning of the term; that is, fully integrated members of society. For Marxists, on the other hand, education ultimately serves the interests of a ruling, capitalist class. This is because schools produce and reproduce the skills needed by employees to carry out production. In addition, they ensure the transmission of the ideology of capitalism, including an acceptance of and respect for ownership, 'freedom', good time-keeping and so on. In this case, childhood is seen as a process through which the next generation becomes 'pro-capitalist' in the full meaning of the term – accepting and agreeing with capitalist ideology and values.

## Exercise 9.7

Write down a list of similarities showing how functionalism and Marxism share a modernist view of both education and childhood.

### Poststructuralism and postmodernism – the role of language in social life

Poststructuralism and postmodernism differ in their approach and focus in understanding society. The former is concerned primarily with cultural meanings and why those meanings might be thought to be unstable and oppressive. Postmodernism, on the other hand, is applied much more broadly, to include, for example, economic issues such as patterns of consumption, developments in culture and identity, the role of the media, the nature of community, education, changes in architectural styles and the rejection of science. However, despite these important differences, poststructuralism and postmodernism tend to share a common philosophical position with respect to the role of language in social life. For this reason, the term postmodernism will be used in what follows to incorporate both the poststructural and postmodern approaches.

As a perspective or theory, postmodernism can be difficult to pin down, and indeed there is a range of quite diverse approaches that have attracted a postmodern label. However, in general terms, the popularity of postmodernism has been associated with a particular view of the role of language in social life – a view that has resulted in scepticism regarding enlightenment principles, and therefore our ability to generate social scientific knowledge based on objective proof.

The postmodern view of the role of language is as follows. The distinctive characteristic of *social* life is that it is meaningful. We socially construct a set of meanings which give sense to our actions and interactions with others within a linguistic and cultural context. All social life is, according to postmodernists, dependent on language. That is not to say that there is no physical dimension to our everyday lives – we need only to attempt to pass through a doorway without first opening the door to realize that is the case! However, society is social only in so far as it has a symbolic existence, in so far as it is meaningful for its members, and meaning resides solely in language. For writers such as Foucault, Derrida and Baudrillard, though different in their theoretical contributions, society is essentially a linguistic construction. Because society has no objective existence, because it exists only in and through language, so it follows that there can be no objective, scientific knowledge of social reality. Instead, we are left with relativism – the idea that, since social reality is essentially constructed, all constructions have equal merit. It is simply not possible to say, as the modernists would wish, that some versions of events are objectively more valid or accurate than others.

A different but related postmodern argument focuses on the claims of social science itself. A belief in social science has its origins in the modern period and, as we have seen, incorporates the idea that we can explain social structures and processes, and that we can demonstrate the validity of our explanations through proof. Sociological theories such as Marxism, Feminism and Functionalism are modernist in this sense. As we know, however, each of these theories describes the nature of society very differently: Marxists talk about class, conflict and exploitation; feminists emphasize gender and patriarchy; while functionalists refer to the conditions for consensus and order. Because we cannot experience or observe structures and processes directly, however, it is impossible to say which, if any, of these theories is correct. As a result, postmodernism argues that the idea that we can judge 'scientifically' between competing explanations of this sort is nonsense. In fact, each theory *constructs* the nature of society in its own image, because there is no single social reality we can understand that is separate from the theories we use to understand it. Instead, there are multiple versions of reality – *relativism* – none of which can be judged 'scientifically' to be better than any other (Brown 1996).

## Postmodernism and education

The postmodern approach has some important implications regarding childhood. The developmental model characteristic of modernism is understood to be just one social construction among many. It has no legitimate claim to represent 'the truth' of what constitutes childhood in any way. The recognition that the organisation of schools and the role of teachers within schools are founded on uncertain principles rather than the 'facts' of childhood allows postmodernists to develop fundamental criticisms of the education system as it is currently experienced.

Education is redefined as 'discourse' – the unity of knowledge and power. Knowledge refers here not to social scientific or objective knowledge, but to construction. In this context, what is meant is the construction of childhood along modernist lines, together with associated beliefs regarding how schools should be organized and what should be taught. Power refers to relations of authority and control that are implicit and explicit in this knowledge. From this point of view, schools are regarded as oppressive institutions, as mechanisms of social control. For example, Foucault's work regarding the role of discipline and control in relation to prison design has been the impetus for other writers to study the role of surveillance in schools. Best (2008) has argued that schools are not just for the regulation of most forms of children's behaviour and habits such as playing sport, eating, walking around school, or addressing teachers, but also the ways in which the curriculum is implemented, assessment takes place and the way the inspection system operates through Ofsted. Best argues that the educational policies of New Labour since 1997 'integrate contemporary surveillance technologies into the life and administrative practices of schools'. Schools increasingly want to know about children's backgrounds, their ethnicity, whether they are entitled to free school meals, how they get to school, why they are absent and so on. Finger-printing has been introduced into some schools as a way of identifying who is entering the school, or for scanning the lunch queue. However, there is no justification for organising education along hierarchical and authoritarian lines. As another example from the postmodern perspective suggests, a national curriculum and its associated national testing are unacceptable because the content and nature of these things are decided on exclusively by 'educational experts' through a process in which children play no part (see Exercise 9.8 below). In the same way, teachers have no particular expertise or moral authority – so the experiences and moral codes of children should be no less valued. The notion that education is something that should be 'done' by adults to children is undermined.

## Exercise 9.8

Describe, in a paragraph, the postmodern approach to assessment within the educational system. What is the purpose of testing and examinations? What should happen to the national curriculum and national curriculum tests from a postmodern point of view?

So what would a 'postmodern school' look like? Given the relativism that postmodernism embraces, the position that no person's views are any better (or worse) than anyone else's, regardless of age, then education should be organized according to democratic principles in which all participants might have a voice. This applies equally to the curriculum, rules regarding behaviour, and the values that underpin such rules (see Exercise 9.9 below to expand on this point). Teachers would not be regarded as professional repositories of wisdom. Instead, teaching becomes a process of facilitating the exploration and development of experiential knowledge for the benefit of all. A postmodern school would be orderly, and would be organized around rules, regulations and a curriculum, but these things would be determined democratically rather than hierarchically. All decisions about how the school is organized, what is studied, and the running of the school day would be made through a process of democratic discussion and debate, with no one person or group having the ultimate right to impose their decision on others. Such an arrangement, say the postmodernists, would be genuinely liberating, particularly for pupils, and this is in stark contrast to the oppressive situation that applies currently.

## Exercise 9.9

Use your experience in the education system – school, college, university – to think about the rules and procedures in the everyday running of an educational institution which affect behaviour. An example might be arriving on time for lessons/lectures and the consequences of poor punctuality. Discuss these points with a group of fellow students how the postmodernist approach could be used to criticize educational practices within schools. To make this more interesting, you could take on the roles of a postmodernist, a Marxist, a feminist or a functionalist to present your argument.

### Postmodernism and education – an evaluation

Some critics of postmodernism regard it as self-evident that a postmodern school would most certainly not be orderly. Instead, it would be inherently unstable with little or no practical worth for teachers, pupils or for society more generally. A situation would develop in which children could more or less do as they liked, with chaotic consequences. While this may (or may not) be correct, it is important to note that this fear is founded precisely on the modernist view of the nature of childhood that postmodernism rejects.

This rejection, as we have seen, is based on a philosophical debate that centres on questions regarding the nature of society, and whether or not we can gain objective, scientific knowledge of it. Some writers have suggested that it is the philosophical nature of the debate that is part of the problem – modernism embraces social science, rationality and truth; while postmodernism promotes constructivism and relativism – and this has lead to diametrically opposed positions regarding childhood, education and schools with no common ground (Edwards and Usher 2001). If, however, we move from abstract philosophical considerations to the political implications of the debate, then both positions have an important contribution to make. Thus, while recognising the powerful influence of modern forms of education, postmodernism's contribution is not as a radical alternative blueprint but rather lies in its capacity as a critical tool that can ask important questions regarding the control of education, what should be learnt, and how schools and classrooms should be organized.

Sociologically too, postmodernism seems to reflect some of the changes that are already occurring within the modern education system and society more generally. For example, the widening participation agenda, which seeks to promote entry to higher education for students from a more diverse range of social backgrounds rather than mainly from the upper and middle classes represents an attempt to break down some of the traditional barriers associated with education, founded on a recognition that current forms of schooling are failing a significant number of young people. These attempts, in part, recognize the need to make curricula and pedagogies less authoritarian in design and more focused on the needs, experiences and learning styles of the students themselves. Another important development that resonates with the postmodern position lies in the expansion of information and communication technologies, and in particular the growing influence of the internet. By its nature, the internet tends to subvert traditional 'mug and jug' arrangements regarding teaching and learning, whereby teachers progressively 'fill' the pupils with knowledge from a jug, and tends to remove the boundaries of what should be learnt. At the same time there is a refocusing of control away from teachers and schools and towards learners of all ages. A third example of postmodernism within modernism might be 'lifelong learning' – an approach to education that is characterized by a multiplicity of curricula and a diversity of organisational frameworks – what Usher *et al.* describe as the 'decentring of knowledge', an acceptance of variety in forms of knowledge with no particular knowledge as central (Usher *et al.* 1997). In addition, the very notion of lifelong learning challenges the developmental model of childhood, the idea that childhood is a learning process that ends when, as adults, we enter the world of work.

The reader's view of education, modernism and postmodernism is, of course, a matter of personal judgement in relation to the debate. What is clear, however, is that it is not inevitable that we arrive at an either/or position based on philosophically opposed positions. Influences that might be characterized as both modern and postmodern can and arguably do coexist in contemporary society, and these should not be ignored.

Michael Apple (1995) argues that it is still important to understand the increasing 'commodification' of education and schools, and the commercial pressures that increasingly affect the curriculum, organization and running of schools. Apple believes that the system in which education takes place is still capitalist, and that point is still the key to providing a sound sociological analysis of the nature and role of education in society.

Generally, postmodernists have been attacked for failing to provide a coherent perspective on the role of education, for being ambiguous in their descriptions of the nature of the system, and ignoring the economic, political and social forces that influence the shape the education system takes.

It is important that you fully understand the differences between modernist approaches to the sociology of education, such as Marxism and Functionalism, and the more recent postmodern critique. There is also a critique of the postmodernist perspective which uses current educational policies such as widening participation and lifelong learning to counter their critique of modernist perspectives.

## Exam Focus

Items A and B and the subsequent questions and answers should assist you to become more skilful, if you underline the places in which the answers are evaluative.

### Item A

Working-class children can be at a disadvantage before they go to school, according to studies of pre-school socialization. Some working-class parents have low expectations of their children, do not value education and do not reward success. Working-class homes have fewer educational books, games and toys for their children, and probably do not have a place to do homework or a stimulating learning environment. The government's Sure Start programme has been designed specifically to target children and families in deprived areas to promote the intellectual, linguistic and social development of young children. The programme also brings together health, welfare, education and parental support in neighbourhood children's centres in service 'hubs' for the under-fives. The aim is to make sure these children start school with some of the appropriate knowledge, skills and motivation to do well, so that the cycle of deprivation is broken.

### Item B

Sociologists have investigated a number of areas which may contribute to the choices pupils and students make in their subjects. Some subjects are perceived to be 'masculine' or 'feminine'. Some subjects have predominantly male or female teachers who may 'channel' pupils into subjects by gender. Peer group pressure seems to have an important role to play in subject choice.

The division along gender lines continues from school through to undergraduate level, with subjects like Engineering and Technology, Physical, Mathematical and Computer Sciences dominated by males, and Languages, Education and the Social Sciences dominated by females.

## Questions

1. Using Item A, outline reasons sociologists have given for the educational underachievement of working-class children. (12 marks)

2. Using material from Item B and elsewhere, assess the strengths and limitations of using ONE of the following methods to study subject choice and gender:

   (a) Unstructured interviews.
   (b) Observation.

   (20 marks)

## Student answers

### Candidate A – answer to question 1

Sociologists have given several explanations for the under-achievement of working-class children in the education system. First, as outlined in Item A, there are factors related to home background that contribute to a child's performance in school. Douglas, in his study *The Home and the School*, found that working-class parents had much less interest in their children's education than did middle-class parents. They were less likely to encourage deferred gratification and encourage their children to do well. According to Bernstein, their language codes are restricted to their community understanding and do not transfer to school, where teachers use a predominantly elaborated code. Working-class children have fewer books, educational games and toys, and therefore are less likely to make the smooth transition into school. Working-class children perhaps have fewer role models who have progressed because of their educational qualifications and therefore see less value in education than do the middles class. This may also be part of the reason why anti-school behaviour can boost the status of working-class children.

However, there are also factors connected to schools that can disadvantage working-class pupils. Hargreaves has shown that the combination of streaming, teacher expectations and labelling have a detrimental effect on the working class, who are likely to be negatively labelled, put into lower streams and expected by teachers not to achieve high grades. Bowles and Gintis, and Willis, have shown how the working class, and boys in particular, may develop an anti-school subculture based on the fact that they cannot achieve high status in other ways, and vent their frustration and aggression against schools and teachers. Becker has shown that teachers make class-based judgements of pupils and positively label children who are more likely to come from middle-class backgrounds seeing working-class children as being impolite, unintelligent and unlikely to be successful.

Several compensatory education schemes have been set up, such as Operation Headstart, and more recently Sure Start, to raise the achievement of children from deprived families. Evidence has shown that these programmes only work on a temporary basis and do not 'break the cycle' of underachievement or have a lasting effect. This may be because of structural inequalities that exist in the wider society which results in the working class having less likelihood of success more generally in work or in terms of income, making educational success somewhat shallow and pointless for them. Sociologists have therefore pointed to factors both inside and outside the school which can contribute to the underachievement of working-class pupils. There are probably a wide variety of contributory factors that affect the educational qualifications achieved by certain groups, and each child will be affected differently by these factors. Not all working-class children under-achieve. However, even the government's widening participation programmes designed to encourage children from lower-class backgrounds to go to university do not seem to have made a marked difference to the overall composition of the intake to higher education.

## Candidate B – answer to question 2

I would choose unstructured interviews over observation to study the reasons behind gendered choice of subjects at school and beyond. It makes more sense to ask people about their choices rather than observe them, as observation may not necessarily reveal the underlying reasons or explanations. Observation is also open to interpretation by the researcher, who may misunderstand behaviour and meaning. Unstructured interviews have the advantage of enabling the researcher both to formulate questions and to allow for a conversation to develop with the respondent talking freely and openly. Some of the same problems of interpretation and misunderstanding can still apply, especially if the researcher has different characteristics to the respondent. Unstructured interviews may make the respondent more relaxed and open to talking about the topic in question, gaining considerable depth and detail. If a rapport has been achieved the respondent is more likely to provide truthful information and thus the research is higher in validity.

However, there are problems with the use of this method to research subject choice. If respondents are encouraged to talk freely they may produce a considerable amount of material that is irrelevant to the study and make analysis of the results complicated and time-consuming, sifting through all the material. The interviewer will need to be trained and skilled – this will add time and costs to the study. Unstructured interviews can be intrusive and therefore limit the material the respondent provides if they feel threatened or intimidated. Furthermore, it is difficult to replicate such studies, so the reliability of the research may be limited, especially over time.

The method could be used in conjunction with existing official statistics regarding choice of subject that are available on government websites such as the DCFS. These are secondary sources of data and can be used to look at patterns and trends over time which can then inform the parameters of a research project.

Unstructured interviews can be closely allied to the interpretivist tradition in sociology whereby researchers are more interested in uncovering the meanings behind behaviour. This is particularly pertinent to a study on subject choice, because the reasons behind actions are often complicated and hidden from obvious view. The means to discover underlying explanations lies in using qualitative methods such as unstructured interviews which delve below the surface of day-to-day interaction. Hence, if sociologists want to find the underlying reasons and explanations for behaviour, research methods must be sensitive, ethical and get under the surface of common sense.

Attempt an answer to the following question:

Outline and evaluate the Marxist approach to the sociology of education. (20 marks)

## Important concepts

socialization • role allocation • pedagogy • social mobility

## Critical thinking

- How relevant is the Marxist approach to an understanding of the modern education system and the development of new qualifications such as the Diplomas and Modern Apprenticeships?
- Is the focus on social class adopted by Marxists failing to pay significant attention to issues of gender and ethnicity when trying to understand educational achievement and performance?
- Has the postmodernist critique of Marxism as a metanarrative brought into question the credibility of the analysis of whole societies?

# References

Aggleton, Peter (1987) *Rebel Without a Cause? Middle Class Youth and the Transition from School to Work* (London: Falmer Press).

Ahier, J., Beck, J. and Moore, R. (2003) *Graduate Citizens: Issues of Citizenship and Higher Education* (London: Routledge Falmer).

Ainley, P. (1993) *Class and Skill: Changing Divisions of Knowledge and Labour* (London: Cassell).

Allan, Philip, Benyon, John and McCormick, Barry (eds) (1994) *Focus on Britain* (Deddington: Perennial Publications).

Althusser, Louis (1972) 'Ideology and Ideological State Apparatuses' in B. R. Cosin (ed.), *Education, Structure and Society* (Harmondsworth: Penguin).

Anyon, J. (1981) 'Social Class and School Knowledge', *Curriculum Inquiry* 11: 1.

Apple, Michael (1982) *Education and Power* (London: RKP).

Apple, Michael (1986) *Teachers and Texts: A Political Economy of Class and Gender Relations in Education* (London: RKP).

Apple, M. (1995) *Education and Power* (London: Routledge).

Arnot, M. (1982) 'Male Hegemony, Social Class and Women's Education', *Journal of Education* 164.

Arnot, M. (ed.) (1985) *Race and Gender: Equal Opportunities Policies in Education* (Oxford: Pergamon Press).

Arnot, M. (2002) *Reproducing Gender? Essays on Educational Theory and Feminist Politics* (London: Routledge Falmer).

Arnot, Madeleine (1991) 'Equality and Democracy', *British Journal of Sociology of Education* 12: 4.

Arnot, Madeleine (1992) 'Feminism, Education and the New Right', in Madeleine Arnott and Len Barton (eds), *Voicing Concerns: Sociological Perspectives on Contemporary Education Reforms* (Wallingford: Triangle).

Arnot, Madeleine and Barton, Len (eds) (1992) *Voicing Concerns: Sociological Perspectives on Contemporary Education Reforms* (Wallingford: Triangle).

Aronowitz, Stanley and Giroux, Henry (1991) *Post-modern Education; Politics, Culture and Social Criticism* (Minneapolis, Minn.: University of Minnesota Press).

Au, W. (2007) 'High-stakes Testing and Curricular Control: A Qualitative Metasynthesis', *Educational Researcher* 36:5.

Avis, James (1993) 'Post-Fordism, Curriculum Modernisers and Radical Practice: The Case of Vocational Education and Training in England', *The Vocational Aspect of Education* 45:1.

Ball, S. J. (1990a) *Politics and Policy-making in Education* (London: Routledge).

Ball, S. J. (1990b) *Education, Inequality and School Reform: Values in Crisis* (King's College Memorial Lecture).

Ball, S. (ed.) (1990c) *Foucault and Education: Disciplines and Knowledge* (London: Routledge).

Ball, S. J. (1995) *Sociology of Education: Major Themes* (London: Routledge).

Ball, S., Bowe, R. and Gerwitz, S. (1994) 'Market Forces and Parental Choice', in S. Tomlinson (ed.), *Educational Reform and its Consequences* (London: IPPR/Rivers Oran Press).

Banks, J. A. (1988) *Multi-ethnic Education: Theory and Practice* (Boston, Mass.: Allyn & Bacon).

Barber, Michael (1994) quoted in Paul Marston, 'A-level Girls Pass Boys for the First Time', *Daily Telegraph,* 25 October.

Barnett, Corelli (1986) *The Audit of War: The Illusion and Reality of Britain as a Great Nation* (London: Macmillan).

Barton, L. and Walker, S. (eds) (1993) *Race, Class and Education* (London: Croom Helm).

Bathmaker, A.-M. (2005) 'Hanging in or Shaping a Future: Defining a Role for Vocationally Related Learning in a "Knowledge" Society', *Journal of Education Policy* 20: 1.

Baudrillard, J. (1983) *Simulations* (New York: Semiotext(e)).

Baxter, J. (2002) 'Jokers in the Pack: Why Boys Are More Adept Than Girls at Speaking in Public Settings', *Language and Education* 16:2.

Becker, H. (1952) 'Social Class Variations in the Teacher–Pupil Relationship', *Journal of the Educational Society*, Illinsis, USA.

Beckett, F. (2007) *The Great City Academy Fraud* (London: Continuum).

Beltz, C. (1985) 'Review of Migrant Education in Australia', *Education News* 19:3 (May).

Bentley, D. and Watts, M. (1987) 'Courting the Positive Virtues: A Case for Feminist Science', in A. Kelly (ed.), *Science for Girls?* (Milton Keynes: Open University Press).

Bernstein, Basil (1975) *Class, Codes and Control: Towards a Theory of Educational Transmission* (London: Routledge & Kegan Paul).

Best, L. (1993) 'Dragons, Dinner Ladies and Ferrets: Sex Roles in Children's Books', *Sociology Review* 2:3.

Best, S. (2008) 'Schools and Surveillance', *Sociology Review* 17:3.

Bettelheim, Bruno (1991) *The Uses of Enchantment: The Meaning and Importance of Fairy Tales* (London: Penguin).

Bevins, Anthony and Nelson, Dean (1995) 'Blacks Stranded at Back of Jobs Queue', *Observer,* 12 February.

Bottigheimer, R. B. (1987) *Grimm's Bad Girls and Bold Boys: The Moral and Social Vision of the Tales* (New Haven, Conn.: Yale University Press).

Bourdieu, P. (1973) 'Cultural Reproduction and Social Reproduction', in R. K. Brown, (ed.) *Knowledge, Education and Cultural Change* (London: Tavistock).

Bourdieu, Pierre and Passeron, Jean-Claude (1977) *Reproduction in Education, Society and Culture* (London: Sage).

Bourdillon, H. (ed.) (1994) *Teaching History* (London: Routledge).

Bowles, S. and Gintis, H. (1976) *Schooling in Capitalist America: Educational Reform and the Contradictions of Economic Life* (New York: Basic Books).

Braverman, H. (1974) *Labour and Monopoly Capitalism* (New York: Monthly Press Review).

Brown, P. (1990) 'The Third Wave: Education and the Ideology of Parentocracy', *British Journal of Sociology of Education* 11.

Brown, P. (1996) 'Modernism, Post-modernism and Sociological Theory', *Sociology Review* 5:3.

Brown, P. and Lauder, H. (1991) 'Education, Economy and Social Change', *International Studies in the Sociology of Education* 1.

Brown, P. and Lauder, H. (eds) (1992) *Education for Economic Survival* (London: Routledge).

Brown, R. K. (1973) (ed.) *Knowledge, Education and Cultural Change* (London: Tavistock).

Burgess, B. (1994) 'Education: An Agenda for Change', in M. Haralambos (ed.), *Developments in Sociology: An Annual Review*, Vol. 10 (Ormskirk: Causeway).

Burke, J. (1989) *Competency-based Education and Training* (London: Falmer).

Burrows, Roger and Loader, Brian (1993) *Towards a Post-Fordist Welfare State?* (London: Routledge).

Buswell, Carol (1991) 'The Gendering of School and Work', *Social Studies Review* 6:3.

Butler, K. (2000) *Performance Based Learning with Style* (Columbia, CT: Learner's Dimension).

Byfield, C. (2008) 'The Impact of Religion on the Educational Achievement of Black Boys: A UK and USA Study', *British Journal of Sociology of Education* 29:2.

Byrne, E. (1978) *Women and Education* (London: Tavistock).

Byrne, E. (1985) 'Equity or Equality: A European Overview', in M. Arnot (ed.), *Race and Gender: Equal Opportunities Policies in Education* (Oxford: Pergamon Press).

Caldwell, B. J. and Spinks, J. M. (1992) *Leading the Self-Managing School* (London: Falmer).

Callender, C. (2001) 'Changing Student Finances in Higher Education – Policy Contradictions under Labour', *Widening Participation and Lifelong Learning* 3:2.

Campbell, B. (1987) *The Iron Ladies* (London: Virago).

Carr, H. (1989) *From My Guy to Sci-fi: Genre and Women's Writing in the Postmodern World* (London: Pandora).

Carter, T. (1986) *Shattering Illusions: West Indians in British Politics* (London: Lawrence & Wishart).

Cassen, R. and Kingdon, G. (2007) *Tackling Low Achievement* (York: Joseph Rowntree Foundation).

Castells, M. (1996) *The Rise of the Network Society* (Cambridge, Mass.: Blackwell).

Castleman, T. and Poole, M. (1990) *Academic Progression, Strategies and Initiatives for Women in Higher Education in Victoria* (Victoria, Australia: Ministry of Education).

Cathcart, H. and Esland, G. (1990) 'The Compliant-Creative Worker: The Ideological Reconstruction of the School Leaver', in G. Esland (ed.), *Education, Training and Employment, Vol. 2: The Educational Response* (Wokingham: Addison-Wesley).

Chapman, S. (2008) 'Is Social Class Still Important?', *Sociology Review* 18:2.

Chitty, Clyde (1993) 'The Education System Transformed', *Sociology Review* 2:3.

Chubb, J. and Moe, T. (1990) *Politics, Markets and America's Schools* (Washington, DC: Brookings Institution).

Cicourel, A. V. and Kitsuse, J. L. (1963) *The Educational Decision Makers* (Indianapolis, Ind.: Bobbs-Merrill).

Clarricoates, K. (1980) 'The Importance of Being Ernest...Emma...Tom...Jane. The Perception and Categorisation of Gender Conformity and Gender Deviation in Primary Schools', in R. Deem (ed.), *Schooling for Women's Work* (London: Routledge & Kegan Paul).

Clune, W. and Witte, J. (eds) (1990) *Choice and Control in American Education*, Vol. 2 (London: Falmer Press).

Coffield, Frank, Moseley, David, Hall, Elaine and Eccleston, Kathryn (2004) *Learning Styles and Pedagogy in Post-16 Learning: A Systematic and Critical Review*, Learning and Skills Research Centre (Trowbridge: Cromwell Press).

Cohen, S. (2000) *State of Denial* (Bristol: Polity Press).

Cole, M. (1988) *Bowles and Gintis Re-visited* (Lewes: Falmer Press).

Cole, Mike (1992) 'British Values, Liberal Values or Values of Justice and Equality', in James Lynch *et al., Equity or Excellence? Education and Cultural Reproduction* (London: Falmer Press).

Colley, H., James, D., Tedder, M. and Diment, K. (2003) 'Learning as Becoming in Vocational Education and Training: Class, Gender and the Role of Vocational Habitus', *Journal of Vocational Education and Training* 55:4.

Collins, C., Kenway, J. and McLeod, J. (2000) *Factors Influencing the Educational Performance of Males and Females in Schools and Their Initial Destinations after Leaving School* (Melbourne: Deakin University).

Collins, R. (1981) *The Credential Society* (New York: Academic Press).

Colson, I. (2004) ''Their Churches Are at Home': The Communication and Definition of Values in Four Aided Church of England Secondary Schools', *British Journal of Religious Education* 26:1.

Connell, R. W. (1986) *Teachers' Work* (Sydney: George Allen & Unwin).

Connell, R. W., Ashenden, D. J., Kessler, S. and Dowsett, G. W. (1982) *Making the Difference: Schools, Families and Social Divisions* (Sydney: George Allen & Unwin).

Connolly, P. (2006) 'The Effects of Social Class and Ethnicity on Gender Differences in GCSE Attainment: A Secondary Analysis of the Youth Cohort Study of England and Wales 1997–2001', *British Educational Research Journal* 32:1.

Connolly, P. (2008) 'A Critical Review of Some Recent Developments in Quantitative Research on Gender and Achievement in the United Kingdom', *British Journal of Sociology of Education* 29:3.

Conroy, J. (2009) 'Preaching to the Pupils', in Clake, J. (ed.) *Britain in 2009* (Swindon: ESRC).

Cooper, P., Upton, G. and Smith, C. (1991) 'Ethnic Minority and Gender Distribution Among Staff and Pupils in Facilities for Pupils With Emotional and Behavioural Difficulties in England and Wales', *British Journal of Sociology of Education* 12:1.

Cordingly, Philippa (1993) 'What About the Class Angle?', *The Times Educational Supplement,* 5 November.

Cosin, B. R. (ed.) (1972) *Education, Structure and Society* (Harmondsworth: Penguin).

Cox, C. B. and Boyson, R. (eds) (1975) *Black Papers 1975: The Fight for Education* (London: Dent).

CRE (Commission for Racial Equality) (1994) 'Training for Real Jobs at Last', *CRE-Connections* 2 (October).

Crozier, G. (2005) 'There's a War Against Our Children': Black Educational Under-achievement Revisited', *British Journal of Sociology of Education* 26:5.

Culley, L. (1986) *Gender Differences and Computing in Secondary Schools* (Loughborough: Loughborough University Press).

Dale, Roger (1985) *Education, Training and Employment* (Oxford: Pergamon).

David, M. (1983) 'Teaching and Preaching Sexual Morality: The New Right's Anti-feminism in Britain and the USA', *Journal of Education* 166.

Davies, P., Adnett, N. and Turnbull, A. (2003) 'Market Forces and Diversity: Some Evidence from the 14–19 Curriculum', *Journal of Curriculum Studies* 34:4.

Davis, K. and Moore, W. E. (1945) 'Some Principles of Stratification', *American Sociological Review* 10.

Dawson, A. (1988) 'Inner City Adolescents: Unequal Opportunities?', in A. Verma and P. Pumfrey (eds), *Educational Attainments: Issues and Outcomes in Multicultural Education* (London: Falmer Press).

DCSF (Department for Children, Schools and Families) (2002) *Youth Cohort Study: activities and experiences of 16 year olds: England and Wales* (London: DCSF).

DCSF (Department for Children, Schools and Families) (2009) *National Evaluation of Diplomas: preparation for 2008 delivery* (London: DCSF).

Deem, R. (1992) 'Schooling and Gender: The Cycle of Discrimination', in J. Lynch, C. Modgil and S. Modgil, *Equity or Excellence? Education and Cultural Reproduction* (London: Falmer Press).

Deem, Rosemary (ed.) (1980) *Schooling for Women's Work* (London: RKP).

De Lyon, H. and Mignolio, F. (1989) *Women Teachers* (Milton Keynes: Open University Press).

Demaine, Jack (1988) 'Teachers' Work, Curriculum and the New Right', *British Journal of Sociology of Education* 9.

Dench, G., Gavron, K. and Young, M. (2006) *The New East End: Kinship Race and Conflict* (London: Profile).

Denscombe, Martyn (1982–96) *Sociology Update* (Annual) (Leicester: Olympus).

DES (Department of Education and Science) (1974) *Work Experience*, Circular 7/74 (London: HMSO).

DES (Department of Education and Science) (1985) *Education for All* (Swann Report) (London: HMSO).

DES (Department of Education and Science), Department of Employment and the Welsh Office (1991) *Education and Training for the 21st Century*, Vols 1 and 2 (London: HMSO).

DES (Department of Education and Science) (1991b) 'Statistical Bulletin', in Martyn Denscombe (1992) *Sociology Update* (Leicester: Olympus).

Desforges, C. and Abouchaar, A. (2003) *The Impact of Parental Involvement, Parental Support and Family Education on Pupil Achievements and Adjustment: A Literature Review* (London: DfES).

DFE (Department for Education) (1992) *Choice and Diversity: A New Framework for Schools* (London: HMSO).

DFE (Department for Education) (1993) *Educational Statistics for the United Kingdom* (London: HMSO).

DfES (Department for Education and Skills) (2003) *The Impact of Parental Involvement, Parental Support and Family Education on Pupil Achievement and Adjustment* (London: DfES).

DfES (2004) *14–19 Curriculum and Qualifications Reform: Final Report of the Working Group on 14–19 Reform* (Annesley, Notts.: DfES Publications).

Donald, James (1992) *Sentimental Education* (London: Verso).

Dore, Ronald (1976) *The Diploma Disease: Education, Qualification and Development* (London: George Allen & Unwin).

Douglas, J. W. B. (1964) *The Home and the School* (London: MacGibbon & Kee).

Dreyfus, H. and Rabinow, P. (eds) (1982) *Michel Foucault: Beyond Structuralism and Hermeneutics* (Brighton: Harvester Press).

Dunne, M. and Gazeley, L. (2008) Teachers, Social Class and Underachievement, *British Journal of Sociology of Education* 29:5.

Durkheim, Emile (1956) *Education and Society* (Glencoe: Free Press).

East, P., Pitt, R., Bryan, V., Rose, J. and Rupchand, L. (1989) 'Access to Teaching for Black Women', in H. De Lyon and F. Mignolio, *Women Teachers* (Milton Keynes: Open University Press).

Edwards, R. (1991) 'Winners and losers: The Education and Training of Adults', in P. Raggatt and L. Unwin (eds), *Change and Intervention* (London: Falmer Press).

Edwards, Richard (1993) 'Multi-skilling the Flexible Workforce', *Journal of Further and Higher Education* 17:1.

Edwards, R. and Usher, R. (2001) 'Lifelong Learning: A Postmodern Condition of Education?', *Adult Education Quarterly* 51:4.

Edwards, T. and Whitty, G. (1992) 'Parental Choice and Educational Reform in Britain and the United States', *British Journal of Educational Studies* 40:2.

Eggleston, J. (1986) *Education for Some: The Educational and Vocational Experiences of 15–18 Year Old Members of Minority Ethnic Groups* (Stoke-on Trent: Trentham).

Elias, P. and Purcell, K. (2004) 'Graduate Careers Seven Years On', Research paper, University of Warwick.

Elliott, B. and MacLennan, D. (1994) 'Neo-Conservative School Reform', *British Journal of Sociology of Education* 15:2.

Elliott, J. and Powell, C. (1987) 'Young Women and Science: Do We Need More Science?', *British Journal of Sociology of Education* 8:3.

Ellsworth, E. (1989) 'Why Doesn't This Feel Empowering? Working Through the Repressive Myths of Critical Pedagogy', *Harvard Educational Review* 59:3.

EOC (Equal Opportunities Commission) (2004) 'Britain's Skills Gap – Challenging Gender Segregation in Training and Work'. See http://www.equalityhuman rights.com.

Esland, G. (ed.) (1990) *Education, Training and Employment, Vol. 2, The Educational Response* (Wokingham: Addison Wesley).

Evans, B. and Waites, B. (1981) *IQ and Mental Testing* (London: Macmillan).

Eysenck, H. J. (1962) *Know Your Own IQ* (Harmondsworth: Penguin).

Feinstein, L. (2003) quoted in Haralambos, M. (ed.) (2006) *Sociology: A New Approach* (Ormskirk: Causeway Press).

FEU (Further Education Unit) (1994) 'Developing GNVQ Science – FEU Evaluation', *FEU Newsletter,* November.

Figueroa, Peter (1991) *Education and the Social Construction of Race* (London: Routledge).

Finegold, D. and Soskice, R. (1988) 'The Failure of Training in Britain: Analysis and Prescription', *Oxford Review of Economic Policy* 4.

Finn, D. (1987) *Training without Jobs* (Basingstoke: Macmillan).

Finn, Dan (1985) 'Manpower Services Commission and the Youth Training Scheme: A Permanent Bridge to Work', in Roger Dale, *Education, Training and Employment* (Oxford: Pergamon).

Finn, Dan (1988) 'Education for Jobs: The Route to YTS', *Social Studies Review* 4:1.

Fitz, J., Halpin, D. and Power, S. (1997) 'Between a Rock and a Hard Place: Diversity, Institutional Identity and Grant-maintained Schools', *Oxford Review of Education* 23:1.

Fitzgerald, M. (2005) 'White Boys Fail Too', *Guardian*, 1 June.

Flew, A. (1986) 'Education against Racism', in D. O'Keefe (ed.), *The Wayward Curriculum* (London: Social Affairs Unit).

Flew, A. (1987) *Power to the Parents* (London: Sherwood Press).

Flude, M. and M. Hammer (eds) (1990) *The Education Reform Act 1988: Its Origins and Implications* (London: Falmer Press).

Foster, P. (1990) ' "Case Not Proven": An Evaluation of Two Studies of Teacher Racism', *British Educational Research Journal* 16:4.

Foster, M., Gomm, R. and Hammersley, M. (1996) *Constructing Educational Inequality* (Lewes: Falmer).

Foucault, M. (1979) *The Order of Things: An Archeology of the Human Sciences* (New York: Random House).

Foucault, Michel (1982) 'The Subject and Power', in H. Dreyfus and P. Rabinow (eds), *Michel Foucault: Beyond Structuralism and Hermeneutics* (Brighton: Harvester Press).

Francis, B. (2000) *Boys, Girls and Achievement; Addressing the Classroom Issues* (London: Routledge).

Francis, B. and Skelton, C. (2005) *Reassessing Gender and Achievement* (London: Routledge).

Francis, B., Skelton, C., Carrington, B., Hutchings, M.,. Read, B. and Hall I. (2008) A Perfect Match? Pupils' and Teachers' Views of the Impact of Matching Educators and Learners by Gender, *Research Papers in Education* 23:1.

Freire, Paulo (1972) *Pedagogy of the Oppressed* (London: Sheed & Ward).

Fuller, Mary (1980) 'Black Girls in a London Comprehensive School', in Rosemary Deem (ed.), *Schooling for Women's Work* (London: RKP).

Furlong, A. and Forsyth, A. (2003) *Losing Out? Socio-economic Disadvantage and Experience in Further and Higher Education* (Bristol: The Policy Press).

Gardner, H. (1983) *Frames of the Mind: The Theory of Multiple Intelligences* (New York: Basic Books).

Garrod, J. and Jones, M. (2009) *Beliefs in Society* (Basingstoke: Palgrave Macmillan).

Gazeley, L. and Dunne, M. (2007) Researching Class in the Classroom: Addressing the Social Class Attainment Gap in Initial Teacher Education, *Journal of the Education for Teaching: International Research and Pedagogy* 33:4.

General Household Survey (1994) *Social Trends*, Vol. 24 (London: HMSO).

Gewirtz, S. (1998) 'Can All Schools Be Successful? An Exploration of the Determinants of School "Success" ', *Oxford Review of Education* 24:4.

Gibson, M. and Ogbu, J. (eds) (1991) *Minority Status and Schooling: A Comparative Study of Immigrant and Involuntary Minorities* (New York: Garland).

Giddens, Anthony (1984) *The Constitution of Society* (Cambridge: Polity Press).

Gilbert, C. (2008) 'Ofsted Addresses Stalled Standards', *Guardian*, 19 May.

Gillard, D. (2007) 'Never Mind the Evidence: Blair's Obsession with Faith Schools', *Forum* 49:3.

Gillard, D. (2007) 'Never Mind the Evidence: Blair's Obsession with Faith Schools'. Available at: www.dg.dial.pipex.com/articles/educ29.shtml; accessed 3 July 2009.

Gillborn, David (1990) *'Race', Ethnicity and Education: Teaching and Learning in Multi-Ethnic Schools* (London: Unwin-Hyman).

Gillborn, D. (2002) *Education and Institutional Racism* (London: Institute of Education).

Gillborn, D. and Mirza, H. (2000) *Educational Inequality: Mapping Race, Class and Gender – A Synthesis of Research Evidence* (London: Ofsted).

Gillborn, D. and Youdell, D. (2001) 'The New IQism: Intelligence, "Ability" and the Rationing of Education', in J. Demaine (ed.), *Sociology of Education Today* (Basingstoke: Palgrave).

Giroux, Henry (1983) *Theory and Resistance in Education: A Pedagogy for the Opposition* (South Hadley, Mass.: Bergin & Garvey).

Giroux, Henry (1994) *Border Crossings* (London: Routledge).

Glanville, J. L., Sikkink, D., and Hernández, E. I. (2008) 'Religious Involvement and Educational Outcomes', *Sociological Quarterly* 49:1.

Goodson, I. (1990) 'Nations at Risk and National Curriculum: Ideology and Identity', *Politics of Education Association Yearbook* (London: Taylor & Francis).

Gorard, S. (2000) 'One of Us Cannot Be Wrong: The Paradox of Achievement Gaps', *British Journal of Sociology of Education* 21:3.

Gorard, S. and Smith, E. (2004) 'What Is Underachievement at School?', *School Leadership and Management* 24.

Green, Andy (1994) 'Postmodernism and State Education', *Journal of Educational Policy* 9:1.

Greenfield, W. (ed.) (1987) *Instructional Leadership: Concepts, Issues and Controversies* (Boston, Mass.: Allyn & Bacon).

Guy, R. (1991) 'Serving the Needs of Industry?', in P. Raggatt and L. Unwin (eds), *Change and Intervention* (London: Falmer Press).

Hallam, S. and Ireson, J. (2006) Secondary School Pupils' Preferences for Different Types of Structured Grouping Practices, *British Educational Research Journal* 32:4.

Hallinger, P. and Murphy, J. (1987) 'Instructional Leadership in the School Context', in W. Greenfield (ed.), *Instructional Leadership: Concepts, Issues and Controversies* (Boston, Mass.: Allyn & Bacon).

Halsey, A. H. (1993) 'Opening the Doors of Higher Education', *Education Economics* 1:1.

Halson, J. (1989) 'The Sexual Harassment of Young Women', in L. Holly (ed.), *Girls and Sexuality* (Milton Keynes: Open University Press).

Hammersly, M. (1981) 'Staffroom Racism', unpublished manuscript, quoted in Robert Jeffcoate, *Ethnic Minorities and Education* (London: Harper & Row, 1984).

Hannan, D. and Boyle, M. (1987) 'Schooling Decisions: The Origins and Consequences of Selection and Streaming in Irish Post-Primary Schools', Paper no. 136 (Dublin: Economic and Social Research Institute).

Hannan, D. and Shorthall, S. (1991) 'The Quality of Their Education', Paper no. 153 (Dublin: Economic and Social Research Institute).

Haralambos, M. (ed.) (1994) *Developments in Sociology: An Annual Review,* Vol. 10 (Ormskirk: Causeway).

Haralambos, Michael and Holborn, Martin (1995) *Sociology Themes and Perspectives* (London: Collins Educational).

Hargreaves, A. (1994) 'Restructuring Restructuring', *Journal of Educational Policy* 9:1.

Hargreaves, A. and Reynolds, D. (eds) (1989) *Education Policies: Controversies and Critiques* (London: Falmer).

Hargreaves, D. (1967) *Social Relations in a Secondary School* (London: Routledge & Kegan Paul).

Hargreaves, D. (2001) *Review of Curriculum 2000* (London: QCA).

Hartley, David (1994) 'Mixed Messages in Education Policy: Signs of the Times?', *British Journal of Educational Studies* 42:3.

Harvey, David (1989) *The Condition of Modernity* (Oxford: Basil Blackwell).

Haynes, J., Tikly, L. and Caballero, C. (2006) 'The Barriers to Achievement for White/Black Caribbean Pupils in English Schools, *British Journal of Sociology of Education* 27:5.

Healey, Nigel (1989) 'Student Loans Versus Grants: The Debate Revisited', *Journal of Further and Higher Education* 13:3.

Hebdige, D. (1989) 'After the Masses', *Marxism Today*, January.

Herrnstein, R. and Murray, C. (1994) *The Bell Curve: Intelligence and Class Structure in American Life* (New York: Free Press).

HESA (Higher Education Statistics Agency) (2006) *Statistics Online*. Available at: http://www.hesa.ac.uk/index.php/component/option,com_datatables/Itemid,121/; accessed 3 July 2009.

Hicks, Lesley (1988) 'Women Teachers', unpublished PhD. thesis, University of York. Quoted in R. Deem, 'Schooling and Gender: The Cycle of Discrimination', in James Lynch *et al.*, *Equity or Excellence? Education and Cultural Reproduction* (London: Falmer Press, 1992).

Hirsch, D. (2006) *What Will It Take to End Child Poverty?* (York: Joseph Rowntree Foundation).

Hodgkinson, Peter (1991) 'Educational Change: A Model for Analysis', *British Journal of Sociology of Education* 12:2.

Hodgson, A. and Spours, K. (1997) *Dearing and Beyond: 14–19 Qualifications, Frameworks and Systems* (London: Kogan Page).

Hodgson, A. and Spours, K. (2003) *Beyond A Levels: Curriculum 2000 and the Reform of 14–19 Qualifications* (London: Kogan Page).

Hodgson, A. and Spours, K. (2007) 'Specialised Diplomas: Transforming the 14–19 Landscape in England?', *Journal of Education Policy* 22:6.

Holly, L. (ed.) (1989) *Girls and Sexuality* (Milton Keynes: Open University Press).

Hoskin, K. (1990) 'Foucault under Examination: The Crypto-Educationalist Unmasked', in S. Ball (ed.), *Foucault and Education: Disciplines and Knowledge* (London: Routledge).

Huddlestone, P. and Oh, S. (2004) 'The Magic Roundabout: Work-Related Learning within the 14–19 Curriculum', *Oxford Review of Education* 30(1).

Hulmes, E. (1989) *Education and Cultural Diversity* (London: Longman).

Hutchings, M. (2003) 'Financial Barriers to Participation', in L. Archer, M. Hutchings and A. Ross, *Higher Education and Social Class: Issues of Exclusion and Inclusion* (London: Routledge Falmer).

Hutt, C. (1972) *Males and Females* (London: Penguin).

Jarvis, F. (1990) 'The Debtor's Bill', *Education* 175:11, 16 March.

Jeffcoate, Robert (1984) *Ethnic Minorities and Education* (London: Harper & Row).

Jensen, A. (1969) 'How Much Can We Boost IQ and Scholastic Achievement?', *Harvard Educational Review* 39:1.

Jones, Anne (1993) 'General, National and Popular', *Education* 26 (November).

Jones, C. and Mahony, P. (eds) (1989) *Learning Our Lines: Sexuality and Social Control in Education* (London: Women's Press).

Jones, L. and Moore, R. (1993) 'Education, Competence and the Control of Expertise', *British Journal of the Sociology of Education* 14:4.

Jones, S. (2004) 'Muslim Pupil Loses Legal Battle to Wear Jilbab', *Guardian*, 16 June.

Jones, Trevor (1993) *Britain's Ethnic Minorities* (London: Policy Studies Institute).

Karabel, J. and Halsey, A. H. (eds) (1977) *Power and Ideology in Education* (New York: Oxford University Press).

Keddie, N. (1971) 'Classroom Knowledge', in M. Young, *Knowledge and Control* (London: Macmillan).

Kelly, Alison (1982) *Why Girls Don't Do Science*, Course U221, Unit 13 (Milton Keynes: Open University Press).

Kelly, Alison (1987) *Science for Girls* (Milton Keynes: Open University Press).

Kelly, Alison (1988) 'Towards a Democratic Science Education', in H. Lauder and P. Brown (eds), *Education in Search of a Future* (Lewes: Falmer Press).

Kessler, S., Ashenden, D. J., Connell, R. W. and Dowsett, G. W. (1985) 'Gender Relations in Secondary Schooling', *Sociology of Education* 58.

Kirby, Mark (1993) 'TECs and the New Vocationalism', *Social Science Teacher* 23:1.

Klein, Gillian (1993) *Education towards Race Equality* (London: Cassell).

Kolb, D. (1984) *Experiential Learning* (Englewood Cliffs, NJ: Prentice Hall).

Kozol, Jonathan (1991) *Savage Inequalities: Children in American Schools* (New York: Crown Publishers).

Labov, W. (1973) 'The Logic of Nonstandard English', in N. Keddie (ed.), *Tinker, Tailor: The Myth of Cultural Deprivation* (Harmondsworth: Penguin).

Lacey, C. (1970) *Hightown Grammar* (Manchester: Manchester University Press).

Laclau, Ernesto and Mouffe, Chantal (1985) *Hegemony and Socialist Strategy: Towards A Radical Democratic Politics* (London: Verso).

Ladner, J. A. (1973) *The Death of White Sociology* (New York: Vintage Books).

Ladson-Billings, G. (2006) 'From the Achievement Gap to the Education Debt: Understanding Achievement in US Schools', *Educational Researcher* 35:7.

Lauder, H. and Brown, P. (eds) (1985) *Education in Search of a Future* (Lewes: Falmer Press).

Livesey, C. and Lawson, T. (2005) *A/S Sociology for AQA* (Oxford: Hodder Arnold).

Lobban, G. (1974) 'Data Reporting on British Reading Schemes', *The Times Educational Supplement*, 1 March.

Lupton, R (2003) *Poverty Street: The Dynamics of Neighbourhood Decline and Renewal* (Bristol: The Policy Press).

Lupton, R., Hempel-Jorgensen, A., Castle, F., Brown, C. and Lauder, H. (2006) 'School Socio-economic Composition and Pupil Grouping in the Primary School', *Times Education Supplement*, 22 September.

Lynch, J. (1986) *Multicultural Education – Principles and Practices* (London: RKP).

Lynch, J., Modgil, C. and Modgil, S. (1992) *Equity or Excellence? Education and Cultural Reproduction* (London: Falmer Press).

Lynch, K. (1990) 'Reproduction: The Role of Cultural Factors and Educational Mediators', *British Journal of Sociology of Education* 11.

Lynch, K. and O'Neill, C. (1994) 'Colonisation of Social Class', *British Journal of Sociology of Education* 15:3.

Mac an Ghaill, M. (1988) *Young, Gifted and Black: Student–Teacher Relations in the Schooling of Black Youth* (Milton Keynes: Open University Press).

Mac an Ghaill, M. (1991) 'Black Voluntary Schools: The "Invisible" Private Sector', in G. Walford (ed.), *Private Schooling: Tradition, Change and Diversity* (London: Paul Chapman).

Mac an Ghaill, M. (1994) *The Making of Men: Masculinities, Sexualities and Schooling* (Milton Keynes: Open University Press).

Mac an Ghaill, M. (1996) 'What About the Boys? Schooling, Class and Crisis Masculinity', *Sociological Review* 44:3.

Maguire, M., Maguire, S. and Felstead, A. (1993) *Factors Influencing Individual Commitment to Lifelong Learning* (London: Employment Department).

Marshall, G. (2002) *Repositioning Class: Social Inequality in Industrial Societies* (London: Sage).

Marsland, D., quoted in J. Demaine (1988) 'Teachers' Work, Curriculum and the New Right', *British Journal of Sociology of Education* 9.

Marston, Paul (1994) 'A-level Girls Pass Boys for the First Time', *Daily Telegraph*, 25 October.

Martino, W. and Frank, B. (2006) 'The Tyranny of Surveillance: Male Teachers and the Policing of Masculinities in a Single-Sex School', *Gender and Education* 18:1.

Mason, M. (2003) 'Religion and Schools: A Human-rights-based Approach', *British Journal of Religious Education* 25:2.

Massey, Ian (1991) *More than Skin Deep* (London: Hodder & Stoughton).

Maughan, B. and Dunn, G. (1988) 'Black Pupils' Progress in Secondary School', in G. Verma, and P. Pumfrey (eds), *Educational Attainments: Issues and Outcomes in Multicultural Education* (London: Falmer Press).

McCarthy, C. and Chrichlow, W. (1993) (eds) *Race, Identity and Representation in Education* (London: Routledge).

McLaren, P. (1991) 'Postmodernism, Postcolonialism and Pedagogy', *Education and Society* 9:1.

McNeil, L. M. (2005) 'Faking Equity: High-Stakes Testing and the Education of Latino Youth', in G. Orfield and M. L. Kornhaber (eds), *Raising Standards or Raising Barriers? Inequality and High-Stakes Testing in Public Education* (Albany, NY: State University of New York).

McRobbie, A. (1991) *Feminism and Youth Culture: From Jackie to Just Seventeen* (London: George Allen & Unwin).

Mehan, H. (1992) 'Understanding Inequality in Schools: The Contribution of Interpretive Studies', *Sociology of Education* 65.

Mickleson, R. A. (1989) 'Why Does Jane Read and Write So Well? The Anomaly of Women's Education', *Sociology of Education* 62.

Middleton, S. (1993) *Educating Feminist: Life Histories and Pedagogy* (New York: Teachers College Press).

Millar, F. (2005) 'A Helping Hand', *Times Educational Supplement*, 4 May.

Miller, D. and Funnell, P. (1991) *Delivering Quality in Vocational Education* (London: Kogan Page).

Mills, M. (2008) 'Being the "Right" Kind of Male Teacher: The Disciplining of John', *Pedagogy, Culture and Society* 16:1.

Mirza, H. (1992) *Young, Female and Black* (London: Routledge).

Mirza, H. and Reay, D. (2000) 'Spaces and Places of Black Educational Desire: Rethinking Black Supplementary Schools as a New Social Movement', *Sociology* 34:3.

Mitsos, E. (2003) 'Racism in Schooling', *Sociology Review* 12:3.

Mitsos, E. and Browne, K. (1998) 'Gender Difference in Education', *Sociology Review* 8:1.

Modgil, S. Verma, G. K., Mallick, K. and Modgil, C. (eds) (1986) *Multicultural Education: The Interminable Debate* (Lewes: Falmer Press).

Moore, D. (1990) 'Voice and Choice in Chicago', in W. Clune and J. Witte (eds), *Choice and Control in American Education*, Vol. 2 (London: Falmer Press).

Moore, R. (1988) 'The Correspondence Principle and the Marxist Sociology of Education', in M. Cole, *Bowles and Gintis Revisited* (Lewes: Falmer Press).

Moore, Rob and Hickox, Mike (1994) 'Vocationalism and Educational Change', *The Curriculum Journal* 5:3.

Morgan, D. (1981) 'Men, Masculinity and the Process of Sociological Enquiry', in H. Roberts (ed.) *Doing Feminist Research* (London: Routledge & Kegan Paul).

Muller, D. and Funnell, P. (1991) *Delivering Quality in Vocational Education* (London: Kogan Page).

Munn, P. and Lloyd, G. (2005) 'Exclusion and Excluded Pupils', *British Educational Research Journal* 31:2.

Murray, Robin (1988) 'Life after Henry', *Marxism Today*, 14–18 October.

Myers, K. (1989) 'High Heels in the Market Place', *Education*, 16 June.

Nash, R. (1973) *Classrooms Observed* (London: Routledge & Kegan Paul).

NCVQ (National Council for Vocational Qualifications) (1995) *Capey Review of GNVQ Assessment* (London: NCVQ).

Nicholson, Carol (1989) 'Postmodernism, Feminism and Education: The Need for Solidarity', *Educational Theory* 39:3.

Norman, F., Turner, S., Granados, J., Schwarez, H., Green, H. and Harris, J. (1988) 'Look, Jane, Look: Anti-sexist Initiatives in Primary Schools', in G. Weiner (ed.), *Just a Bunch of Girls* (Milton Keynes: Open University Press).

O'Donnell, Mike (1991) *Race and Ethnicity* (New York: Longman).

O'Donnell, Mike (1992) *A New Introduction to Sociology* (Walton-on Thames: Nelson).

O'Keefe, D. (ed.) (1986a) *Anti-Racism: An Assault on Education and Value* (London: Sherwood Press).

O'Keefe, D. (ed.) (1986b) *The Wayward Curriculum* (London: Social Affairs Unit).

O'Reilly, J. (1992) 'Where Do You Draw the Line? Functional Flexibility, Training and Skill in Britain and France', *Work, Employment and Society* 6:3.

Ofsted (Office for Standards in Education) (1993) *Unfinished Business: Full-Time Educational Courses for 16–19 Year Olds* (London: HMSO).

Öhrn, Elisabet (1993) 'Gender, Influence and Resistance in School', *British Journal of Sociology of Education* 14:2.

Palmer, F. (ed.) (1986) *Anti-Racism: An Assault on Education and Value* (London: Sherwood Press).

Parekh, B. (1986) 'The Concept of Multi-Cultural Education', in S. Modgil *et al.* (eds), *Multicultural Education: The Interminable Debate* (Lewes: Falmer Press).

Parmar, P. (1989) 'Other Kinds of Dreams', *Feminist Review* 31.

Parsons, Talcott (1959) 'The School Class as a Social System', *Harvard Educational Review* 29.

Pearce, S. (1986) 'Swann and the Spirit of the Age', in F. Palmer (ed.), *Anti-Racism: An Assault on Education and Value* (London: Sherwood Press).

Platt, A. and Whyld, J. (1983) 'Introduction', in J. Whyld (ed.), *Sexism in the Secondary School* (London: Harper & Row).

Plowden Report (1967) *Children and Their Primary Schools* (London: HMSO).

Power, S., Whitty, G. and Edwards, T. (2006) 'Success Sustained? A Follow Up Study of the 'Destined for Success' Cohort', *Research Papers in Education* 21:3.

Punter, D. (1986) *Introduction to Contemporary Cultural Studies* (London: Longman).

Raffe, D. (1993) 'Participation of 16–18 Year Olds in Education and Training', *Education Economics* 1:1.

Raggatt, P. (1991) 'Quality Assurance and NVQs', in P. Raggatt and L. Unwin (eds), *Change and Intervention* (London: Falmer Press).

Raggatt, P. and Unwin, L. (eds) (1991) *Change and Intervention* (London: Falmer Press).

Ramsay, P. (1983) 'Fresh Perspectives on the School Transformation–Reproduction Debate: A Response to Anyon from the Antipodes', *Curriculum Inquiry* 13:3.

Ranson, S. (1990) 'From 1944 to 1988: Education, Citizenship and Democracy', in M. Flude and M. Hammer (eds), *The Education Reform Act 1988: Its Origins and Implications* (London: Falmer Press).

Ravitch, D. (1990) 'Diversity and Democracy: Multicultural Education in America', *American Educator,* Spring.

Read, B. (2008) ' "The World Must Stop When I'm Talking": Gender and Power Relations in Primary Teachers' Classroom Talk', *British Journal of Sociology of Education* 29:6.

Reay, D. (2001) 'A Useful Extension of Bourdieu's Conceptual Framework? Emotional Capital as a Way of Understanding Mothers' Involvement in Children's Schooling', *The Sociological Review* 48:4.

Reay, D. (2005) quoted in Livesey, C. and Lawson, T., *AS Sociology for AQA* (London: Hodder Arnold).

Reay, D. (2006) 'The Zombie Stalking English Schools: Social Class and Educational Inequality', *British Journal of Educational Studies* 54:3.

Reay, D. (2007) 'Unruly Places: Inner-city Comprehensives, Middle-class Imaginaries and Working-class Children', *Urban Studies,* Special Issue on The Geography of Education 44:7.

Renter, D. S., Scott, C., Kober, N., Chudowsky, N., Joftus, S. and Zabala, D. (2006) *From the Capital to the Classroom: Year 4 of the No Child Left Behind Act* (Washington: Center on Education Policy).

Riddell, Sheila I. (1992) *Gender and the Politics of the Curriculum* (London: Routledge).

Rist, R. (1970) 'Student Social Class and Teacher Expectations', *Harvard Educational Review* 40:3.

Robbins Committee (1963) *Report on Higher Education* (London: HMSO).

Roberts, H. (ed.) (1981) *Doing Feminist Research* (London: Routledge & Kegan Paul).

Rorty, R. (1982) *Consequences of Pragmatism* (Brighton: Harvester Press).

Rosenthal, R. and Jacobson, L. (1968) *Pygmalion in the Classroom* (New York: Holt, Rinehart & Winston).

Rust, Val (1991) 'Post-modernism and Its Comparative Education Implication', *Journal for Comparative Education Review* 35:4.

Rustin, Michael (1994) 'Flexibility in Higher Education', in Roger Burrows and Brian Loader, *Towards a Post-Fordist Welfare State?* (London: Routledge).

Sadker, M., Sadker, D. and Klein, S. (1991) 'The Issue of Gender in Elementary and Secondary Education', *Review of Research in Education* 17.

Saunders, Peter (1994) 'A Social Divide Based on Merit', *The Independent,* 25 October.

Savage, M. (2003) 'Review Article: A New Class Paradigm?', *British Journal of Sociology of Education,* 24:4.

Schagen, I. and Schagen, S. (2005) 'The Impact of Faith Schools on Pupil Performance', in R. Gardner, J. Cairns and D. Lawton (eds), *Faith Schools: Consensus or Conflict* (London: Routledge Falmer).

Schultz, T. W. (1977) 'Investment in Human Capital', in J. Karabel and A. H. Halsey (eds), *Power and Ideology in Education* (New York: Oxford University Press).

Scott, D. (1990) *Coursework and Coursework Assessment in the GCSE* (CEDAR: University of Warwick).

Scraton, S. (1987) 'Gender and P.E.: Ideologies of the Physical and the Politics of Sexuality', in S. Walker and L. Barton (eds), *Changing Policies, Changing Teachers* (Milton Keynes: Open University Press).

Scruton, R. (1986) The Myth of Cultural Relation', in D. O'Keefe (ed.), *Anti-Racism: An Assault on Education and Value* (London: Sherwood Press).

Scruton, Roger (1984) *The Meaning of Conservatism* (London: Macmillan).

Self, A. (ed.) (2008) *Social Trends 38* (Basingstoke: Palgrave Macmillan).

Self, A. and Zealey, L. (eds) (2007) *Social Trends 37* (Basingstoke: Palgrave Macmillan).

Senese, G. (1991) 'Warnings on Resistance and the Language of Possibility: Gramsci and a Pedagogy from the Surreal', *Educational Theory* 41.

Sharpe, Sue (1976) *Just Like a Girl: How Girls Learn to Be Women* (Harmondsworth, Penguin).

Sharpe, Sue (1994) *Just Like a Girl: How Girls Learn to be Women: From the Seventies to the Nineties* (London: Penguin).

Short, G. (2003) 'Faith Schools and Social Cohesion: Opening up the Debate' *British Journal of Religious Education* 25:2.

Siegal, F. (1991) 'The Cult of Multiculturalism', *The New Republic,* 18 February.

Sieminski, Sandy (1993) 'The "Flexible" Solution to Economic Decline', *Journal of Further and Higher Education* 17:1.

Simkins, Tim (1994) 'Efficiency, Effectiveness and LMS', *Journal of Educational Policy* 9:1.

Simon, Brian (1988) *Bending the Rules: The Baker Reform of Education* (London: Lawrence & Wishart).

Skeggs, B. (2004) *Feminism after Bourdieu* (Oxford: Blackwell).

Skidmore, C. (2008) *The Failed Generation – The Real Cost of Education under Labour* (London: The Bow Group).

Smith, E. (2003) 'Understanding Underachievement: An Investigation into the Differential Attainment of Secondary School Pupils', *British Journal of Sociology of Education* 24:5.

Smithers, A. (1993) *All Our Futures – Britain's Education Revolution* (London: Channel 4 Publications).

Smyth, J. and Garman, N. (1989) 'Supervision as School Reform: A Critical Perspective', *Journal of Educational Policy* 4:4.

Sowell, Thomas (1981) *Ethnic America: A History* (New York: Basic Books).

Spear, M. (1985) 'Teachers' Attitudes towards Girls and Technology', in J. Whyte, R. Deem, L. Kant and M. Cruickshank (eds), *Girl Friendly Schooling* (London: Methuen).

Spender, D. (1982) *Invisible Women: The Schooling Scandal* (London: Writers and Readers Publishing Cooperative).

Spours, Ken and Young, Michael (1988) 'Beyond Vocationalism: A New Perspective on the Relationship between Work and Education', *British Journal of Education and Work* 2:2.

SSEC (Secondary Schools Examination Council) (1943) *Curriculum and Examinations in Secondary Schools* (The Norwood Report) (London: HMSO).

Stake, J. E. and J. F. Katz, J. F. (1982) 'Teacher–Pupil Relationships in the Elementary School Classroom: Teacher-Gender and Pupil-Gender Differences', *American Education Research Journal* 19:3.

Stanton, G. (1990) 'Curriculum Implications', in J. Burke, *Competency-based Education and Training* (London: Falmer Press).

Stanworth, M. (1983) *Gender and Schooling* (London: Hutchinson).

Strand, S. (2008) *Minority Ethnic Pupils in the Longitudinal Study of Young People in England*, University of Warwick.

Summerfield, C. and Gill, B. (2005) *Social Trends* 35 (Basingstoke: Palgrave Macmillan).

Sutton Trust (2005) *The Educational Background of the UK's Top Solicitors, Barristers and Judges* (London: Sutton Trust).

Swale, J. (2006) 'Meet the NEETs: Media Accounts of the Underclass Debate', *Sociological Review* 15(2), February.

Sylvester, D. (1994) 'Change and Continuity in History Teaching', in H. Bourdillon (ed.) *Teaching History* (London: Routledge).

Taylor, G., Shepard, L., Kinner, F. and Rosenthal, J. (2001) *A Survey of Teachers' Perspectives on High-Stakes Testing in Colorado: What Gets Taught, What Gets Lost* (Boulder, Col.O: CREST/CREDE).

Taylor, H. (1989) 'Romantic Readers', in H. Carr, *From My Guy to Sci-fi: Genre and Women's Writing in the Postmodern World* (London: Pandora).

Taylor, M. J. (1981) *Caught Between: A Review of Research into the Education of Pupils of West Indian Origin* (Windsor: NFER/Nelson).

Taylor, Monica (1988) *Worlds Apart? A Review of Research into the Education of Pupils of Cypriot, Italian, Ukrainian and Vietnamese Origin, Liverpool Blacks and Gypsies* (Windsor: NFER/Nelson).

Theodossin, E. (1986) *In Search of the Responsive College* (Bristol: Further Education Staff College).

Thompson, J. (1984) *Studies in the Theory of Ideology* (Cambridge: Polity Press).

Thompson, Paul (1983) *The Nature of Work: An Introduction to Debates on the Labour Process* (London: Macmillan).

Tikly, L., Caballaro, C., Haynes, J. and Hill, J. (2004) *Understanding the Educational Needs of Mixed Heritage Pupils* (London: DfES).

Tizard, B. and Phoenix, A. (2002) *Black, White, or Mixed Race? Race and Racism in the Lives of Young People of Mixed Parentage* (London: Routledge).

Tizard, B., Mortimore, J. and Burchall, B. (1981) *Involving Parents in Nursery and Infant Schools* (London: Grant McIntyre).

Trowler, P. (2003) *Education Policy: A Policy Sociology Approach* (London: Routledge-Falmer).

Usher, Robin and Edwards, Richard (1994) *Postmodernism and Education* (London: Routledge).

Usher, R., Bryant, I.and Johnston, R. (1997) *Adult Education and the Postmodern Challenge* (London: Routledge).

Vasquez, James (1992) 'Locus of Control and Academic Achievement', in James Lynch et al., *Equity or Excellence? Education and Cultural Reproduction* (London: Falmer Press).

Verma, G. and Pumfrey, P. (eds) (1988) *Educational Attainments: Issues and Outcomes in Multicultural Education* (London: Falmer Press).

Wakeling, P. (2005) 'La noblesse d'état anglaise?: Social Class and Progression to Postgraduate Study', *British Journal of Sociology of Education* 26:4.

Walford, G. (1990) 'British Education and Privatization', in G. Walford, *Privatization and Privilege in Education* (London/New York: Routledge).

Walford G. (2008) 'Faith-based Schools in England after Ten Years of Tony Blair', *Oxford Review of Education* 34:6.

Walker L. (1989) *Australian Maid: Sex, Schooling and Social Class*, Dissertation, PhD Behavioural Sciences (Sydney: Macquarie University).

Walker, S. and Barton, L. (eds) (1987) *Changing Policies, Changing Teachers* (Milton Keynes: Open University Press).

Walkerdine, V. (1981) 'Sex, Power and Pedagogy', *Screen Education* 38.

Ward, L. (2004) 'Pupils at Good Schools Gain 18 Months', *Guardian*, 9 August.

Warren, S. (2005) 'Resistance and Refusal: African-Caribbean Young Men's Agency, School Exclusions and School Based Mentoring', *Race, Ethnicity and Education* 8:3.

Watson, I. (1993) 'Education, Class and Culture: The Birmingham Ethnographic Tradition and the Problem of the New Middle Class', *British Journal of Sociology of Education* 14:2.

Weiner, G. (1985) *Just a Bunch of Girls* (Milton Keynes: Open University Press).

Weiner, Gaby (1990) 'What Price Vocationalism – The Feminist Dilemma', *British Journal of Education and Work* 4:1.

Weiner, G., Arnot, M. and David, M. (1997) 'Is the Future Female? Female Success, Male Disadvantage and Changing Gender Patterns in Education', in A. H. Halsey, P. Brown and H. Lauder, *Education, Economy, Culture and Society* (Oxford: Oxford University Press).

Weis, L. (1990) *Working Class Without Work: High School Students in a Deindustrialising Economy* (New York: Routledge).

Weis, Lois (1992) Disproportionality, Education and Social Justice', in James Lynch et al., *Equity or Excellence? Education and Cultural Reproduction* (London: Falmer Press).

West, Cornell (1993) 'The New Cultural Politics of Difference', in C. McCarthy and W. Chrichlow (eds), *Race, Identity and Representation in Education* (London: Routledge).

Whitty, G. (1989) 'The New Right and the National Curriculum: State Control or Market Forces?', in M. Elude and M. Hammer (eds), *The Education Reform Act 1988: Its Origins and Implications* (London: Falmer Press).

Whitty, G. (2002) *Making Sense of Educational Policy* (London: Paul Chapman).

Whitty, G., Edwards, A. D. and Gerwirtz, S. (1993) *Specialisation and Choice in Urban Education: The City Technology College Experiment* (London: Routledge).

Whyld, J. (ed.) (1983) *Sexism in the Secondary School* (London: Harper & Row).

Whyte, J. (1984) 'Observing Sex Stereotypes and Interaction in the School Lab and Workshop', *Educational Review* 36:1.

Whyte, J., Deem, R., Kant, L. and Cruickshank, M. (eds) (1985) *Girl Friendly Schooling* (London: Methuen).

Wilkinson, H. (1994) *No Turning Back: Generations and the Genderquake* (London: Demos).

Wilkinson, L. C. and Marrett, C. B. (eds) (1985) *Gender Influences in Classroom Interaction* (New York: Academic Press).

Williams, F. (1989) *Social Policy: A Critical Introduction* (Cambridge: Polity Press).

Willis, Paul (1977) *Learning to Labour* (Farnborough: Saxon House).

Willis, Paul (1983) 'Cultural Production and Theories of Reproduction', in L. Barton and S. Walker (eds), *Race, Class and Education* (London: Croom Helm).

Woods, P. (1983) *Sociology and the School: An Interactionist Viewpoint* (London: Routledge & Kegan Paul).

Working Group on 14–19 Reform (2004) *14–19 Curriculum and Qualifications Reform; Final Report of the Working Group* (London: DfES).

Wright, Cecile (1987) 'School Processes – An Ethnographic Study', in J. Eggleston *et al., Education for Some: The Educational and Vocational Experiences of 15–18 Year Old Members of Minority Ethnic Groups* (Stoke-on Trent: Trentham Books).

Wright, D. (1986) 'Racism in School Textbooks', in D. Punter (ed.), *Introduction to Contemporary Cultural Studies* (London: Longman).

Yates, L. (1985) 'Is Girl-Friendly Schooling What Girls Need?', in J. Whyte, R. Deem, L. Kant and M. Cruickshank (eds), *Girl Friendly Schooling* (London: Methuen).

Young, M. F. D. (1971a) 'An Approach to the Study of Curricula as Socially Organised Knowledge', in M. F. D. Young (ed.), *Knowledge and Control* (London: Collier-Macmillan).

Young, M. F. D. (ed.) (1971b) *Knowledge and Control* (London: Collier-Macmillan).

# Index

# *Titles in the*
# Skills-Based Sociology *series*

978-0-333-68763-5    978-0-230-21782-9    978-0-230-21781-2

*Designed to cover the key concepts, issues and contemporary debates in Sociology*

978-0-333-96889-5    978-0-230-21792-8

## To order visit www.palgrave.com